Advance Praise for *The S*

"Michael Ward's book presents a realistic   y
AIDS epidemic in Boston. I was especially ....   of
love and loss expressed at Mark's memorial service."
—Jerome Groopman, MD,
staff writer in medicine and biology for *The New Yorker*

"Over three decades ago, just when we were all learning about AIDS, Michael Ward and his lover experienced firsthand the uncertainty, fear, and heartbreak of the disease. It is essential that we not forget these early days of the AIDS crisis. Thank goodness Michael is here to remind us of the human cost of those days in this moving, deeply personal, and beautifully written book."
—Ken Harvey, author of *A Passionate Engagement* and
If You Were With Me Everything Would Be All Right

"*The Sea Is Quiet Tonight* is about so much more than life and death. It's a story about how relationships survive when death is close. It's a story about community. I felt as if I knew all of the characters personally. A real stand-out is the characterization of Aunt Pearl, and both sets of parents are given good and honest space on the page. Michael Ward and Mark Halberstadt are present— visually, emotionally, realistically. While no relationship is without its difficulties and challenges, this wonderful memoir presents a searingly honest portrayal of life and love, of decency and strong ties. It asks all the right questions within the frame of a fraught relationship. The writing is tight and clean, and the prose is never maudlin. Michael Ward has written from the heart about a wonderful, terrible time in his life, and in so doing he's honored Mark Halberstadt's memory."
—Catherine Parnell, Senior Associate Editor, *Consequence* magazine

"*The Sea Is Quiet Tonight* is beautifully written, a deeply affecting story."
—Helene Atwan, Director, Beacon Press

"Sometimes what matters most is the story under the story. Maybe you think you know the story of the AIDS crisis and its devastations in this country. But inside that story are the kind of guiding, soul-level stories we need so much now: about how to be a true friend, how love takes apart our fondest dreams of what's supposed to happen, and ultimately how to grow up as human beings. Michael Ward's *The Sea Is Quiet Tonight* gives us both the outside and the inside stories. I read it in two sittings, riveted, nourished by the honest, sad, funny, beautiful truth of what unfolded for the author and his beloved and their friends and family. I won't forget this book."

—Sherry Ruth Anderson, author of *Ripening Time: Inside Stories for Aging with Grace*

"Profoundly evocative of a time when hilarity and high camp gave way to unimaginable horror. Enter into these pages, if you dare. For those of us who lived to tell the story, Michael Ward calls forth the memory of the beauty, the dread, the terror, and the extraordinary ways we cared for one another."

—Rev. Kim K. Crawford Harvie, Senior Minister, Arlington Street Church (UUA), Boston

The Sea Is Quiet Tonight
A Memoir

Michael H. Ward

With a Foreword by Mitchell Katz, M.D.

Querelle Press
New York, NY

Published by Querelle Independent, a division of Querelle Press
PO Box 2808 Broadway #4
New York, NY 10025

Library of Congress Cataloging-in-Publication Data

Ward, Michael H., 1944—
The sea is quiet tonight : a memoir / Michael H. Ward
1st edition
189 p., 23 cm.
ISBN 978-0-9967-103-3-6 (paper)
ISBN 978-0-9967-103-4-3 (digital)
1. Ward, Michael H., 1944—   2. Halberstadt, Mark, 1942—1984. 3. AIDS (Disease) – Patients – United States – Biography. 4. Gay men – United States – Biography. I. Title.
RC607.A26 W37 2016
616.9792—dc23 [B]   2016947238

Printed in the United States of America

Cover by: Linda Kosarin, The Art Department

www.querellepress.com

"All sorrows can be borne if you put them into a story or tell a story about them."

—Isak Dinesen

FOR

MARK HALBERSTADT

AND

MAURICE MELCHIONO

Mark at the helm of *The Dancing Bear*, May 1982

Table of Contents

Foreword

Love and death. For a generation of gay men, love and death were inextricably intertwined. To love, in the age of AIDS, was to mourn.

For Michael Ward and Mark Halberstadt, who fell in love at the beginning of the epidemic in 1981—when so little was known, and so little could be done—there was barely a second between those first heady days of falling in love and having to let go. Yet their story, told touchingly in this memoir by Michael, is full of emotion and insight. Their time together was intense, as if somehow they knew, from their first encounter, that they had to hurry.

The elements of their love affair—lust, passion, vulnerability, commitment, frustration—are the themes of any love affair. Still the themes are fresh and potent as we watch them play out in the lives of these two very different men. Mark is reserved, contained, stoic, and has no strong aspirations; he hopes to spend his days sailing around the Caribbean. Michael is outgoing, emotional, accessible, and always has a task. Even his leisure activities—running, working out, the occasional sexual romp—have an element of achievement. He wants to build a steady practice at work and have a few dollars in the bank.

Although the differences between them would make for an interesting love story at any moment in time, this was not just any moment. Mark and Michael are part of the generation of gay men who came of age post-Stonewall. The seventies were a time of struggle to overcome the negative ideas that society held about gay men—ideas that many of us held about ourselves—that there was something wrong with us, that we were defective in some way. Buoyed by the strength of the civil rights movement and women's liberation, many of us came out to our friends and families and found acceptance. Others less fortunate were severed from their families or lost their jobs. And there were those who remained in the closet, not risking the alienation and discrimination that came with coming out, in this era when it was widely legal to discriminate by sexual orientation.

So gay men in the early eighties varied greatly in how open they felt able to be about their orientation. Michael notes he had "come out to the whole planet" by 1981, which may only be a mild overstatement; Mark, while not closeted, was more circumspect, as he was about everything. At the same time, gay male culture celebrated sexual expression. Going to the baths, having multiple partners, pushing limits, and pushing aside taboos were celebrated as forms of liberation. And we were certain that no harm could come of it, or at least no harm that couldn't be cured with a penicillin injection.

AIDS changed that. It again made sex between men, even liberated men, feel wrong and dangerous, because it actually was dangerous, something that could, in fact, kill you. Yet even as AIDS created a new reason for people to fear gay men (I remember a middle-aged patient telling me that she was worried about my being her doctor because she knew I took care of so many AIDS patients), the ultimate effect of the epidemic was to push gay rights forward, not back into the closet.

Family members, including Mark's family, saw how their sons were loved by their partners, friends, and the broader gay community. Thirty years before the U.S. Supreme Court validated same sex marriage, AIDS forced families, hospitals, mortuaries, and religious institutions to acknowledge and, in many instances, accept same-sex partnerships. AIDS also propelled openly gay and lesbian doctors, nurses, psychologists, and other professionals to come out and care for the sick and dying. As we watched people fight for their lives against a cruel and terrifying illness, we rethought the fears that kept us in the closet.

These changes reached beyond those in the caretaking professions: the lawyers who wrote the wills, the teachers who wrote the curricula, the legislators who wrote the laws, including those that provided health insurance for domestic partners, a legal category that presaged gay marriage. Without the AIDS epidemic, I do not think gay rights and marriage equality would have made so much progress in these last thirty years. A surprising silver lining in a very dark cloud.

I met Mark when he was hospitalized for his first bout of *Pneumocystis* pneumonia in 1983. I was a medical student at the time and one of the founding members of the AIDS Action Committee in Boston. I was paired with Mark by the director of the committee, Larry Kessler, who believed that two nerdy, introverted Jewish New Yorkers would surely get along, which we did, right from the start. Mostly we met for lunch. I would bring him a sandwich and we would sit and talk about AIDS treatments, or the weather, or gay culture, anything other than death. Following Mark's death, I cared for hundreds of patients with AIDS. I spent two decades examining them, writing prescriptions, trying to keep them out of the hospital, talking to their partners and family members—and ultimately watching them die. Death is not something you get used to. It's the opposite. Each death reminds you of the others that have preceded it.

And then things changed. In 1996, protease inhibitors came on the market. Before that, the drugs we wielded, while more effective than anything we had had for treating Mark in the early eighties, just delayed the inevitable. But protease inhibitors brought people back to life. From the edge of death, people regained weight, regained strength, went back to the gym, and went back to work. It was the most amazing thing I had ever seen, a joy spoiled only by remembering those, like Mark, who died before these drugs became available.

There is still no cure, but in 2016 there are many effective and safe medications to fight HIV. As long as people take their medicines, they will live out life spans almost as long as those who are uninfected.

So we have great victories to celebrate: the development of better and better treatments for HIV, the growth of the political power of the LGBT community, the victory of same-sex marriage. But we can't forget what we have lost—a whole generation of gay men. One of them, a very special one, was Mark Halberstadt. The world is poorer without Mark's dry wit and urbane sensibility. In this beautiful book, Michael Ward has captured their story, our story, so that we won't forget. And for that I will always be grateful.

—Mitchell Katz, M.D.
Director, Department of Health Services
County of Los Angeles, California

Preface

I'm in the visitor's lounge on the ninth floor of the Deaconess Hospital. Dusk is approaching in late September and the brightness is beginning to fade from the sky. I'm alone in the room, standing near the pay phone, and I watch through the long windows as the lights gradually blink on in the buildings downtown. I need to phone Mark's elderly parents, who know he has been hospitalized for tests but do not know his diagnosis. Mark and I have had lunch at their home on Long Island a couple of times, but Mark is resistant to discussing his private life with them, and I'm a big part of that life. It's 1983, and the acronym AIDS has barely come into common usage. The *New York Times* has been reporting on a "rare cancer" that has been detected in gay men in the U.S. Most of my friends in Boston believe the reports are over-hyped, the media's latest attempt to demonize gay sex. All I know for sure is that gay men in New York and San Francisco are being diagnosed and dying at a frightening rate. How do I explain to Mark's parents what is wrong?

Ida, his mother, answers the phone and we exchange brief pleasantries. She says, "Did Mark's tests come back?"

I take a deep breath and say, "Yes, he's been diagnosed with a type of pneumonia. It's called PCP."

His father, Eddie, is on the other phone by now and says loudly, "What is it? P what?"

"PCP, Eddie." I speak slowly and clearly, forcing my voice to be steady. My stomach is in knots. "They call it *Pneumocystis.*"

"Who gets pneumonia at his age?" he says irritably. "He's only forty-one. Only old people get pneumonia."

We're all quiet. My mind goes blank as I continue to gaze out the window. I feel surprise at how bright the lights of downtown Boston have become in just a few short minutes, the sky still blue but fading fast. Pulling myself back into the conversation, I say, "This is a special kind of pneumonia, Eddie, and they're going to treat it with a new medication of some kind. Doctor Groopman seems confident that they can cure it."

Another moment of quiet. The visitor's lounge is nearly dark now. Then the words that I'm dreading are spoken. Ida says, "Is this that bad pneumonia that young men have been getting in New York?"

"Yes, it is." I feel tears forming but keep my voice neutral, trying not to alarm them. "I'm sorry, but we're hopeful that medication will take care of it."

Eddie says, "Does Mark want us to come up?"

"No, he asked me to give you his love and said that he'll call himself when he feels a little better. I'll be here with him, and I'll call you if there's any change." I can hardly breathe now and feel like I've left my body. The conversation, the experience of talking to these people I know in only a superficial way, is surreal.

Eddie then says loudly, "That's good, Mike, he'll be home soon. You'll call us. Ida, hang up the phone now, tell Mike goodbye."

Ida's voice is shaky when she says, "Thank you, Mike, thank you for being there. You'll call us."

"For sure, Ida. I promise." I hang up the phone and lean against the wall, resting my cheek against the cool tile, grateful for the darkness. *How will I ever get through this*, I wonder. It feels impossible to grasp the enormity of what's happening. Clearly, nothing will ever be the same. I open the door and pass into the bright hospital hallway. The light stuns me back into my body. Suddenly alert again, I find my way back to Mark's room.

PART ONE

Chapter 1

Gay men in the seventies and early eighties saw Fire Island as a combination of Mecca and Oz. There is even a wooded area between the adjacent communities of Cherry Grove and the Pines that is commonly referred to as Judy Garland Memorial Park. It's also known as the Meat Rack.

In early September of 1981, I drove from Boston to Long Island and took the ferry to Cherry Grove. Friends had rented a one-room efficiency apartment for the season in a house facing the bay and had invited me to use their unit for a week. I was ecstatic. I'd been to Fire Island a few times as a guest, but never for a week on my own.

A woman I had worked with a few years earlier in Princeton, New Jersey, had called to say she'd be staying with friends in the Pines at the same time. Why didn't I come down to Tea Dance that first day? Meeting a small handful of new people seemed far easier than confronting hundreds of sweaty, dancing strangers by myself. I said I'd love to.

I walked down the beach that links the Grove and the Pines on the east side of the island, feeling more excited than nervous. I was still getting over the final breakup with my former partner, Frank, and I was feeling insecure and vulnerable about getting into the gay male scene. I wasn't much of a sexual adventurer, though I'd had my share of one-night stands and "affairettes," as a friend called them. But the idea of outdoor cruising or the baths freaked me out. Despite our problems as a couple, Frank and I had enjoyed the security of a loving relationship. On my own, I faced the uncertainty of my prospects, bad first dates and rejection. I was attractive enough, thirty-seven, dark Irish, tall and lean. But I was insecure and felt far less experienced than the crowds of gay New Yorkers who thronged Fire Island. Surely years of marching in Gay Pride parades and coming out to everyone on the planet had prepared me for something more passionate and engaging than I had yet known. I longed for something fuller and more real.

From the beach I could hear Taana Gardner's "Heartbeat" thumping loudly from the Pavilion as I made my way across the narrow boardwalks to the west side of the island. Powerboats bobbed in the water off shore, and the Fire Island ferry had just docked, a hundred or more gay men with backpacks and rolling suitcases spilling down the gangway. Rounding the corner to the deck of the Pavilion, I spied my friend Gena in the midst of the throng on the dance floor. She grinned and waved me over, and I fought my way through the mêlée to meet her at the bar. The music was ear-splitting, the deck jammed with sweating men in shorts and tank tops. As we turned to order a Blue Whale, a man appeared at her elbow. Gena shouted his name twice before I understood what she said: Mark Halberstadt, a friend from Peace Corps days.

I was immediately taken by his looks. He was short, maybe five foot six, wearing khaki shorts and sandals and a navy blue polo shirt. I was struck by his outfit, a little more put-together and less flamboyant than most of the other men on the deck. He had tight, dark, curly hair and a handsome, chiseled face; brown eyes with wire-rimmed spectacles, a small mustache, and perfect teeth. He was lean and muscular, and he had a very cute smile. I felt a pleasant lurch inside. This was someone special.

Since it was impossible to converse without shouting, the three of us danced to a couple of songs and then Gena went back to the bar. Mark cupped his hand to my ear and said he'd bought a new camera and wanted to take some pictures. Would I go for a walk with him? I was aware of his touch, the warmth of his lips moving against my ear. Why not? We wandered the boardwalks as he snapped pictures, first of the ocean and the beach, then a few of me. We talked easily about his love of sailing, which he said was "almost like a religion" to him. I shared my love for my work as a psychotherapist in Boston, one topic flowing into another, and an hour passed quickly. When he invited me to dinner, I was thrilled. He was staying in a big, rambling house in the center of the Pines with a deck looking out to the ocean. I felt like I was on a movie set. There were handsome men milling around, a lot of clever conversations and good-natured ribbing, and Mark organized a handful of us to prepare dinner and set the table on the big deck. I was excited to be in the thick of it.

*

Hours later, having abandoned the others to clean up the dishes, we're in bed, and there are candles lit around the room. I'm lying on my back, he's sitting astride my hips. We're exhausted from the evening and from making love for hours. I understand by now that Mark, while reserved and thoughtful in speech, is completely liberated sexually. I find his confidence and responsiveness a turn-on. He's looking down at me, grinning, a faun or satyr, and for the first time in my life I feel completely and passionately unselfconscious. It's as if my body is connected to a rheostat, and he has found the switch to turn me on, making me brighter and more alive. It's his grin I remember, so vulnerable, a look of triumph, as if he'd gone fishing and unexpectedly landed a very big fish. Given that I'm six foot three and outweigh him by thirty pounds, I am indeed a big fish.

A series of warm early September days followed, full of buttery sunlight, lolling on the beach, and endless walking. Everything we said, everything we did seemed funny and charming and special. I'd never experienced this kind of connection to a man. I spent most of the time that week in the Pines with Mark, abandoning the little studio in the Grove. I have photos of us from those days together, just a few, and my favorite shows the two of us lying on our stomachs with our arms folded under our chins. We're looking up into the camera and someone must have said something funny, because Mark and I are both laughing, eyes crinkled, with expressions that are achingly openhearted. It's so clear, looking at that picture, that we were smitten.

Back in Boston the next week, I repeatedly shook my head, as if to wake up. Had this event really taken place? Had I actually fallen in love? Distracted and vulnerable, I try not to talk about him endlessly to my roommate, Ed, with whom I'd moved into an apartment just three days before I went to Fire Island. I tell myself I am a sensible person, a psychotherapist. I'm mature, I have a career and a busy life. Mark had given up his teaching job in New York City and was completing his work for his license as a boat captain, living in the city some of the time and in Florida the rest, moving sailboats and taking deckhand jobs for experience. While only two years older than I, he had freed himself from the teaching career his parents had wished for him, and was committed to living a sailor's life, ultimately hoping for his own wooden yacht and sailing in the warm waters of the Caribbean. I had never set foot on a boat and was water-phobic from nearly drowning in childhood, but my rapture made his life sound utterly romantic and desirable. It was easy to imagine being side by side with him on that wooden boat, which in my fantasy I named *Safe Harbor*.

In the days before cell phones and email, it was more of a challenge to communicate long-distance. Because he was transitioning to living in Florida, Mark had canceled his landline in New York. When I left him in Manhattan on Sunday to drive home, we tentatively planned for him to come to Boston on Friday afternoon, when I would be free from work. He said he'd "drop a note." I started looking for the note on Tuesday and found only bills. I felt certain it would be in the mailbox when I got home on Wednesday, but the box was empty. Waiting, I found that I couldn't eat, and slept poorly. Normally level-headed, I found myself obsessing about him in every spare moment. I felt foolish, had never been "sick with love," as the psalmist said. But on Thursday, opening the mailbox with fear and trepidation, I saw a small envelope with a pale blue gridded pattern and a matching small piece of stationery inside, upon which was written: "Arriving Back Bay Station 4:00 p.m. Friday. Amazing, feel stunned and so very happy. Alive, at last . . ." I let out a whoop of joy and exclaimed, "That's the perfect name for our boat!"

*

At the appointed hour on Friday I paced on the platform of the train station, my thoughts a jumble of hopes and fears. I was afraid to let go and free fall into my emotions, afraid I'd exaggerated what I'd felt when we met. The specter of rejection lurked. Back Bay Station on a late Friday afternoon is close to pandemonium, and I reflected on the crowd at our meeting at the Pavilion only two weeks earlier and smiled to myself. Then I saw him alight, searching the crowd for my face, and his serious expression turned to sunshine when he made eye contact with me. After a quick embrace we headed for the Green Line C train to take us out to my apartment on Bay State Road.

Mark stayed for four days, much of which we spent either in bed or in the kitchen. Mark had lived in Paris his sophomore year in college, studying at the Sorbonne and taking cooking classes on the side. He was a masterful chef and talked about Julia Child with the reverence that others might have used for Mother Teresa. One of his many gifts was mimicry, and he could do long monologues from Julia's show, *The French Chef*, nailing her voice and mannerisms. He stood at the kitchen counter preparing breakfast, wearing only an apron with a print of Michelangelo's *David* on the front: "No no no! This hollandaise is *not* behaving. More egg yolk? Ahhhh. Much better!"

Our appetites for both food and sex were unquenchable. One of his favorite radio shows as a kid growing up in New York had been *Breakfast with Dorothy and Dick*, in which Dorothy Kilgallen and her husband, Dick Kollmar, would broadcast comments about the previous evening's social events from their sixteen-room apartment in Manhattan. "Hi, darling . . . Hi, sweetie . . . Here we are at home in little old New York ready to visit with our radio friends . . ." Mark would awaken me with these words each morning, and then, switching between Dorothy's voice and Dick's, narrate the "social events" of our previous night, including what occurred at home in the bedroom. I'd only known him a month, but I was entranced, besotted, sore from lovemaking, and the happiest I had ever been. I had to drag myself away from him to go to the office and counted the hours one by one until I could go home.

Mark had to prepare to help move a sailboat from Long Island to Florida, so he returned to New York early on Tuesday morning. Our working lives could not have been more different. His was more like a fisherman's, dependent on time and tide. Mine was highly structured, seeing clients for fifty minutes at a time four days a week, leading therapy groups, attending training sessions and supervision groups. Our communication styles were different as well. While we were both raised in working-class homes, his family was Jewish, mine Irish. He had one brother, I had five brothers and two sisters. He was intellectual and clever but private. I was outgoing, verbal, and emotional. Neither knew exactly what to do with the other. Once we had to rely on phone calls and notes, I struggled to feel connected. I wanted more from him, more reassurance and contact. He was able to provide enough of those things when we were together. But when we were separated by time and space, I felt disconnected, from myself and from him, and I was left full of longing.

Chapter 2

On the last Friday of September, Mark and I arranged to meet in Stamford, Connecticut, at a boat show. I was raised in Nebraska. I had never been to a boat show, or even been in a canoe that I could remember. Since his world was sailing and sailboats, I wanted to make a good impression, so I dressed carefully, unaware that the last thing one wears to a boat show is cowboy boots. I felt humiliated when Mark greeted me at the gate to the marina by looking at my feet and murmuring, "Oh, dear. You can only wear soft-soled shoes like docksiders on deck." We explored five big yachts, me having to yank off the boots at boarding and awkwardly pull them back on as we exited the gangway. I tried to enjoy myself but was filled with embarrassment, like a farmer way out of his comfort zone. The boats were amazing, however, and Mark beamed as he explained nautical terms and rhapsodized about knots. I could tell it would be a steep learning curve for me, beginning with learning how to swim. "Oh, dear" indeed.

From there we drove to Syosset, Long Island, to spend the night with my closest couple friends, Betts Collett and Gerry Ente. I was excited about introducing Mark to them and I was not disappointed. Betts had made a wonderful dinner, *soupe de poisson* and an elegant fresh raspberry cheesecake. Betts and Mark *kvelled* about Julia Child. Wine and laughter flowed. We had a wonderful time, despite being tired from a long week, and all four of us fell asleep in front of the fire after dinner.

The next morning Mark and I drove to the coastal town of Center Moriches to meet the men Mark would be sailing to Florida with in ten days. His sailor friends were in their late sixties, very tanned and lively, and they enjoyed showing me their fifty-foot yacht, the *Skua*. It was quite impressive, and I was considerably more relaxed than I had been at the boat show. I was also wearing sneakers. These men were living the life Mark longed for, with a house on Long Island, a house in Jupiter, Florida, and an elegant sailboat to carry them back and forth. Mark was clearly happy to introduce me as his boyfriend, the first time I had heard him use that word. Considering his natural reticence, that felt like a public announcement to me and I'm sure I was beaming.

At last we headed for our fourth and final destination, Bellport, which was less than thirty minutes away. It was a glorious day, sunny and cool, and we were looking forward to three days in the house of friends of Mark from the city. They were traveling, so we had the house to ourselves. The owners were interior designers, and the house was both simple and stunning: an open floor plan with a living/dining/kitchen area, a beamed cathedral ceiling, and wide wooden stairways on either side of the main room leading to the upper floor. Everything was painted white, and the light in the room was dazzling. There were French doors on two sides, one pair opening out onto a large deck, the other to a garden area dense with shrubbery that contained a small pool and a Jacuzzi.

"Paradise," I cried, and Mark laughed.

"Pretty amazing, huh?" he said.

"I'm speechless. This house is a dream."

We went upstairs to unpack but started horsing around before we were halfway finished, pushing our bags to the floor to clear the decks. The stress and fatigue of the previous week evaporated as we tore off our clothes and rediscovered each other's bodies. Despite having had sex with a significant number of men over the preceding eighteen years, I had never had the experience of falling in love with someone who could so fully abandon himself to the pleasures of the body. This bookish New York intellectual became transformed by desire into a being of passion, and I happily surrendered for the ride.

"I love your build," he said, sitting cross-legged beside my outstretched body, "how big and yet lean you are. And I love that you're so willing to be passionate with me. I go to the baths frequently, I've always enjoyed sex, but in these weeks between our visits I haven't gone out looking."

I felt delighted. "Are you telling me that I'm enough?" I teased.

"More than enough," he said. At night we would rinse off in the outdoor shower and slide into the Jacuzzi, then into the pool, lying on our backs looking up at the stars. I had never felt so open and free.

Our time in Bellport, brief as it was, marked a shift in our relationship. On Sunday night Mark had prepared *coq au vin* with a little green salad, and ripe peaches with ice cream for dessert. Out of the blue he said, "Will I scare you away if I use the F word?"

"Considering our daily activities, do you have to ask?"

"Not *that* F word. The future! I'm wondering about our future. And if you think I'm rushing things, say so, please."

Suddenly feeling sober, I looked at his face, which had become serious. I loved his mouth and the thin line of his moustache, his perfect white teeth. I brushed the back of my fingers along his jaw line, and he reached up to take my hand.

I said, "Sorry, I get distracted when I look at you. I feel totally present when

I'm with you and lost when I'm not. My whole life has been turned upside down."

"Mine too." He began kissing the palm of my hand.

"Oh no," I said, "you're not going to distract me. So what about the F word? What are you thinking?"

Releasing my hand, he said, "I guess I just wanted to get it out on the table. There's something about you that makes me feel hopeful. Maybe I could manage a committed relationship. I don't have a great track record, but when we're together, I begin to feel like anything is possible." He caught himself and stopped, then asked, "Do I sound melodramatic?"

I leaned across the table and kissed him. "Not by half. You can say things like that all night if you want to. I'm easy."

"So we both feel that there is something here, yes? And we can move forward and see where life carries us?"

"Nicely said." I was flushed with pleasure. "But you have to promise to stay as connected to me as possible."

"What do you mean?"

"I can't imagine being separated for a month. I'm someone who needs connection. Don't forget about me when you're moving the *Skua* to Florida."

Over breakfast the next morning we agreed to meet in Fort Lauderdale at the end of October. I was returning to Boston to work, he was going to be helping provision the *Skua* and then be on the water for two to three weeks, depending on weather. He would try to call me on the ship's radio, and also when they went in to shore for gas or provisions. It was hard to leave the fairy tale house, the pool and Jacuzzi, but I had a deeper sense of Mark as a person and felt hopeful that something might actually develop from these encounters.

*

Mark's trip on the *Skua* lasted slightly more than three weeks. They ran into bad weather that frequently made sailing impossible, and also had to take the boat into shore for engine repairs. As it turned out, he was only able to call twice, once on the ship's radio, once from the shore. From the ship he sounded as if he were talking in a wind tunnel, and each time either of us was finished talking, we had to shout, "Over." It was bizarre. The call from shore was marginally better, a clear line but a painfully stilted conversation. After three weeks of little contact, I felt completely disconnected from him.

A few days later I flew to Fort Lauderdale, wishing I had planned only a weekend rather than eight days. He greeted me at the airport with a quick hug, and we searched for conversation as we waited for my bag. At last we headed to the home of friends for whom he was housesitting. It took several days of sunshine and good food and dancing at the Copa before I felt myself begin to relax. Sex was frequent and passionate, but I longed for a deeper emotional connection. Very gradually, that began to emerge as well.

Early in the visit Mark introduced me as his "main man" to his Florida friends, Dick and Ed, who were also "boat people." I found it curious how deeply involved they all were with sailing. Most conversations centered around two subjects: boats and boys. There was a discernible population of older, wealthy men with younger, unemployed men, referred to as "twinkies," who shared bed and board and who provided amusement and companionship. This put me off at first, but Mark pointed out that these relationships were mutually beneficial and voluntary. I couldn't argue with that.

Dick and Ed, who owned a boat called *Ilovit*, invited us to go out for a day of recreational sailing. It was a large yacht, with a full galley and sleeping spaces for four people below-decks. This was my virgin voyage. If I hated it or got seasick, I feared our future was doomed. Mark promised that if the seas were too choppy, we'd cut the time short. In addition to the two of us and our hosts, there were four or five twinkies, in their late teens and early twenties, who carried shoulder bags stuffed with sunscreen and emollients of all kinds, as well as bottles of water and juice.

There was a light wind and bright sunlight, a perfect day. As soon as we pulled away from the dock, the boys stripped down to the briefest of Speedos and oiled each other before spreading out and taking up most of the available deck space. Someone tuned into a disco station on a portable radio. Mark had agreed to serve as captain, leaving Dick and Ed to entertain the young men, so we settled in at the helm.

Mark watched me carefully, checking in as we moved through the Intracoastal Waterway to Port Everglades, where we would enter the ocean. He asked me, "Are you doing OK?" so often that I finally said, "Stop! If I get nauseous, it will be obvious from my green gills!" Meanwhile, Dick and Ed made big pitchers of screwdrivers and began plying the twinkies with drinks. Mark and I declined. The noise level increased, the disco music got louder. I felt relatively indifferent to the babble but noticed Mark's jaw tightening. We spoke in low tones.

"Are you upset?" I asked, moving close to him on the seat.

"I love sailing. It feels essential to me. And this day is so perfect. I wanted your first trip to be special for you, and our hosts and their friends might as well be by the pool at the Bimbo Bar."

I laughed. "It's fine, Mark, really. You might not be able to tell from looking at me, but I'm feeling ecstatic. I'm not even remotely seasick. It's amazing: the air and the sun on the water and the gulls and pelicans circling." I couldn't stop grinning.

He smiled then, and kissed me full on. "Thanks for that. Now I feel hopeful again."

From behind we heard catcalls. "More kissing," a boy shouted. "Give us a show!"

Mark steered the *Ilovit* out into the ocean, and gradually the waves became bigger, causing the boat to rock. The wind picked up a little, and there was some general scrambling for towels and windbreakers. Dick helped Mark unfurl a second sail while I held the wheel and we picked up speed, plowing through the troughs of water. I found the experience exhilarating. *Not bad for a Midwesterner,* I thought, sailing on a beautiful boat with a handsome sailor. And I was hungry! Mark cautioned me about preparing lunch, said the galley was narrow and might be hard to navigate. I went below anyway and found that my size was an advantage in wedging myself securely between the counter and the bulkhead behind me. In short order I made tuna salad sandwiches for the whole party. But when I climbed back to the deck, I realized only Mark and our hosts would be joining me for lunch: a few of the younger set were leaning over the railings, regurgitating their breakfasts. The rest huddled out of the wind, clutching their windbreakers and looking miserable. Mark grinned at me.

"You'll make a hell of a sailor," he said.

"Let's get these landlubbers back to port, Captain," I replied.

"Aye aye."

The next morning, before I headed for Boston, we once again looked at our calendars and figured out when we could meet: three weeks from the next Thursday, in Puerto Rico, where I had booked a trip a month before I met him. It would only be for four days, and they would have to last us for at least a month or more. We were quiet riding to the airport. I was grateful to have settled into the comfort and merged bliss of our connection. I asked him to drop me off at departures, knowing it would be easier than lingering together, and he agreed. When I leaned across to kiss him goodbye, he said, "I'll be thinking of you. I love you." It was the first time he'd said it, simple and sweet. I felt myself flush with pleasure. "I love you too," I said.

*

Mark and I talked on the phone frequently, but we also wrote letters that could be read and reread. He was a wonderful writer, and he took more emotional risks in articulating his feelings for me on paper than he did on the phone. He told me he loved me far beyond what he'd thought he was capable of. He said he'd never felt these feelings, the loss of boundaries, the longing. I hadn't either, not at this depth or with this level of passion. But it was newer for Mark, who was not only introverted by nature, but had also spent a lifetime armoring himself against his mother's intrusiveness. His vulnerability was well protected.

Just before we were to meet in Puerto Rico, Mark called, clearly distressed.

Usually we talked briefly, but this call lasted nearly an hour. He had moved his things out of storage and into his friend John Batson's house, but he hadn't unpacked. He said, "I feel very unsure of my direction. When I moved my stuff down here over a year ago, I thought I was going to be living here. But now . . ."

"Would it help if I said I'm yours, heart and soul?"

"That's a good start," he replied, his voice softening. "I think I'm feeling scared."

"What's the worst that could happen?"

"That I'll give you all of myself, and it won't be enough."

I marveled at his directness and said, "I'm afraid of the same thing, you know."

"Come on! You seem so sure of yourself, you're . . ." He searched for the right words. "You're more emotionally mature. You've been in long-term relationships. You've been in years of therapy. I've had a ton of sex and a few boyfriends, but I've never even lived with someone."

"Look, Mark. We're both scared. One big difference in our lives is that I'm working and have my identity as a therapist to hang on to. You've left teaching behind and are placing all your bets on a whole new path." I sounded more sure of myself than I felt. "I have no idea how we can bridge these two worlds, but I'm really in love with you. And I'll give this relationship all I've got."

I could hear him sigh on the other end of the phone, and his voice relaxed. We began to talk about Puerto Rico, what the gay bed and breakfast would be like, how wonderful it would be to once again be in swimsuits and have hours together. We finally said goodbye with a promise to continue the conversation over piña coladas on the beach.

*

We met at the Beach House a few days later. Boston already had snow on the ground when I left, and I saw a different world as I looked out the airplane window during our descent into San Juan: sunlight glinting on bright blue seas, long white beaches, dense stretches of green foliage. Old San Juan was smaller than I expected, but we were staying on Condado Beach, which was packed with hotels, guesthouses, and large private homes.

Since he and I first met, every greeting and parting had been different for Mark and me, and this one was no exception. He had arrived at the hotel before me and was already settled in. It was a lively place, small and brightly decorated, run by a wonderful woman named Rae who had an all-gay staff and a mostly gay clientele. She was businesslike but warm, and within minutes I felt like I'd been there for days. We had a cabana tucked into dense palms that afforded some privacy, and the atmosphere was completely open. Other than San Francisco, I had never been anywhere where I felt less inhibited about being gay. While we still needed to maintain social distance with each other on the streets and at the beach, we could be openly affectionate in all parts of the hotel. That was an enormous relief, and we took full advantage, holding hands across the table at lunch or cuddling in front of the TV in the lobby to watch the stateside news.

Our time was brief, but we made each day last. The lovemaking was addictive, my orgasms so intense they felt like blackouts. Our activities were apparently so enthusiastic that, at brunch one morning, we were greeted by applause when we showed up in the little breakfast room on the terrace. Roberto, our favorite waiter, brought us juice and coffee and wagged his finger at us.

"*Sinvergüenza,*" he said. Shameless! "What would your mommies say?"

"I learned this from my mommy," I told him.

Roberto threw his hands in the air in mock horror and said, "Blessed Mother of God, help your poor children!"

Mark and I roamed the beach. We read in the shade of the umbrellas under tall palm trees and I found quiet spots to write in my journal. Like Bellport, it was paradise.

On our third night we had dinner at a restaurant called Scotch and Sirloin, situated on a lagoon across from Old San Juan. We sat at a table near the end of the terrace, right on the water, and drank in the view of the city at night, lights twinkling, a breeze making the candles on the tables flicker. We ate almost without speaking, then Mark intoned, "A massive meal for manly men," using the voice of Walter Cronkite as he finished his last bite of a huge filet mignon. "I'm stuffed." We watched the small boats moving across the lagoon, and I felt the beauty and power of this place, a perfect moment.

"Where do we go from here?" I wondered aloud.

"I wish it were simple," Mark said, "but it's not. It's hard for me to imagine relocating to Boston." His new line of work depended entirely on connections, and he had none in New England. He also had to complete his supervised hours before he could take the certification exam to be captain.

I said, "What do you live on? I assume you don't have a trust fund."

He explained that, several years earlier, he and seven others had invested in the McIntyre Building on 18th and Broadway in Manhattan. It had originally been used for manufacturing, but he and his partners had converted the building to loft spaces. He owned the 9th floor, which contained three lofts and a storage space. With most of the renovations complete, he had quit his teaching job and decided to follow his heart into sailing.

But there was a glitch. The owners were waiting for their Certificate of Occupancy, and one of Mark's tenants had been withholding his rent for many months over a dispute about rent control versus rent stabilization. It was an issue affecting all the units in the building, so the process in the courts would take time. He said, "Without the income from that tenant, I'm barely clearing enough money to cover expenses."

"Thank you," I said. "That's a much fuller picture. I've experienced some tension in you when we talk about spending money but had no idea what it arose from."

"What about you?"

"I've spent the last two years building a psychotherapy practice in Boston. When I moved up from Princeton, I had to start from scratch, so I lived on my savings until very recently. Only in the last few months have I actually earned more than what will cover my expenses." I hesitated for a moment, then said, "Financially, this would be a disastrous time for me to move away from Boston."

We sat quietly, then I touched his forearm with two fingers and rubbed it lightly, making eye contact. Deciding where to live together was clearly going to be a challenge. "Mark, for now let's concentrate on both Boston and New York. I realize you'll need to travel for work, but let's try to normalize some kind of relationship."

"It's daunting," he said. "But I know I love you." He hesitated for a moment, then said, "I thought it was too late for me to find a relationship like this. I'll do my best not to disappoint you."

We awoke Sunday to more fine weather. We were both scheduled to leave on Monday afternoon, him for Miami, me for Boston. We had an easy day, quieter than the previous three, and sweetly companionable. We slept and cuddled a lot. We had moved to some level of clarity. It seemed possible to me, for the first time, to imagine having an intense and passionate relationship and to pursue my work and my own interests as well. Love and autonomy. It wouldn't be easy, but wasn't that what we'd been fighting for politically? Equal opportunity for happiness.

Then we had a scare on Sunday evening. While we were beginning to pack after dinner, Mark developed pains in his stomach. Soon he had a fever that reached 102 degrees. He alternately felt burning hot, then shuddered with chills. I was very frightened and talked to Rae, who said she'd be glad to take us to the hospital if we wished. Mark wanted to wait, saying, "It's probably just an exotic bug," so I settled myself down. I made sure that I had his Blue Cross Blue Shield card and that I could call upon Rae at any time.

Sitting in a wingback chair at the head of the bed, I watched Mark doze, wiping the perspiration from his forehead and giving him 7Up from time to time. In those hours it dawned on me that, after only three months, I felt deeply committed. Eventually the fever began to diminish, and Mark asked if I'd read to him, a novel by P. G. Wodehouse that he'd brought with him. I read several chapters, investing Bertie Wooster's lines with my best British accent, and Mark laughed himself to sleep.

We both awoke early, him on the bed and me in the chair. He was not 100 percent better, looking small and vulnerable in the big white bed all alone, but he clearly felt better. And damned if he didn't seduce me when I came back from a last walk on the beach, looking for shells and feeling downhearted about separating.

"You can't be serious. You were practically comatose last night!"

"Don't be a spoilsport," he teased, snapping the elastic on his little white shorts.

"No," I said. "I'm too worried about you."

With a smile and a wriggle of his hips, he slipped off his shorts and said, "It's not necrophilia yet, darling."

Against my better judgment, hormones took over and I slipped into bed beside him.

Chapter 3

New Year's Eve, 1981, was cold and clear in Boston. Mark and I arrived back at the apartment on Bay State Road within an hour of each other. I had just come back from spending Christmas week with my family in Omaha, and Mark had been in Florida working. My roommate, Ed, was visiting friends in Maine for the weekend, so we had the place to ourselves. I noticed with some amusement that Mark and I had unpacked, settled in, and bought groceries instead of immediately getting romantic. It was late in the afternoon by then and already getting dark.

"Do you think the bloom is off the rose?" I asked with a smile.

"Why?"

"We didn't jump into bed as soon as we saw each other."

"Oh." Mark had been headed to the kitchen to start a beef stew for dinner, but detoured back into the bedroom where I was sitting at my desk. He massaged my shoulders for a minute and asked, "Am I neglecting you?"

"No, silly goose, I'm teasing. I'm just noticing that we're getting more settled. You have clothes here now, and books. Your duffel bag is unpacked and stowed in the basement. This is beginning to look like a relationship." I reached for his hands on my shoulders. "That feels very good."

"The massage or the relationship?"

"Both," I said. "Now go make my special dinner." It was, after all, our first New Year's Eve together. He gave my shoulders a final squeeze and went into the kitchen.

We sat in front of the fire, eating bowls of stew and crusty French bread and ice cream. We had been apart for several weeks and had a lot to catch up on. He was feeling good about his time in Florida. He had lined up a few boat-moving jobs, and he enjoyed staying with his friend John Batson.

"However," he said, "my heart is with you. Missing you is actually painful."

"You sound surprised. Haven't you ever missed anyone before?"

"Yes," he replied, "but not in this way, this kind of achy feeling. I feel foolish talking about it."

"What's foolish about loving someone?"

"It's hard feeling so open. I've avoided any kind of commitment for a long time."

I watched his face in the firelight. I thought of a conversation I'd had with my mother only the morning before, sitting at the breakfast table in Omaha. We were talking about Mark and me, about what she termed "your homosexual relationship," and she kept cautioning me to go slowly.

I told Mark, "My mother thinks I move too fast in relationships, that I fall in love too easily, then feel trapped."

"Wasn't she supportive of us?"

"It's really about me. She believes I have a problem with commitment. She's said it so often I wonder if it's the truth or if it's become a self-fulfilling prophecy."

"But you've had all kinds of relationships. And you were with Frank for four years. What does she want?"

"Her baseline is her marriage. They're going on fifty years. There's never been a divorce in my family or in the extended family. People get married and stick it out, whether they're happy or not." I started stacking the dishes on the table, preparing to move toward the kitchen. "She said we've spent all of our time in romantic places and don't know the nitty-gritty of everyday life, the boredom of it."

Mark was sitting up straight now, no longer in the soft and vulnerable place of a few moments earlier. "Well, that's why we're here, isn't it? We want to find that out. It's risky, for both of us. How about being optimistic?"

I laughed as I leaned over to kiss him. "I always look on the bright side."

We moved to clear the table and load the dishwasher, realizing with a start that it was 11:30 and the new year would soon be upon us. Grabbing coats and scarves and gloves, we headed for the Harvard Bridge on Massachusetts Avenue, only a few blocks away, and arrived in time to watch the fireworks over the harbor. We opened a split of champagne and drank from the bottle, kissing as the rockets exploded over our heads, laughing at the noise and the exhilaration of being outdoors so late. When things quieted down, Mark surprised me by pulling a harmonica from his coat pocket and playing "Auld Lang Syne." The lights of downtown shone brightly against the black night sky and the wind was cold. I was acutely aware of the moment, a new year, and a great adventure unfolding.

*

The weeks flew by. My work at the office was stable, and Mark seemed quite content to read, cook, and do projects. He had brought an amplifier up from New York and disassembled it, replacing parts and installing it into my existing stereo system. It was a great improvement and I was impressed with his skill and patience. Mark and Ed found several things to tackle together, repairing broken hinges on cupboards, replacing the works in the toilet tank. These small jobs connected them, and Ed seemed relaxed with Mark there. Since he traveled in his work, Ed was gone as much as he was home.

In late January we went to New York for the weekend. We had a theater date with Robert Kirkpatrick, called "Kirk," someone Mark had met at the baths a year or two earlier. After that brief encounter, they had developed a close friendship. Kirk was ten years younger than we were, tall and bright, and clearly devoted to Mark. The three of us went to see Caryl Churchill's play *Cloud 9*, which struck me as funny and irreverent until I unexpectedly started crying in a scene in which there was a painful relationship breakup.

After the show Kirk and Mark teased me for crying, Mark saying, "You mustn't give in to maudlin impulses." I felt thin-skinned with these sophisticated New Yorkers, who had a smart remark for everything. I then met Craig Jackson, Mark's former boyfriend, who had invited the three of us to his apartment for a late light supper after the theater. He was handsome and engaging, an interior designer with a spectacular apartment filled with artfully arranged boughs of flowering cherry and tiny vases of paperwhite narcissus. There were oversize pieces of abstract art on the walls. Feeling vulnerable from the play and completely outclassed, I was quiet until Craig took me into the kitchen and, in the course of conversation, told me he had been born and raised in Omaha. He also was Irish Catholic, and he had attended elementary school in St. Margaret Mary's parish, where my brother Tom was the pastor. We marveled that Mark could have found two boyfriends who came from Omaha. By the time we rejoined Mark and Kirk in the dining room, we were chatting like old friends, and Mark raised his eyebrows.

"Have you two been talking about me out there?" he asked.

"No, darling," Craig said, "we were discussing the night life in Omaha. We tricked with some of the same people!"

Kirk jumped in. "You dogs! Does everyone leave Omaha right out of high school or college?"

"They do if they're gay," Craig responded. "And speaking of dogs, who is the one man in the room that everyone else had sex with on the first date?"

"I wouldn't call meeting someone at the baths a date, Craig," Kirk replied. "But Mark did invite me back to his apartment afterward."

We ate pecan waffles and drank two bottles of champagne without a single pause in conversation. Mark seemed very happy, if a trifle embarrassed to be the center of attention.

As we walked back to his building, I asked Mark why the relationship with Craig had lasted only six months. He said, "We were interested in different things."

"How so?"

"We wanted to spend our free time in different ways. Craig's work calls for a lot of formal events and entertaining. I'm drawn to a quieter life."

"Was the breakup hard for you?" I asked.

"No. I could see it coming." Then he said with some pride, "We never fought, never had a single unpleasant conversation."

I didn't think of that as something to aspire to, but I let it pass.

In March we had another New York visit, this time staying in #901, Mark's original unit in the McIntyre Building. He shared the co-op with a friend, a magazine photographer who sometimes used the space for fashion shoots. It was stunning, only about 900 square feet but with ceilings twelve feet high. Mark's was the only floor that had enormous arched windows on three sides. The light was remarkable, as were the views, looking north, west, and south. In the rear of the unit was a small galley kitchen with upscale appliances and the entrance to a loft space, which contained both a small seating area and, on a slightly higher level, a platform bed. I loved the light and openness. I would lie on the sofa, my head in his lap, and daydream. I was, on this late winter afternoon, dozing.

"I have a bit of a plan," he said.

I murmured, "Uh huh," and he continued.

"You know the space down the hall on the left? The storage room?"

"Uh huh."

"And the laundry room next to it?"

I sat up and rubbed my eyes sleepily. "Yes, dear. Where is this going?"

"I want to turn it into a *pied-à-terre* for us."

I was instantly alert. "Tell me more."

He explained that the storage unit was only ten by fifteen feet, but it had a high ceiling and a long window looking north. "We could put in a loft bed like we have here, and a fabulous, tiny kitchen. And . . ." He paused for effect. "We could convert the laundry room back into a bathroom."

He was glowing, and I could barely breathe from excitement. Our own place in New York! Then my heart fell. "But where would all that money come from?"

"I think the work could be done for ten to fifteen thousand dollars. My parents are worried about me not having my own space in the city, and they're considering giving me the money."

"I can't believe it. How long have you been sitting on this?"

"Long enough to believe that it's possible. I'll bet Craig Jackson would do the interior, too." I had never seen him so animated. *This is what he looks like,* I thought, *when he's not preoccupied about money or sailing or where our relationship is headed.*

Later that evening, after a romantic dinner in a Japanese restaurant, we continued to talk about having our own small space in the building, until Mark fell asleep. Restless, I crept down the three steps from the bed to the sofa and sat looking downtown. The city, as always, was brilliant with light, and I marveled at the course that had led me from my loneliness in Boston, to meeting Mark on Fire Island, to sitting here in the dark with New York City spread out at my feet. A little of my lifelong anxiety arose: *What's the catch here, where's the trick?* But those feelings faded as I burrowed back under the blankets with Mark and drifted off to sleep.

*

The end of March in Boston was bitterly cold, and Mark was restless, wanting to be in Florida, but not wanting to be too far from me or from his "business" in New York, which from my perspective looked like a lot of worrying without much change in his financial circumstances. He was preoccupied and often remote. I was busier than usual, having started to lead a training seminar that required extra attention. Our styles in dealing with stress were so different: I verbalized, he withdrew. Most of the time this was not a problem, but when our needs conflicted, tension rose.

We had our first fight, which included a little door slamming on my part, over my weight. I had weighed 185 when I met him and had gained 10 pounds since then. Some of the weight was attributable to winter and not being able to run as much or as far; some from seven months of eating his cooking, which, being mostly French, involved an abundance of butter, cream, eggs, and pastry. He began to tease me about "losing my figure," then to suggest that I eat smaller portions, or go for a run on days when the weather was more moderate. The first time or two I took it in stride, but I could feel myself pulling away. Really, was 10 pounds all that important? I knew I'd lose it when the weather got nice again. Who did he think he was, to feign solicitousness when what he was really feeling was disgust? I was working up quite a head of steam prior to our friend Deborah Haynor coming over to dinner one Saturday night with her girlfriend, Wendy.

Mark and I had been distant most of the day. He shopped for groceries and prepared the meal while I managed to get in a workout at the gym and did a pile of paperwork. He was making *boeuf en croûte*, a very elegant but time-consuming preparation of filet baked in pastry. I had looked forward to seeing Deborah and Wendy for weeks, but that afternoon I'd fallen into a black hole when Mark said, "Tut tut tut!" as I opened a package of Milano cookies. Door slam number one. I left to run some errands and came back feeling moderately better, put on the disco version of *Evita* as I prepared to shave and take a shower before the guests arrived. Mark came into the bedroom from the kitchen and said parentally, "Do you think we could listen to some grown-up music for dinner, like Cole Porter?" I said, "Put on whatever you want." Door slam number two. We barely spoke before the guests arrived.

Deborah is a very close friend, funny and openhearted, and my bad mood dissipated while the women were there. When we had a moment alone in the kitchen, Mark asked, "Can we declare a truce until we're alone?" I nodded. We managed to be cordial with each other and the evening went smoothly. But after they left I stayed in the kitchen to clean up and he went to bed. By the time I finished the dishes, Mark was asleep and I hugged my side of the bed, his "tut tut tut" repeating endlessly in my head.

The next morning he continued to tinker with the amplifier while I made breakfast and set the table in front of the bay window. I made a fire and then called him in to eat. Once we were seated, we talked quietly, seeking to find our way back to each other. He said he'd liked Deborah and Wendy very much, that I had such nice friends. I said that dinner was, as always, sublime. We were quiet for a few moments, then he cleared his throat.

"Is one allowed to discuss difficulties at breakfast?" he asked wryly. I shrugged. He said he had hated my withdrawal for the past twenty-four hours, didn't know what he'd done wrong but wanted to sort it out. I could feel my anger resurfacing, but he was so hesitant that I felt a glimmer of affection instead.

"I hate your remarks about my weight gain, which only make me anxious and angry and want to eat more. I miss the nice things you used to say. I know the first rush of romance is over, but you seem mostly either quiet or critical where I'm concerned."

He held my gaze for a long moment. "I'm sorry I've been razor-tongued," he said. "I'm not good at dealing with feelings. I want you to be happy with me. And I hate when you make me invisible."

I told him that I had a hard time dealing with anger myself, that when I felt shamed I withdrew into a black space inside and felt ugly and powerless. As I spoke, I felt relief looking at his face and seeing his concern. It was a challenge to forgive completely, but the tension began to dissolve.

He asked if we could try to be more direct, said that it wasn't easy for him either. "Please, tell me when I hurt you." Then added, "But not by slamming doors!"

That same Sunday morning, Mark's friend Kirk called from New York to suggest that we take a sailing trip together. We telephoned John Batson in Fort Lauderdale, who agreed it was a great idea, and the four of us committed to a week in May. We would "bare boat," which meant that Mark would be the captain and we would crew. No outsiders, no strangers. It sounded like heaven. Mark and Kirk located a company in the U.S. Virgin Islands and arranged for a Saturday-to-Saturday rental out of St. Thomas. Mark would be the responsible party in terms of the contract, and he would also prepare most of the food ahead of time, heat-seal it, and pack it in dry ice for the trip. The provisions, like rack of lamb, would be considerably nicer than the hard tack and beef jerky eaten in days of old. In exchange for this work, John, Kirk, and I would be responsible for the cost of the boat rental.

Mark left for ten days of work in Florida and I went through my usual withdrawal: moody, restless, and hungry all the time. Gone were the days of not being able to eat when he left. Now I wanted to eat night and day. Worse, I had to face the reality of the upcoming sailing trip and learn how to swim. All that water! I had promised Mark I would take lessons, and I signed up for a course at UMass Boston, taught by a coach who specialized in working with "fearful adults." I arrived for the first class weighing 199 pounds and numb with fear.

Etienne St. Onge, whom we were invited to call "Coach," turned out to be a terrific guy, a native of Trinidad with a musical accent and a warm, reassuring manner. On the first morning, the ten of us students sat in a circle on the floor by the pool, wrapped in our towels, and shared our histories of dealing with water. I told of my experience of being thrown off a dock by classmates at a public swimming pool at age twelve and nearly drowning before a lifeguard fished me out. I gagged for long minutes on the beach, then fell asleep for two hours in the noontime sun, getting a second-degree sunburn before it occurred to my classmates to wake me up. My fellow swimming students shared their stories as well, and the coach murmured sympathetically before having us splash around in the shallow end of the enormous pool that the university maintains. Day one: check.

Over the course of ten weeks, I never missed a session, despite feeling sick to my stomach every Monday morning before driving to the pool. We first learned to float, which came easily to me, then we learned the crawl. I could not get the hang of it and panicked as soon as I knew I had reached the deep water, but Coach seemed always to be there, slipping a hand of support under my stomach or my legs, talking quietly as I sputtered and flailed. Mark was inordinately proud of me, praised my progress and telephoned on the Mondays he was not in town to see how the class had gone.

By the fifth week, half the class had dropped out. I mastered swimming on my back much more quickly than on my stomach, and finally could do a passable breaststroke by class nine, though I never really learned that graceful "turn the face, breathe, turn the face, breathe." To graduate, we had to swim the entire length of the pool, first on our bellies, then on our backs. Only four of us completed the task, and I felt like I'd won an Olympic gold medal when Coach gave me my certificate and a hug.

Midway through the weeks of lessons, friends who lived in a one-bedroom apartment four doors down the street announced that they were moving to New York and asked if we wanted their apartment. Since Ed was planning to move into a place of his own, Mark and I were faced with a major decision. Their one-bedroom was on the top floor of a four-story brownstone and had a better view than we had where we were, and the rent was cheaper because the space was smaller. Mark had once told me that he didn't believe lovers should live together, that separateness provided more mystery and the couple would become bored with each other less quickly. All I could think of was my mother, who would have said, "That's so shallow, people need to become real to each other, go through everything together." There was truth in each position, but in my heart I longed for commitment. After wrestling with the idea for a few days, Mark assented. He believed that the resolution to his court case was imminent. I offered to pay the rent until he had more income, and he agreed to pay the utilities. We were set.

My fears were more about the emotional commitment. As neutral as Ed's presence was, having a third person around at least some of the time titrated my connection to Mark. I had not forgotten how trapped I had felt in the last half of my relationship with my former partner in New Jersey, but I held out hope for the success of romantic love. And where better to explore that love than in a tiny aerie high above the Charles River? We agreed: one year, we'd commit for one year. It wasn't the way our parents had done it, "till death do us part," but one year felt like an important step nonetheless.

Chapter 4

Finally, it was spring. One Sunday morning in April, Mark and I drove from Manhattan to Queens. I was going to meet his parents, something I had been lobbying for since the preceding fall. We had been very involved for nearly eight months, and I felt like it was more than time. He frequently answered the phone in the apartment when my mother called and had taken to "visiting" with her, which mostly meant listening rather than talking. (My mother once said to me, "He's very bright, dear. But so quiet!") Mark, on the other hand, almost always called his parents rather than vice versa, so I lacked that casual connection with them.

Mark's father had worked at a car dealership as a clerk, and his mother had been a school secretary. They were in their mid-seventies by this time and had been retired for several years. His father took up the piano at seventy-two (Mark learned as a child and played beautifully). His mother was a rabid, left-leaning Democrat. They both loved to read. My parents also had working-class backgrounds (Dad an assistant superintendent in a milk-bottling plant, Mom a housewife) and also loved to read. But they were Catholics first and Democrats second. When I talked about my family, I felt relaxed and open. When Mark talked about his, I frequently sensed an underlying tension.

I asked, "What more should I know about your parents before I meet them?"

"Not much. My mother talks a lot. Dad is pleasant. You'll be fine."

"What do they know about me?"

"What do you mean?" he asked.

"I *mean*," I said, "what do they know about our relationship?"

"That we're friends and that I stay with you in Boston from time to time."

"C'mon, Mark! Do they know the *nature* of our relationship?"

He looked at me sideways as he drove my car across the Brooklyn Bridge and navigated his way onto the Long Island Expressway. "You mean, do they know we fuck?"

"Don't be a pig. Do they know we're more than friends?"

"Maybe," he replied. "In my family we don't talk about such things. I was supposed to grow up and give them grandchildren like my brother, Bert, did."

"You're thirty-nine years old. Isn't it odd that you haven't brought a girl home yet?"

He continued driving, fiddling with the radio station, and changed to the inside lane on the Expressway. He said, "When I was in college and grad school, my mother would say, 'So? Have you met anyone?' And I'd say no. She'd say, 'So? When are you going to bring a girl home?' And I would shrug and change the subject. Finally, one day ten or twelve years ago, I was visiting them and Mom screamed at me, 'You're a homosexual, aren't you! I know you are. Just admit it!' I stood up and said, 'If you ever ask me that question again or ask me anything about my personal life, I'll never come back here.' And I left."

I was stunned. "What happened?" I asked.

"She never asked me again."

"And nothing has been said in the last ten or more years about it?"

"No. When I was seeing Craig, the four of us had dinner one night in the city, but nothing was said, and then he was out of my life."

"Sounds like she really took you seriously."

He smiled grimly. "I was serious." We were off the Expressway and onto Main Street, heading down to 122nd Avenue. My stomach was in knots. "Just relax," he said. "There won't be any scenes. They're just very . . . Jewish."

"OK," I said, putting on a bright smile. "My friends' mothers have always liked me. Maybe your mother will too." But I felt a sense of dread.

We arrived at the house, a half-house really, on a block with identical brick side-by-sides. The day had heated up and I was perspiring, regretting that I had worn a light blue polo shirt and hoping there wouldn't be sweat stains under the arms. We parked the car in the driveway and went up the steps to the front door, me carrying a bakery box of *rugelach* that I'd gone all the way uptown to Zabar's to buy. Mark's dad opened the door and hugged Mark, pulling him into the house, and then looked up at me.

"Well! Michael, is it? Mark says you originally come from Nebraska. They grow them tall there, huh?" He was about five feet three inches tall. I handed him the bakery box, and he took me by the arm and walked me into the living room. The shades were pulled partway down and there was an air conditioner humming in a high window in the adjacent dining area. Mark's mother rose from her rocker and came toward me. My eyes were adjusting to the dim light and I realized she was even smaller than Eddie, five feet tops. She also had severe osteoporosis, with what my mother called "a dowager's hump," so she had to tilt her head sharply back to make eye contact. Taking my right hand in both of hers, she looked up. "Michael," she said. "He didn't tell me you were a tree." I started laughing and knew we were going to be friends.

"Come in, darling," she said, still holding my hand. "Sit here on the sofa near me so that we can talk. I want so much to know you." She had very black hair, on the short side, combed back and sprayed to the density of Chinese lacquer. She wore harlequin-shaped glasses, black, with thick lenses. I hadn't seen a pair of those in decades. I asked to use the restroom before we sat down and was led to a tiny bathroom off the kitchen. When I came out and turned back into the dining room, I noticed that the table was set for five. As I moved to rejoin Mark and his parents in the living room, the doorbell rang.

"Mark, that will be Pearl," Ida said. Then to me, "My sister Pearl lives just on the next block and she's joining us for lunch." I remained standing, uncertain what to do. Mark opened the door and in came Pearl.

"Mark, darling!" She pulled him to her bosom, holding him tightly. She was two or three times the size of Ida and as blond as Ida was brunette, but with much bigger hair. She was slightly taller but seemed gigantic in comparison to Mark's petite parents. She wore a white sundress printed with bright flowers, white sandals, lots of makeup, and a little hat with a bit of veil and a tiny white rose on it. Her hearing, like Eddie's, was diminished. Suddenly the three older people were all talking at once and at top volume, a condition I came to consider normal whenever I was with them. Mark gave me a look and, *sotto voce*, said, "Welcome to my world."

I enjoyed myself enormously, although I found some of their behavior unnerving. Not only did they talk very loudly, they interrupted each other constantly, and everyone had an opinion on everything. A *strong* opinion. Ida put out a plate of nuts, dates, and dried apricots. Eddie insisted we have a cocktail before lunch. It was past noon by then and I would have loved to have a beer, but Eddie only drank Manhattans, and Ida only allowed him to have one when there was company. So in the spirit of fellowship Mark and I both had Manhattans. When I declined the maraschino cherry, Eddie put it in anyway, declaring it wasn't a real Manhattan without one.

In decent weather, lunch with company apparently always involved Eddie making burgers on the grill. He had an entire ritual involving getting the grill and utensils from the garage and the charcoal from the pantry ("It gets damp in the garage"). He then donned a white butcher's apron meant for someone significantly taller than he, so that the ties went around his buttocks and the hem to the tops of his shoes. Soon the burgers were sizzling. Mark and I sat on a bench in the yard, and father and son talked about brother Bert's two boys and how Bert's law practice was doing. Eddie repeatedly called Mark "Junior," which I found touching. Soon we were carrying a platter of hamburgers and toasted buns into the dining room, where Ida and Pearl had brought out sliced cheese, potato salad, coleslaw, pickles, and condiments.

Eddie sat at the head of the table, Ida at the opposite end. Mark and I were on one side, Pearl on the other. The older people, seated at a slightly greater distance from each other than they had been in the living room, spoke even more loudly than before. There was much talk of politics, both national and local. Both parents had been in unions before their retirements, and Ida was still active in hers. Pearl had not worked outside the home, but her late husband, Sam, had belonged to the plumbers and pipefitters union. This was a union family. I gained status in the group when I revealed that I had put myself through college and graduate school by working in the bottling plant where my dad worked and had been a Teamster for six years.

I was completely taken by how intelligent they were. They could back up their arguments with facts, and they challenged each other with authority. Mark, however, participated little, except to disagree with his mother. They clashed heatedly in their opinions on threatened strikes in the city schools, but Ida backed off, seeming to want his approval more than she wanted to win. I was seated near the upright piano, which was covered with framed photographs, and I reached for a picture of Mark, hoping to ease the underlying tension. In the photo he was about four years old, leaning his chin on his crossed arms, which were resting on a tabletop. He was adorable, a heartbreaker even then, grinning impishly. His mother had placed a second, much smaller photo into a corner of the frame, this one of an infant who bore no resemblance to Mark. Before I could ask, Ida said, "He was not a pretty baby at all, but he was a nice-looking little boy." Mark took the photo from my hand and looked closely.

"Mom, this homely baby isn't me. It's a girl!" He grasped the edge of the photo from the frame and removed it, examining the back. "It's Uncle Nate's daughter Sylvia. Maybe she was the daughter you always wanted!" His annoyance was clear. He handed the framed photo of himself back to me, leaving Sylvia stranded on the table, and we resumed eating our lunch as the conversation moved on to other topics.

One of my favorite moments occurred when I asked Ida to pass me the mustard, which I lathered onto my hamburger. When I set the jar down, Pearl asked me to hand it to her. Ida said, "What do you want mustard for, you don't use mustard."

Pearl held out her hand and replied, "Just pass me the mustard, Michael. I like mustard."

Ida pulled the jar out of Pearl's reach, and said, "You only want it because Michael used it. You don't even like mustard!" Then she slammed the mustard down on the table in front of Pearl.

Unfazed, Pearl said, "Thank you, darling." And to me she said, "Don't you love Gulden's?"

I was openmouthed by this point. Mark nudged me and we changed the subject to books, which I hoped would be a more neutral topic. I learned over time that Ida and Pearl were utterly devoted to each other but had been fighting like this since they were small children. Ida, two years Pearl's senior, felt superior in all ways. Pearl held a different view.

Eddie told me he had taken up the piano since his retirement and was "catching up to Mark in skills." His teacher, Hetty Levine, had also been Mark's teacher, so father and son discussed Eddie's current lesson and what he was learning. Ida suggested that Eddie play something for us while she and Pearl cleared the table and made coffee. Mark and I sat on the sofa and Eddie played "Edelweiss." It was painful to my ear, but Mark lavished him with praise, saying, "It used to be that I was called upon to play for company. You're the star now, Dad." Eddie squirmed with pleasure. It was easy to imagine Mark at six or seven, performing at the same piano. Eddie played "Edelweiss" once again before Ida and Pearl served the coffee and *rugelach* and we returned to the table.

After dessert and coffee Eddie initiated a conversation with Mark about what was happening in the McIntyre Building. Mark was noticeably vague about details on the legal problems, especially concerning his tenant, but he brightened when Eddie raised the possibility of funding the tiny apartment for Mark on the 9th floor. Ida jumped in.

"We want that for you, Mark. You need your own place down there."

Eddie said, "Even a little place in the building would be better than none. I still don't understand why you're renting all three of your units."

"Dad, you know why. That's how I'm supporting my shift to another career."

Eddie's jaw set. "What kind of a *career* is sailing? Why don't you just teach again, or finish your dissertation and get your doctorate? There's a lot you could do with a Ph.D. in Arabic studies. You were so close, Junior. "

Mark kept his voice even. "Dad, we've been over this territory a million times. I don't want to teach junior high kids anymore. And to finish the dissertation I would have had to go back to Tunisia to complete my fieldwork. I don't want to live outside the country any more. I'm almost forty. I want a different life from what I wanted in my twenties."

"Your twenties! How about your sixties!" Eddie's voice rose. "How will you support yourself sailing around the Caribbean in your sixties!"

Mark stood up and looked at me. "I need to use the bathroom before we go," he said, and left the room. Ida and Pearl were both looking miserable, Ida twisting her napkin in her lap.

Pearl tried to salvage the situation, jumping in to tell me how her husband Sam had installed the bathroom in Mark's co-op and what a headache it had been. But the tension remained in the room. When Mark came back, we made small talk for a few minutes and then said our goodbyes.

We were quiet as we left the neighborhood. Mark was obviously upset and I was grateful to be surrounded not by conversation but by the sounds of the traffic. Finally, on the expressway heading toward the Whitestone Bridge, I said, imitating his mother's voice, "So? How do you think it went?"

He laughed, visibly relaxing, and said, "You first. What did you think?"

"I had a great time, despite the dramatic finale. I never thought I'd see the day that I would call my family restrained, but in comparison to yours, oy! I love their grittiness, how bright they are, that they read and talk about what they read. And I adore Pearl."

"Me too," he said. "Pearl was my salvation growing up. Mom and Dad always had expectations, wanted perfect grades, felt I should be the best in everything I did. Pearl lived a block away, and she and Sam had no children. I spent a lot of time over there and they thought I was ... not perfect, but fine, just the way I was."

"What was your dad so upset about? Surely the topic of your unfinished dissertation is old news."

He expelled a long breath. "Here's the short version." He explained that his parents had wanted to help him with his investment in the McIntyre Building. He initially agreed, but then his father had an opinion on everything: how the investors divided the spaces, how the negotiations were handled. One night Mark blew up at him and said, "I don't want your help. This is my project, not yours!" And he floated the money he needed through the teachers' credit union and from friends. His parents were devastated.

"One more thing," he said. "We've run into many more problems with the conversion of the building than we anticipated, and my funds are very tight. Mom and Dad want me to return to teaching and I can't stomach the idea." He added plaintively, "I just want to sail!"

Despite the noise of the traffic on the expressway, the car suddenly felt very quiet. It was rare to see Mark flooded by feelings. I bided my time, then put my hand on his shoulder as he stared straight ahead.

"Well," I said, "I'm really happy I met them. I see the challenges, as you will see with my parents. But I know you better now. And that Pearl is a pip!"

He smiled and said softly, "Thank God for Pearl."

Chapter 5

We arrived in St. Thomas early on a Saturday afternoon. Though it was only mid-May, it was already very hot, a shock to those of us still recovering from the winter in New England. Mark and I had taken a 6:00 a.m. flight to San Juan, where we met our boat mates, Kirk and John, then took a puddle jumper to St. Thomas. I had expected it to be lush, like Puerto Rico, but much of the island was rocky, more desert than jungle. The small airport was crowded with both locals and tourists, the latter identifiable by their expensive clothing and dazed expressions. The space was noisy and felt pleasantly foreign.

Mark took charge and commandeered a taxi. He had been to St. Thomas many times and knew exactly what needed to be done. After we piled our luggage and the Styrofoam containers of food into the boot of the jeep, the driver took us out to the marina and deposited us near the dock. Mark and Kirk then went on with the taxi driver to a market to buy fresh fish, milk, eggs, and produce. John and I stayed with the gear, moving everything via the long wooden walkways to our rental boat, the *Dancing Bear*.

She was a beauty, forty-three feet long, a heavy two-masted vessel with a wishbone rig that allowed the sails to be trimmed to suit the wind. Her decks gleamed white in the bright sun. Everything was clean and polished, including the wheel. Below-decks there was a galley, a crawl space for the engine, two berths forward where John and Kirk would sleep, and a tiny aft cabin where Mark and I bunked. I found the arrangement of space below claustrophobic, but I figured it would be manageable, given that presumably we would spend every waking hour on deck.

After stowing all our gear and the many bags of groceries Mark and Kirk brought back, we had a quick lunch and met with the leasing agent. Mark demonstrated his knowledge of handling the boat and paid the balance of our deposit. His signature on the contract made him completely accountable for the yacht and its passengers. Since both John and Kirk had some experience with sailing, they acted as crew. Knowing practically nothing about the tasks at hand,

I tried to stay out of the way as we cast off from the dock and threaded our way through the marina. At last we headed out into the great blue sea.

We sailed for at least several hours every day, rain or shine, moving from one area to another: Trunk Bay, Robbins Bay, Great Bay. The vistas were even more beautiful than I had imagined. The Caribbean is filled with tiny islands, some just large outcroppings of rock, scrubby, mountainous, and dry. Brown-green shapes rose in the distance as we flew along in our boat. Mark used the engine as little as possible, except when it rained or there was no wind. The sun was fierce, especially in the late afternoon, and we kept the canopy up much of the time. We rarely wore more than our swimming trunks from one end of the day to the other. It felt sybaritic to me, so much flooding my senses: heat, light, the air on my skin as the boat cut through the waves.

Each day began with checking the anchor, which Mark did several times during the night as well, to make sure it had held and that we had not drifted. He then spent time poring over the charts to see where we might head and how the weather looked. We ate breakfast and did chores, then checked the lines, the supplies, and the engine before leaping off the boat into the sea.

At first, the others did the leaping, and I would climb down the ladder with my life vest on and reach out for a hand before I would let go of the ladder. I loved the feeling of the water, the color and all the life in it, but I still carried years of phobia about drowning. Both Mark and John stood in for Coach St. Onge, encouraging me, supporting my body when I would sputter. Snorkeling did not come naturally to me, despite my daily attempts to master it. John had a fit when he saw the fins Mark had encouraged me to buy, big heavy rubber things that were meant for scuba diving. Mark, being thrifty, said he hoped we would scuba one day; John, being pragmatic, knew that I would learn to snorkel a lot faster wearing the lightweight blue silicone fins he had, and he insisted I use them throughout the trip. No matter where we swam or snorkeled, I was hyperconscious of where I was, and for the first few days I was relieved when the adventure was over and I could clamber back up the ladder to the relative safety of the boat.

Kirk had more experience than John with sailboats, so he assumed the role of first mate, which meant, among other things, that he helped with securing the anchor. At the end of each sail, as we prepared to settle into a new bay for the night, Mark would recheck the charts and then station Kirk at the helm while Mark lowered the anchor from the front. Kirk had to move the boat very slowly forward and back until Mark felt the pull that indicated the anchor had set. This was a hit-or-miss proposition, as we soon found out. Mark would call out "forward" or "reverse," and Kirk would respond with the boat in gear, then Mark would yell, "No, no, Kirk, too far! Stop!" When Mark did this the second time, Kirk lost it.

"Goddamn it, Mark, stop yelling at me! You said 'Forward'!"

"I know I said forward, but I only meant a little bit forward, not ten feet."

"Well, how the fuck am I supposed to know how much forward you mean? Might you be a little more *precise*?"

John told me the first afternoon that our job during anchoring was "to look pretty and stay out of the way." He also dubbed this daily event "the anchor snit." John and I were both averse to conflict, so after that first day we would go down to the galley and begin cocktail hour during the anchor snit, no matter the hour, emerging onto the deck with a large pitcher of rum punch once the yelling had abated. There never seemed to be any bad feelings between Mark and Kirk, so everyone could move happily into the next phase, which lasted several hours.

We played music on the cassette player during cocktail hour, ranging from Ella Fitzgerald and Dinah Washington to Peter Allen and Bette Midler. Mark usually swam a bit, a break from being in charge, and then set about preparing meals, ably assisted by Kirk. They both loved fine food. Mark had purchased excellent cuts of meat in Boston and prepared vegetables and stews, which he had heat-sealed and frozen, and to which they added fresh produce. They also grilled the fish from the shopping expedition in St. Thomas. Our breakfasts and lunches were usually simple, but each dinner was an event. There was the occasional cooking snit when Mark made a preparation choice that Kirk disagreed with or vice versa. Nevertheless, dinner was generally my favorite time of day. The late afternoon and evening on a sailboat in good weather is as close to heaven as I imagine I will get in this life. Rum punch was plentiful, as well as wine with dinner, and the food was superb.

I announced one night at dinner, "You know what? This is male bonding! Drinking, farting, gross jokes, peeing off the side of the boat. I love it."

"Darling," Kirk said, "straight men would never put the effort into food that Uncle Mark and I have done." We had taken to calling each other "Uncle" for some reason that no one could remember.

"Then it's gay male bonding," I replied. "And straight men don't call each other 'darling,' Uncle Kirk."

"Not unless they're giving or receiving a blow job," John chimed in.

And so it went. John and I did all the cleanup, starting with dishes and ending with scrubbing the grill, which got a lot of use. Kirk and Mark would kick back and relax, Mark often dropping off to sleep in my lap when I'd sit down with them after KP duty. We'd watch the sunset fade, then clouds move across the face of the moon, which was waxing into fullness during our week on the water. Mark and I were both Cancerians, and I felt caught between moon and sea in a delightful way. The universe felt very large.

I had spent limited time with Kirk and John before this trip, and I discovered that they could not have been more different from each other. Kirk was high-strung, funny, and quick-witted, but prone to taking offense and flying off the handle. John had an ever-present grin, a silly sense of humor, and an easygoing nature. He exuded an effortless maleness that I found both disarming and attractive. Mark was the link to each of us, and there was a moment at dinner early on when Kirk and I realized, as we had at Craig Jackson's apartment, that we had each slept with Mark at the starting point of the relationship. After teasing Mark a bit about "flaunting his tail feathers," we agreed that most friendships we had with other gay men had begun as sexual encounters. The Stonewall riots in New York City in 1969 had galvanized gay men and lesbians to fight police oppression and to organize politically. By this time the four of us had all been involved in the movement for years and had a defiant attachment to sexual freedom.

As our captain and chef, Mark felt the weight of his responsibilities. He didn't sleep particularly well and was always ready to tuck in soon after dinner. Kirk would usually go below when Mark did, and their banter carried to the deck as they brushed their teeth. I wondered if Kirk had a crush on Mark. There was an emotional intimacy to their spats and their easy laughter. The thought made me more curious than jealous. In some subtle way we seemed to have paired off, Kirk with Mark and John with me. After John and I finished cleaning up the dishes, we would lie on the upper deck, still in swimsuits, watch the stars, and drink more rum, Anejo this time, a Bacardi rum that tastes almost like liqueur. We would make jokes about the anchor snits or other amusing things that had happened during the day, and we also lay in companionable silence watching the night sky. My father and John's mother had both been severely alcoholic when we were growing up. In obvious and not-so-obvious ways, our lives had been shaped by this fact. We traded stories from childhood, both painful and funny. Until late in the evening we lay under the stars, brilliant in the Caribbean sky, sipping our Anejo. By midweek I had a terrific crush on John, the adolescent version, supported by his mischievous humor and unfailing thoughtfulness. And he was handsome as the devil.

This kind of time with other men was new for me. From the age of fourteen I had worked after school and on weekends to earn the money for my school clothes, books, and tuition to a Jesuit boys' high school. I had never been to camp, played team sports, or joined clubs. I had no idea how "normal" boys bonded in those situations. My sexual attraction to other boys isolated me in high school, and tortured me. While my nature is essentially social, the person I presented and the person I experienced myself to be were very different from each other. On the boat I felt a familiar discomfort in not knowing exactly how to belong. What were the rules in this "club"? I knew how to be in a couple with Mark in our ordinary life, but what about here, where our foursome was our whole world for a week, and in this club, in which the boys were gay and Mark had previously had sex with both John and Kirk?

For months I had anticipated that the trip would be very romantic with Mark, but the reality of four adults on a medium-sized sailboat meant that privacy was nonexistent. And Mark was preoccupied with all he had to manage. We had sex a few times early in the morning, but in a haphazard kind of way, more for relief than romance. We were good-humored and easy with each other but not emotionally intimate. I began to wonder if something had changed, if in the natural course of being together we were becoming "buddies."

I was also aware of the deep level of respect I felt for Mark's leadership. He was competent and tireless, managing the boat, getting us from one bay to another, supervising meals and cleanup. I could easily envision how this could be a career and a way of life for him, but where I might fit into that felt uncertain. Over the week I developed some skills in helping with the sails and taking my turn at the wheel. But the experience felt exotic, something to do occasionally and enjoy with friends but not what I could imagine as a lifestyle. This was something else to ponder: How could we possibly construct a future that worked for both of us?

Midweek we crossed from the American to the British Virgin Islands. That morning John, Kirk, and I left Mark aboard the *Dancing Bear* and rowed into Road Town, on Tortola, where we had our passports stamped and paid duty to the British. The Customs House was unprepossessing, an old building with bales of hay stacked against an outside wall and a goat wandering around the dusty yard. An officious woman named Miss Meyers told us in her clipped British accent that, before she could perform her duties, we were to "make a neat line in front of the kiosk," even though there were only the three of us and one man from another boat. We then walked around the area, enjoying the odd sensation of regaining our land legs. Kirk, who had visited the island as a child, surprised us by reciting verbatim the words on a plaque commemorating the visit of Her Majesty, Queen Elizabeth II, to Tortola in 1966.

By the time we rowed back out to the boat, clouds were gathering. Mark had used the time we were gone to reorganize the lines on the deck and straighten out the galley. He looked preoccupied and encouraged us to "step on it" as we came aboard.

"Tie the dinghy securely," he directed. "We're going to have some weather. I want you to make sure your things are secure below, and let's get out our raingear."

John, Kirk, and I said, "Aye aye, Captain!" in unison, which garnered a laugh from Mark, and we scurried below. We emerged back on deck promptly, all wearing ponchos, as the wind began to pick up. Mark took the helm as Kirk released the anchor and we headed into the wind toward Robbins Bay.

Soon the rain began pelting down, and Mark and Kirk frequently shifted sails to maximize using the wind. Once underway, we huddled under the canopy and discussed what we'd seen in Tortola, making jokes about Miss Meyers and her goat. Very slowly the wind died down, but the rain continued to fall in sheets. Mark increased the motor and we continued on our way for several hours. I made sandwiches and brought them on deck. Then Kirk went below to read, John to nap, so Mark and I had a little time to ourselves.

"Do you get nervous when it rains like this?" I asked. Mark seemed surprised at the question.

"Do I look nervous?" he asked.

"No, I guess not. You actually look very cute with your hood up. Sexy, even."

"Men!" he said, quoting a familiar line from my mother. "You're all alike. Are you nervous?"

"Not in the least. It's weird how secure I feel with you. It's as if, as long as you're in charge, I don't have a thing to worry about."

"Well, there's nothing to worry about today, that's for sure. Are you having a good time?"

"Absolutely. I've loved every day." While that was an oversimplification, this didn't seem like the time to open a discussion of my ruminations.

"That makes me very happy," Mark said. "I want you to learn to love the water like I do."

We motored for another hour or so. The rain eased up, and I called Kirk to come help as we entered Robbins Bay. By the time we anchored, the rainsqualls were intermittent.

It remained overcast and humid through the evening and night. We had to have dinner below, Mark heating a stew he had prepared in Boston, Kirk parceling out what we had left for salad. It was hot and sticky in the cabin and we all got cranky. John had the patience of a three-year-old and kept irritating Kirk, interrupting and teasing him. Finally John and I were able to clean up from dinner and return to the deck, sprayed with Cutter repellent to fend off the mosquitoes, and drank rum while Mark and Kirk read below. "Another night in paradise," John said as we clinked glasses and watched the moon try to poke through the clouds. The air was cooling off and I was aware of John's body lying next to mine on the upper deck. I wondered idly what he would do if I initiated something, but despite copious amounts of alcohol, common sense said, "Don't fuck up a good thing." Mark and I had an open sexual contract with several agreed-upon limits, which included not sleeping with each other's friends and not doing anything that would embarrass either of us. *Clear breach of contract here*, I thought to myself, and sighed. At least I was spared the risk of rejection.

The next morning was Friday, the beginning of our sixth and last full day on the boat. We all awoke early and were greeted by a luscious sunrise, layers of gray-blue changing to pink, then an intense orange-red. Dozens of pelicans were diving for fish. They looked prehistoric, long skinny birds with a huge wingspan. They would circle and circle, then—*splat!*—plummet into the water to snatch up a fish in their beaks. As they swallowed, they wiggled their tail feathers like hoochie-coochie dancers.

After a quick swim we ate breakfast and decided to head back to Peter Island, our favorite spot from the week. The wind was up and we had a spectacular sail. I'd been taking a turn at the helm for several days and felt thrilled on that day to be sitting in the captain's seat, wheel in hand, skimming across the water as the others adjusted sails or lay in the sun reading or dozing. I reflected on my last few years in Princeton before I moved to Boston, how constrained my life had felt. I never imagined that this feeling of freedom was possible.

Great Harbor and Peter Island did not disappoint. We anchored early in the afternoon and had plenty of time to read, chat quietly on the deck, and swim. By this point we were unselfconscious about being naked in front of each other, and John asked me to put suntan lotion on his back and the backs of his legs before he put his swimsuit on. It was briefly painful, a moment full of desire on my part, but in no time we were all jumping off the deck into the sea.

I never did fulfill my hope of snorkeling without the life jacket, but I did swim without it, both on my stomach and back. Even without masks we could see the remarkable variety of ocean life beneath us, brain and fan coral in fantastical shapes, fish darting in and out of their crevices. I jumped off the boat over and over and even made one aborted dive, which ended as a belly flop. It made no difference. We were all sublimely happy, and my mates praised my progress.

For our final dinner Mark grilled a butterflied leg of lamb, the last of the food prepared and frozen in Boston. It was perfectly tender and flavorful, as were the grilled potatoes. Kirk mixed up the last of the vegetables and we celebrated the feast with wine and music, Peter Allen belting out the lyrics to "I Could Have Been a Sailor" and Mark finally leading us in the old sea shanty, "Blow the Man Down," eliciting a few bawdy changes to the lyrics.

As the full moon rose, John, Kirk, and I each made a toast to our captain, who was tired and happy and only a little drunk. "Bravo!" we cried, pouring more rum, and we vowed to repeat the trip together in a year. We stayed up late, finally and with great care making our way down the ladder to brush our teeth and crawl into our berths for the last time. I curled around Mark, tucking him against my body. Just before I fell asleep I realized I had not had a last Anejo with John on the deck. I thought of having applied the suntan lotion to his legs and smiled to myself. At least that was something.

The following morning we were slow to move, feeling the effects of the heavy dinner and alcohol. We took turns working on deck and working below, cleaning and securing what remained and packing what went with us. Kirk pulled up the anchor for the last time and we headed toward St. Thomas, less than two hours away. Very little was said as we enjoyed a cool, clear morning, finally finding our way back into the marina.

Mark went to the office to complete the business of returning the boat, while the rest of us unloaded the gear and carried it up to the gate. Our original plan was to stay in St. Thomas overnight, then fly back to Puerto Rico for our flights home. But after looking at the dusty and crowded streets of Charlotte Amalie, Mark said, "I have an idea. Let's go to San Juan for the night." The crew cheered. Mark made a phone call to the airport and had us on a Prinair flight in slightly less than ninety minutes.

When we entered the airport in San Juan, we were buffeted by noise and stimulation. Other than our brief encounter with Miss Meyers, we had spoken to no one but each other for a week. Here at the busiest airport in the Caribbean, there were thousands of people, all seeming to talk at once. It felt like the Tower of Babel. We made our way to the baggage area, having no idea where we would go from there.

I called the Beach House from a pay phone, but they were completely booked, so we looked in a gay guide that Mark had brought and chose Arcos Blancos. It was also on Condado Beach, but the atmosphere was totally different. The two large white houses with arches were protected by a high security wall, which prevented passersby from seeing the swimming pool where gay men swam or sunbathed, many of them naked. There was a bar and restaurant, open to the breeze from the ocean on the beach side, that was very crowded and cruisy. After a week sailing, the whole scene was a shock to the system.

Mark and I showered together, luxuriating in the abundance of hot water, shampooing each other's hair to remove errant bits of sand and salt. He then lay down on the bed and instantly fell asleep. I was tempted to crawl in next to him but could hear the call of disco music, so I went out to the bar, where I found John and Kirk. They had conveniently positioned themselves so that they could see both the sunbathers and swimmers at the pool and also the muscle boys walking along the beach. A handsome Latin waiter appeared at my elbow with a piña colada and purred, "Welcome to Arcos Blancos."

In retrospect I would probably have benefitted more from the nap, but the three of us drank and laughed our way through a few pleasurable hours of cocktails and cruising. By the time Mark appeared, it was time to organize for dinner. We changed clothes and took a taxi to Old San Juan, where we savored our favorite moments from the trip over a great meal in the courtyard of Los Galanes. By the time we got back to Arcos Blancos I was exhausted. John and Kirk wanted to go dancing, and I made a weak effort to talk Mark into it, but I knew there was no chance. He graciously suggested that I "have a night out with the boys," but I followed him to our room and fell upon the bed, still fully clothed. He helped me undress and we talked briefly about seizing the moment, but this moment was clearly about sleep.

We made up for that lost opportunity early the next morning. I had worried that the buddy connection I'd felt with Mark on the boat was a transition in the relationship to something less intimate, that maybe my expectations for a deeper relationship were too high. But our lovemaking was intense and passionate, with all the elements of lust and affection that made sex with Mark unique. Once again I was flooded with love.

The four of us had a quick brunch on the patio at the guesthouse and headed back to the airport. The goodbyes to Kirk and John were good-humored and sweet. After just twenty-four hours back on land, I was an adult again, not a fifteen-year-old boy with a crush. When I hugged John goodbye, I felt simply affection. Mostly.

Mark's flight for Miami left an hour or so after mine to Boston, so he came with me to my gate. It felt odd to be without our crewmates, odder still to be in such a noisy and public place together. I wanted badly to hold his hand, but a kid on a bicycle had yelled, "Faggot motherfuckers!" as we'd loaded our luggage into the taxi at Arcos Blancos, and I felt self-conscious and mildly paranoid in this crowd of people.

"We seem always to be saying hello and goodbye," I said.

"We're still just getting to know each other," he replied. "I learned some new things about you on this trip."

"Like . . . ?"

"How silly you can be."

"I assume that's a reference to screaming and camping with John?" I felt myself tense a bit.

"Yes. And you don't need to ask: I love you more for it. It's a part of you that I don't seem to bring out."

I laughed. "Your sense of humor is more refined, I think."

"Either that, or I'm too tightly wound." There was a little silence, then he quoted Popeye: "I yam what I yam."

"You're a wonderful man, Mark Halberstadt. I really love you, and I'm beginning to trust the love, that it's got a life of its own. I still don't have the faintest idea how we're going to work this thing out, where we'll live or what we'll do, but I want it."

A woman's voice announced my flight over the loudspeaker and we stood up. I had teased him earlier about kissing me goodbye at the airport, never imagining he'd actually do it, but he leaned up and kissed me firmly on the lips.

"I want it too," he said.

Chapter 6

When I returned from the great boating adventure, I weighed under 190 for the first time in six months. I was full of energy and had even gotten the Irish version of a tan, more ruddy than brown. For eight days I'd been with three other men 24/7. Now even Ed was away, in the Midwest visiting his ailing grandmother, so I had the apartment to myself. Having gone from constant contact to none, I felt unanchored. However, the workweek was full, and I didn't hit a bump until Friday afternoon, when I had to meet with my attorney, Tom Patton, to finalize my financial separation from Frank Mahood.

I had left Frank more than three years earlier, and we'd tried a number of times to reconnect. We saw each other for the first time about six months after I moved out and immediately fell into each other's arms. The breakup had been painful for both of us, and I felt like a drowning man being offered a life preserver. But I was moving to Boston soon, so this reconnection was tempered by our knowledge that he was staying in Princeton and I was leaving. He helped me to pack and move, and we talked about having a long-distance relationship and seeing what happened.

However, I was moving to Boston to start a new life. I had grown sick of being a "country mouse." I wanted to live in a city and experience the full range of options available to gay men in 1979. In my fantasy, that meant a lot of sex. Frank and I had had a monogamous and loving but not passionate relationship, and at thirty-five I believed my shelf life was rapidly expiring. I desperately longed for "liberation," though I was uncertain how that translated into practice. Once in Boston I met a handsome man while volunteering at *Gay Community News* and started an on-again, off-again affair. It became clear that I couldn't fit Frank into this picture, even though he did everything he could to adapt. There was a period of negotiation, unsatisfying to all parties, and then a final, difficult telephone conversation. I said I needed time off to digest what was happening and figure out what I wanted. In a rare burst of bitterness, Frank said, "That's what you do, Mike. You chew people up, *digest* what you can, and spit out the rest. That's what you're doing now. You're spitting out what's left of me." And he hung up the phone. Within a week I received a letter from an attorney in Princeton, stating that the settlement of our common property would be conducted without Frank being involved and suggesting that I get an attorney. Enter Tom Patton, who had helped many gay couples resolve disputes. Here we sat, several meetings and many months later, with him holding a check for my share of the house.

"Have you read through the agreement thoroughly?" he asked.

I had barely scanned it but said, "Yes, it's fine."

"Do you have any questions, Mike?"

"Not unless you're a marital counselor as well as a lawyer."

He straightened the papers he was holding and set them neatly on the desk. "This is a difficult moment for everyone. It's hard for us to let go of whatever the struggle was about. But at least the legal struggle is over."

"You *are* a marital counselor!" I said. "I feel such a mishmash of feelings, Tom, angry and hurt. I felt guilty for the last two years because I knew the relationship wasn't working and I didn't have the guts to leave." Tom looked sympathetic, sitting in his chair behind the big desk, and simply nodded. I continued. "Frank and I met in the heat of what we liked to call 'the revolution,' post-Stonewall. We helped create a local gay organization and settled into a tiny house that we filled with things—rugs, pottery, artwork. At first I felt snug and safe. But after a couple of years I felt suffocated, all the routines and television programs and little dinner parties. Ugh. It felt like a parody of what I'd ridiculed in heterosexual marriages, believing they were complacent and empty." I took a long breath and he nodded again, which this time made me laugh. "You're a good listener, Tom. I'm almost done. Will you hear one more thing that you've probably heard before?"

"Of course."

"I'm feeling bad because of *how* it ended, not *that* it ended."

After a moment we stood and shook hands, traded checks, and I headed for home.

When I spoke to Mark that night, still mulling over the breakup with Frank, I hoped to talk about the stirrings of anxiety I felt in committing to another relationship. But he had a bad cold, was busy packing up his things in Florida, moving some to New York and some to Boston, where we would store them until we moved into our own apartment. He said he felt like he'd failed in his intention, had spent two years in Florida and had little to show for it. I said, "You've almost got your captain's license." He said, "Yes, and I almost had my Ph.D." Clearly it was not the time to talk about my fears. By early June, Mark had completed the move from Florida and was splitting his time between Boston and New York.

June was the rainiest month in memory, and cold. Mark was miserable whether in New York or Boston. His two favorite pastimes, riding his motorcycle and sailing, were seriously curbed by the weather. He had said at the outset of the month, "This is going to be the greatest summer ever!" We had a long car trip planned, which included a stop in Nebraska to visit my family, but this greatest summer was supposed to include sailing frequently on the Charles at Community Boating and riding his motorcycle between Boston and New York. The weather did not help our relationship. I was working hard and felt resentful coming home and listening to him complain about the rain. The scene was set for fight number two.

"What do you want me to do about it?" I asked.

"Well, you could at least sympathize. I thought you were supposed to be a therapist." He smirked. I pushed past him and went into the living room.

He said, "I was just kidding."

"Not funny." I surprised myself by bringing up something that had happened when our friends Deborah and Wendy were over for dinner a few nights earlier. Deborah had talked about having epileptic seizures in childhood and how fear of losing control had shaped her early life. I had teared up several times, as had she. Later that night, while we were doing dishes, Mark had referenced the conversation. I expected him to say something sympathetic but instead he said sarcastically, "Did you have teary sessions like that with Frank?" I was furious but let the remark pass.

I said, "Let me start with 'I was just kidding.' You frequently do things that feel hostile to me. The crack about 'you're supposed to be a therapist.' And how snide you were about Deborah and me welling up at dinner. You say hurtful things and then say, 'Oh, it was just a joke.' I grew up on that with my older brothers. I won't live with it."

He looked embarrassed. He said, "My family deals with feelings by screaming. I don't like tears, my own or anyone else's. They make me uncomfortable. I like things pleasant." After a moment, he said, "Craig also criticized me for being sarcastic. I think I'm being clever, but it cuts."

There didn't seem to be anything else to say. But the knots in my stomach began to dissolve. I became aware of the quiet in the room and the sound outside of the ever-present rain. "Peace?"

"Yes," he replied. After a moment he added, "I'm afraid that one of these days you're going to say, 'Go back to Florida where you belong.' I feel so unsettled here." I wondered what it cost him to be so honest about his fear.

"We're both unsettled right now, Mark. It's going to take time." I wanted to be more reassuring but was beginning to wonder myself if we were moving too quickly.

*

At the end of June, we spent the weekend in New York and I ran my first race, the Gay Pride Run in Central Park. It was a 10k and I was as nervous as a cat. Once we started, it took me several minutes to settle into a steady pace, then I felt carried along by the cheering crowd and the beautiful day. Someone called out, "You're looking good," and I flew over the finish line, Mark yelling, "You look great, honey, you look great." For someone who had avoided sports as a kid at all costs, it was a liberating moment.

My good spirits lasted until the Gay Pride March the next day when, in the midst of tens of thousands of people, I passed Frank Mahood not once but twice, and he cut me dead both times. I thought he simply didn't see me the first time, but the second time he had to completely turn away to avoid making eye contact. I hated myself for caring.

We spent the first week of July in Cherry Grove. Fire Island was as rainy as everywhere else, but our spirits were lifted by being with our own kind. On my birthday, Mark made me breakfast in bed: eggs, cantaloupe and strawberries, muffins and coffee. We had a space heater on high to keep the chill at bay. I opened my card from him, not "Happy Birthday" but a thank you card that said, "Thank you for letting me love you on your birthday." Then he made me close my eyes, and when he said "Now!" he was holding up an antique kilim rug from Afghanistan, a village rug with a complex and colorful design. I was thrilled. Knowing that he had purchased it years earlier when he lived abroad did not diminish the pleasure I took in the gift.

We talked endlessly about our future. He would ask if I thought I would like living in New York. "What if you started a practice there?" In the bungalow on Fire Island, the idea seemed possible, including living in one of his units once the lawsuit was resolved (in his favor, of course). We could begin by my keeping a practice three days a week in Boston but living in New York the other four and beginning to build a network. My friend Betts worked there and she said she'd be happy to refer clients to me, as would other therapists I knew in the city. I might even be able to share office space with her. But back home, I would remember that it took me two full years to support myself when I moved to Boston. What were we going to live on if I was part-time in Boston and he didn't have a job? How would I pay for housing in two places? When I queried Mark, he said optimistically, "I'll be fine by then. You can count on it." But I had doubts.

Toward the end of our week in Cherry Grove, Mark got a phone call that Boyd Morrow had died. Boyd was one of his partners in the McIntyre Building, in his forties, and had gotten sick in March. Mark had originally been told that Boyd had cancer, but friends later said that the doctors never did give a clear diagnosis. Bizarrely, Boyd was the second relatively young person Mark knew who had died in two months. I had never seen him so upset, his face completely drained of color. He said, "How could this be? He's my age. And David from the house in the Pines died suddenly too. It's so weird." I moved to sit next to him but he held up his hand to stop me.

"I need to pull myself together."

"OK," I said. "Will you let me hold you?"

"I just need a minute. Boyd was only forty-one. How could he die so quickly?"

I could think of nothing to say. The death of relatively young people was not in my experience. In a moment Mark said, "Will you sit with me now?" I moved to the small sofa and put my arm around his shoulders, which were rigid, letting him settle against me. He talked a bit about Boyd, how sensible he had been, how committed to buying the building and creating something that would serve them all financially. And now he was dead. A few days later, Mark headed into the city to join friends who were flying to Florida for Boyd's funeral, and I drove back to Boston alone.

I returned to work, as usual feeling supported by the routine and the sense of value that I drew from the sessions with my clients. Mark's birthday fell thirteen days after mine. To celebrate we went sailing on the Charles in the afternoon, a beautiful, cloudless sky and the heat a welcome relief. I still felt mildly anxious on the water but enjoyed witnessing Mark's ease with handling a boat, albeit a very small one, and we chatted quietly about our upcoming trip to the Midwest. Then Mark lapsed into silence, and I imagined he was thinking about Boyd. Earlier he had said that what he wanted for his birthday was a nice dinner out, so I had invited a friend of his from college, Arnie Kruger, as well as Kirk and Ed, to Icarus, where we had a delicious if subdued meal. Mark was still melancholy, and our efforts to rib him about turning forty fell flat.

*

I had never taken all of August off, as many therapists do, but this year I was taking three and a half weeks, beginning in mid-July. The weather remained fine as we prepared to drive cross-country, planning to end the trip in Colorado and then fly back from Denver. We made brief stops along the way, camping or staying with old friends, and finally reached Omaha to experience another round of "meeting the parents," but in reversed roles.

I had come out to my parents in 1974, and they dealt with my sexual orientation as best they could. Mom talked about it to my older siblings but not to her sisters. Dad didn't talk about it at all. Frank had been to Omaha with me once, so they'd already had the experience of my bringing home a boyfriend. They were very relaxed and welcoming to Mark, Mom talking a mile a minute and Dad smiling in the background. We were given the room I'd shared with my brother John, chastely sleeping in twin beds.

I drove Mark around Omaha, showing him my childhood home ("three bedrooms, eight kids, one bathroom!"), St. Bernard's Elementary School, Creighton Prep High School, the University of Nebraska at Omaha. I wondered what it looked like to a native New Yorker, but he was warm and responsive on the tour. We had a beer at the Diamond, a cheerless gay bar with a handful of men sitting on bar stools and country-western music on the jukebox. I became mute, flooded with unhappy memories of the years I felt isolated in Omaha as a young gay man. I had been terrified that I would be trapped there, buried alive. Mark put his arm around me and murmured, "Relax. You don't live here anymore." The muscles in my jaw eased as I leaned into his shoulder.

Mom made pancakes, bacon, and eggs on our last morning, and Mark managed to get Dad to talk about his career at Roberts Dairy. It was not a job that he was proud of, but his alcoholism had diminished his capacity to complete a college degree at night and find another path. Mark and Dad were sitting at the kitchen table chatting companionably, and Mom and I smiled at each other over the stove. "He's a keeper, sweetheart," she said. Later, when they stood on the front stoop waving to us as we pulled away, Mark murmured, "You really are lucky to have them."

The drive to Colorado went by without incident. We finally arrived in the town of Snowmass, where I took part in a professional conference. Mark spent his days reading and hiking while I attended meetings. There was partying every night and we got very little sleep. Betts was there as well, and her husband, Gerry, arrived as the conference ended. The four of us drove to the H Bar G Ranch, which is set on the lip of a deep, oval-shaped valley. It felt like we were sitting just inside the rim of a large gravy boat, though in this case the contents were evergreens, quaking aspens, and green fields dotted with roan horses and Holstein cattle. Below us, at the far side of the valley, lay the town of Estes Park.

We came to the H Bar G because Mark had done his Peace Corps training here in the 1960s. The place was filled with good memories for him and as he showed us around and reminisced about the months he had spent there and the friends he had made, I was reminded of his energy when we were sailing with John and Kirk. This was a place where he had felt competent and happy, where he learned the skills that helped him to succeed teaching English for three years in a mountain village in Tunisia. I felt a pang, wishing that there were something in his life in Boston and New York that could reconnect him to his self-esteem.

We spent four nights on the ranch, hiking every day, horseback riding, and picnicking. On our last day we went rafting on the Colorado River, one of the sweetest and most joyful memories I have. The day was hot and sunny. There were four rafts with eight people each, all wearing life jackets, and we initiated spirited water fights with the people in the other rafts. At two different points we slid off the side of our boat into the icy cold river. Betts yelled for us to float on our backs and hold hands, forming a circle like spokes on a wheel, and we were carried by the current, turning in lazy circles as we looked skyward at the mountains surrounding us. That night at dinner we agreed that it was "the best ever," not only the rafting but the vacation in general, and we toasted to many more vacations together. Mark and I sat on the porch of the cabin before going to bed, the sky loaded with stars, and counted our blessings.

I took his hand. "You seem so alive and open here."

"Everything I love is here: you, good friends, being in nature. I miss my Peace Corps buddies and wish I'd gone to more reunions, but my memories are good ones."

"Didn't the Peace Corps offer you a job when you came back?"

"Yes," he replied, fiddling with a stick that was lying on the porch. "I could have worked in Washington, or even come back here to train new recruits, but grad school was calling. Mom and Dad were pushing me to get a doctorate. I loved the Peace Corps, though, the promise of making a difference."

"The road not taken."

"Exactly. I had no idea what I would do with a Ph.D. It was hard to imagine being an academic. At Ann Arbor I was itchy to get back to New York, but I wasn't clear what I wanted to do. I began teaching junior high in the city as a way to support myself, and the years passed. And passed."

I felt the weight of his choices bearing down on him. Hoping to comfort him, I said, "So you have a new dream now, sailing the world in a wooden boat."

"With you," he said. "You're an important part of that dream."

"I have that dream as well, a dream of a shared life. But sometimes it looks like a long way from where we sit to where we hope to land."

I put my arm around his shoulders as we took a last look at the amazing sky, the Big Dipper right over our heads, and crept back into the cabin and into our single bunk. The following morning we all departed from Denver Airport, me to Boston and the others to New York. I had to get back to work, and our move to the new space was only fifteen days away.

I had done as much packing as possible before the trip, but the enormity of the move hit me when I got home. Anxiety permeated my days. I was full of fears and doubts about the choice to move, though I tried valiantly to remain upbeat. Ed had already found an apartment in Jamaica Plain and begun his transition, so boxes were everywhere. I soon felt as if I'd never been on vacation.

When Mark returned a week before the move, I settled down again, grateful for his good-humored participation. We arranged to meet with the neighbors down the street whose apartment we were moving into. On a late August evening we gathered in the bay of our second-floor window with a bottle of wine, looking down onto the street. The late summer light was fading. As they all discussed moving-day details my mind wandered, exhausted from packing. I listened quietly to bits of conversation that drifted up from the pedestrians walking below.

Suddenly we all jumped at once. There had been a panicked cry, and something bulky plummeted past our window onto the cement stairs leading into the building. Three floors above us, on the roof, we could hear people shouting. Mark, who was nearest the view of the front stairs, said quickly, "Don't look." But we already had. A young man's body lay crumpled on the steps, blood pooling under his head. A dozen people thundered past our door and crowded out onto the landing. A girl began screaming. An ambulance was there in moments, but the man was already dead. A group of newly arrived students had had a party on the roof, an activity explicitly forbidden by the landlord because the roofs had no railings. Unaware of how near he was to the edge, the young man had stepped backward, lost his balance, and fallen.

Even after the body had been taken away and the partygoers had dispersed, the four of us were in shock. We said very muted goodbyes and agreed to meet again on moving day. I decided to take a short walk before bed, hoping to clear my head, and came upon our maintenance man scrubbing blood from the steps. He said only, "It's so sad."

Moving day was chaos. Our new apartment was on the fifth floor. The building had a tiny elevator in the lobby and no front stairway, though there was a narrow flight of stairs at the back of the first floor. Many bulky items of furniture had to be hauled up these stairs. With the help of two movers and a few friends, we accomplished the job in six hours, and I went back to clean the old apartment alone, taking a last look at what felt like my old life. Mark and I left for Fire Island a day later.

On September 2 we celebrated our anniversary in Cherry Grove, observing our first year together "back at the scene of the crime." We were lying in bed early in the morning when he used those words, and I jumped on top of him, threatening immediate criminal acts. However, we were both filled with aches and pains from the move, and we fell back asleep before anything else could develop. Later we walked down the long beach from the Grove to the Pines in the surf, carrying our sandals, and arrived at Tea Dance in time to note the exact moment of our meeting. It was Labor Day weekend and the Pavilion was a madhouse, the usual mob of sweaty men flailing their arms to "It's Raining Men." We laughed about the volume of rain early in the summer and thanked our stars for the change in July to hazy, hot, and humid. At least we weren't cold. We meandered down Aeon Walk and passed the house where we had spent our first night together. A different group of people had rented the house this summer, and we reminisced as we continued on, sitting on the top step of the stairs leading down to the beach.

"Do you remember that first night?" he asked.

"As I recall, it was very romantic. I thought you were refined."

"I wouldn't characterize some of those positions as refined, darling."

"Oh well, I'm a farm boy at heart. Exposure to breeding animals and all that."

I had never been on a farm in my life.

The breeze picked up as the sun began to set behind us, the light over the ocean gradually dimming. I put my arm around him and pulled him close. "Here's to us, kiddo. What a time this has been. I had no idea how glorious or how hard falling in love could be."

"I had given up on love," he said. "Doesn't that sound corny? But it's true. At best I had hoped for a companion to warm my bed. You've offered so much more."

"We have a lot of work ahead," I said. I felt troubled by the thought of the apartment, full of boxes, the uncertainty of Mark's financial circumstances, all the unknowns.

He took my face in his hands and kissed me. "Shoulder to shoulder?"

"Of course. And belly to belly!"

We walked back up the beach to Cherry Grove as darkness fell, into another year.

PART TWO

Chapter 7

The new apartment at 27 Bay State Road, the top floor of a five-story brownstone, was about half the size of the one I had shared with Ed. It had much better views of the Charles River, stretching west toward Watertown and east all the way to Charlestown, including the Harvard and Longfellow bridges and the Esplanade. The elevator opened directly into a tiny foyer that led into a living room with a working fireplace, a large bay window, and an alcove with its own window facing the river. There was a decent-sized kitchen and an interior room adjacent to the kitchen that contained a skylight. We briefly considered using it as a bedroom, but the view from the living room won out, and we put the bed in the alcove so that we could wake up to see the sun rise over downtown.

The room off the kitchen had to serve many functions: closet, dressing room, study, guest room. Mark had dozens of old cardboard boxes, chock full, that had been stored in the damp recesses of the basement in the McIntyre Building, as well as dozens of Delta Airlines boxes that were a gift from a flight attendant with whom he had had a brief liaison. The latter boxes contained all that was important to him and were referred to by his friends in Florida as "Mark's Delta Airlines collection." Initially all the boxes got piled into the multi-purpose room.

Among other things that Mark had moved up from New York was a harpsichord that he had built from a kit when he was in graduate school. It was a lovely instrument, about the size of a spinet piano, painted black. When the lid was propped open, there was a vivid pastoral scene painted on the inside, complete with blue sky, clouds, and chubby angels. He laughed when I was dumbstruck; I had never seen anything like it.

We continued to unpack, and it became clear rather quickly that we had nearly twice as much furniture, artwork, kitchenware, and boxes as we could possibly keep in the apartment. There were also half a dozen rugs of various sizes from his sojourn in Tunisia, stored for years in the bowels of the McIntyre Building. It felt like Christmas, unrolling these colorful carpets, trying them out in different areas to see what would work. We figured out how we would organize the rugs and the furniture, then rolled the rugs up again. The musty smell was making both of us sneeze, and we put taking them to be cleaned at the top of our long list of things to do.

After the summer I was back to working four long days, doing individual and couples sessions, leading three groups, and running a training seminar. Mark said he would take charge of getting us settled, but he seemed oblivious to the mess. In the room off the kitchen, he was content to create a desk for himself out of an old table, adding a cardboard filing cabinet in which to file his bills and the documents relating to the lawsuit. I applauded his desire to organize his papers but was unhappy that he didn't seem to have any plan for getting rid of the stacks of boxes, as well as the suitcases and clothes that would not fit into the single closet. The louvered doors into this room were mismatched and badly hung; and after I threatened to write "Abandon hope, all ye who enter here" over the lintel, we referred to the room simply as Hell.

I came home from work one day to find that Mark had purchased white, heavy-duty plastic shelving, which he bolted to the walls on two sides, and upon which boxes were stacked up to the skylight. Luggage and sundry objects having no other place rose from the floor to the bottom of the shelves. This was not my idea of decorating a room. The entire apartment was still a mess, and I wanted to cry.

"Mark, really, is this going to be our permanent solution? Now it looks like the inside of a storage unit. Where can we put a bed for guests?"

"It's not permanent. But we have to get things stacked up so we can move around. I'm thinking about how we can maximize using the space."

I'm sure I looked doubtful. He continued. "Look, Mike, here's a chance for us to practice how we'll use space in our little *pied-à-terre* in New York. Let's be creative. It's like a dry run."

He was sitting on the floor sifting through old bills and records, and he had a smear of grime across his right cheekbone. I sat down on the floor next to him and rubbed his smudged cheek with the sleeve of my shirt.

"OK, I'll be patient. But I hate mess. Please be diligent."

"Cross my heart," he said.

After a few weeks of moving things from one place to another in the apartment, I started taking boxes to the office. My colleagues and I had a bathroom with a separate tub room that was never used. They graciously allowed me to stack things floor to ceiling in the bathtub. But I still found myself dreading going home after work. Pictures remained unhung, books in boxes. I felt trapped and suffocated in the apartment. Mark, who spent no significant time with other people unless I was around, began to get listless. I cringed one day when my friend Betts referred to him as "your wife." Intimate conversation became less frequent, and our sex life sputtered.

At dinner one night, a meal notable for its lack of conversation, he said, "We need to figure out how you're going to make more money."

I stared at him. "Why do I need to make more money?"

Misinterpreting my annoyance for interest, he launched into a narration about an article he'd read in the business section of the *Times* on the relative merits of renting versus buying.

"Real estate prices are favorable right now," he said. "You really should be putting the money you're spending on rent here into a condo. We need to figure out how you could save for a down payment."

I was paying all of the rent on the new apartment until he either started earning some money or the court case was resolved. I was aware of his eagerness and desire to help, but I felt furious that he was home all day while I trudged off to the office. "I'm doing as much as I can," I said. "And I'm not going back to working five days in order to save for a condo. I'd love to own a condo. But *we* can't do it on my income alone."

Silence. I looked at him. He looked out the bay window at the lights of Cambridge. Finally he said, "What do you want me to do? Work in a coffee shop? Do day labor?"

"It doesn't matter to me what you do," I said. "But I want you to think about how you might earn money instead of thinking about how I'm going to make more money."

"I didn't mean to offend you. I know you're working hard. I just thought you'd be interested in the article." He got up to clear the dishes, and I put my hand out to stop him from taking my plate. "I'm not trying to piss you off. If I were independently wealthy, I'd be happy to support you while you sort out your options. I know you don't know anyone in the sailing community here. But you're not doing anything to meet them. And I know you don't want to go back to teaching, but you could at least investigate substitute teaching in the private schools. You have great credentials and experience. I'm going further into debt every month, and we need to address that problem before we're both broke." He resumed clearing the dishes and we lapsed back into silence.

During the following week Mark did make some phone calls and also found a listing for "gay sailing enthusiasts" in the *Gay Community News* classifieds. I took a carload of clothes and a few pieces of furniture to Goodwill. There was modest progress, but the distance between us remained.

On the last Friday of September a friend of a friend in San Francisco called to say that he was visiting Boston and wondered if we could meet. Mark suggested we invite him to dinner on Saturday, and we decided to invite Arnie Kruger, Mark's old friend from college, to join us. Arnie asked if he could bring someone with him, and we said that would be fine.

Saturday began well. I was moderately good-humored after clearing more things out of the apartment the day before, and I took a long run along the river. Mark spent most of the day in the kitchen, while I hung pictures and reorganized the built-in bookshelves. I picked up the rugs from the cleaners and felt a rush of pleasure when we put them on the floor, in some places layering them. The room took on the flavor of a North African bazaar, and we both felt delighted. Late in the afternoon I soaked in the bathtub with a glass of wine, then dressed carefully. I still had some color from our time on Fire Island and from running outdoors. My weight was well under 190 and I was pleased with how I looked. I found Mark's friend Arnie more than a little acerbic, and I wanted to make a good impression on the strangers from out of town.

The guests were expected at 6:30, and Terry Hudson from San Francisco arrived ten minutes early. He was bright, talkative, and cute, a museum designer who was in Boston to have a consultation at Harvard for a museum he was creating in Dubai. I liked him right off, appreciated his directness and lack of attitude. I made him a drink and we sat in the living room and talked about our mutual friend in San Francisco and about other museums he had installed. Mark was still busy in the kitchen, his dinner preparation taking longer than he had planned. He came into the living room about 6:30 and asked Terry, "Will you forgive me if I jump in the shower before the others get here? Arnie is always late, and I'm roasting!"

Terry replied, "Of course. Maybe Mike will show me the view from the roof. This is the top floor, isn't it?" Mark and I looked at each other. We were still shaken by the memory of the young man falling only weeks before.

Mark said, "Yes, this is the top floor, but we had to agree when we signed the lease that we would go up on the roof only in case of emergency. If you do go up, please don't stay long. And be careful!" He went into the bathroom and we could hear the shower start.

I stood up and said, "C'mon, Terry, it's Saturday night. No one will be around to report us." We went out the kitchen door and up a short flight of stairs, arriving in time to watch the sun move lower in the sky over North Cambridge. The colors were glorious. Terry gave my shoulder a squeeze before turning back toward the door.

"We'd better beat it before you lose your lease," he said, and we slipped back downstairs before Mark was out of the shower.

Arnie and his friend Max finally arrived about 8:00, by which time Mark was beside himself, afraid that dinner would be ruined. Terry and I were on our third drink, feeling no pain, and I shepherded our guests to the dining table. Max lit a joint and began to pass it around. I helped bring in the food, noting to Mark in the kitchen that Arnie had offered no apology for being ninety minutes late. Mark just rolled his eyes. I opened the first bottle of red wine and seated myself.

The meal, as always, was sumptuous. There was a starter of *pâté* and slices of crusty French bread, followed by a rich *boeuf bourguignon* that Mark served over homemade noodles. Mark always liked to follow the entrée with a light green salad, then the guests moved from the table to the sofa while I cleared and Mark made espresso. We finished up with chocolate mousse and coffee at the table. The lights downtown shone brightly in the early darkness. The room was filled with candlelight. It was a beautiful night, and we were all in high spirits.

Max was adorable. It was as simple as that. He was twenty-five, more than ten years younger than any of the rest of us, and worked for Andy Warhol in Manhattan as a film promoter. He was wearing tight plaid slacks, a white shirt, and a red, white, and blue bow tie. He had large brown eyes and thick dark hair and a smile that gave me palpitations. I was deeply sorry that I had drunk so much before Arnie and Max arrived, because I could barely take my eyes off him.

We had a wingback chair to the left of the harpsichord. To its right was a long sectional sofa with an extra seat on either end, creating what was then called a "conversation area." Terry sat in the wingback chair, Mark and Arnie to his left on the sofa, and I sat on the other end of the sofa near the window. We were all drunk and stoned by this point, and the guests began one-upping each other with tales of their encounters with the rich and famous.

Max came back from the bathroom and lit another joint, then arranged himself next to me, but with his legs over the back of the sofa and his head resting on the edge of the seat cushion near my knee. Through the haze of pot and alcohol, his behavior seemed completely unsurprising. By this time he had dispensed with his bowtie and unbuttoned the top four buttons of his white shirt, exposing a lovely, hairy, well-shaped chest. The others continued their animated conversation about Noël Coward, Stephen Sondheim, and Maurice Sendak, while Max placed a pile of decorative pillows on his stomach. He asked me where they were from, and I lifted them with my left hand, one by one, and made up a story about the provenance of each. The other men, seated as they were at the other end of the sofa, were unaware that my right hand was free to roam beneath the pillows. Max was hard as a rock beneath my touch; but we never looked at each other, and we maintained a steady conversation about home decorating.

I finally could bear the tension no longer and stood up. I went to the window and feigned interest in the view. Arnie, Mark, and Terry were still talking and Mark poured more wine. Max came and stood in front of me, asking about different buildings across the river as he found ways to push against me and touch me, showing his perfect teeth and pink tongue. I said over and over to myself, *Don't make a fool of yourself! Stop this!* But I was lost.

Then I noticed that the conversation behind me was lagging. Terry was quieter, and I could see his candlelit face reflected in the bay window, eyes watchful. I moved away from Max and tried to look nonchalant. I was painfully aroused and wished only to escape, but there was no escape. Then Terry said,

"Max, why don't you have Mike show you the view from the roof?" Before I could demur, Max moved toward the kitchen and Terry told Mark and Arnie how pleasant it had been to watch the sunset spread across the sky.

I prayed that no one would follow us up, and indeed, we had about five minutes of uninterrupted lust, Max pushing my hand down the back of his slacks while unzipping my pants to insert his other hand. My tongue searched his mouth, heart pounding. I never took my eyes off the door to the roof, knowing that eventually someone would follow us. Fortunately it was Terry, the devil's handmaid, who joined in the sexual mêlée for a few moments before we all went downstairs.

The party was over. I tried hard to pretend that everything was normal, but clearly it wasn't. Mark was distant. Arnie was alert, eyes moving from one to another of the returnees. Someone suggested that we go dancing, but Mark made it clear he wanted only to walk the guests to their car. Arnie offered Terry a ride to his hotel, so we gathered ourselves together for the trip down in the elevator. As the others moved into the foyer, I leaned down to kiss Mark. He looked me in the eye and whispered a single word: "Tacky." My face flushed with shame, but I moved away from him as if I hadn't heard and entered the elevator. On the sidewalk, as we made our way to Arnie's car, Mark walked on my left and Max on my right. Even in this moment I couldn't stop myself from brushing against him, and he hooked his thumb in the belt loop behind my back as we walked along the street. The five of us said animated goodbyes at the car, pledging friendship forever, and Mark and I walked silently back home.

We were both drunk and exhausted, and I suggested he go to bed and let me clean up the wreckage of the party. I put on my headphones, Sylvester screaming, "You make me feel mighty real!" as I scraped plates and put them in the dishwasher. It was a relief to be absorbed in such a concrete task, but I was flooded repeatedly by the memory of the sexual intensity I'd experienced with Max. I wanted only to be back on the roof with my hand down his pants. After more than an hour of rinsing and scrubbing, the kitchen was clean enough to turn off the light, and I collapsed into sleep next to Mark.

In bright daylight I awoke to Mark cuddling me, the first time in many days, and we made love. The previous night felt like a fever dream, and the lovemaking with Mark was familiar and sweet. Still, there was much that needed to be said. He got up and made coffee, then came to the sofa and sat down. I got my own coffee and joined him, having a hard time making eye contact. He said evenly, "I don't think it's in our contract for you to flirt with our dinner guests and take them up to the roof."

Quoting the contract, I said, "No sex with mutual friends, and don't do anything that would embarrass the other person. The only rule I didn't break was to take his last name and phone number. You were right about what you said last night. My behavior *was* tacky."

Mark gave the smallest of smiles. "He was terribly cute."

"And I was like a bitch in heat," I replied. "I am so sorry, my dear. I've done some pretty inappropriate things in my life, but this may take the cake." I was filled with shame and remorse. I wondered briefly if he knew what had happened on the sofa, and what he imagined had happened on the roof. But I didn't volunteer any information and he didn't ask. I continued. "I'm especially sorry it happened with Arnie. I know you've been trying to jumpstart that friendship again, and I must have embarrassed you terribly."

"It was awkward," he said, "especially with Terry here. Arnie said to me when you were on the roof, 'Oh darling, do you mean to tell me that you've been together over a year and this is the first time Mike's acted up? Good for you!'" Mark sounded sour, a rare moment in which he dropped his guard and I could see his hurt. I felt a stab of hatred for Arnie.

I said, "I'll call him later today and apologize."

"That would be good," he said. "What do you Catholics call it? Penance?"

"Yes," I said, feeling like what I really deserved was a day in the stocks. Public shaming. I got up to refill our coffee cups. I asked from the kitchen, "Do you ever wonder if I'm an alcoholic?" I had never asked that question of myself, let alone him. It was a secret from my conscious mind, a little inchoate fear that floated in the darkness. Mark waited until I returned to the sofa.

"We all drink a lot socially. You smoke more marijuana than I do. Are you worried about it?"

"Not exactly," I said. "I just don't think I ever would have done what I did last night if I hadn't been drunk."

"And maybe you wouldn't have been so drunk if Miss Kruger and Mr. Warhol's protégé hadn't been an hour and a half late for dinner." Mark stretched and yawned. "A last word on the subject. I did feel hurt. I did feel angry. But these things happen. Let's put it behind us." He went out into the kitchen to make breakfast and called out, "And thanks for doing all the dishes!" I realized I was off the hook, but I still felt miserable.

The weather was warm and golden in October, and little by little the apartment got settled. The landlord gave us a minuscule storage closet in the hallway going up to the roof, and we packed it so tightly that we were afraid to open the door for fear of an avalanche. I read and discarded several boxes of letters, many of which I'd received during the two years I'd taught school overseas on military installations after graduate school. In rereading some of them I was reminded of both the excitement of those days and the acute loneliness of being a closeted gay civilian on remote military bases during the Nixon administration. I found a photo of myself standing on the tarmac of the airstrip in Goose Bay, Labrador, ready to board a C47 cargo plane that would take me to my next assignment in Iceland. I looked windblown and very young at twenty-four, but there was a certain hopefulness in my expression that made my heart ache.

Sitting on the floor with the letters scattered around, I could hear my mother asking me her perennial question when I was out of sorts as a teenager. "Honey, what in the world do you *want*?" From as early as I could remember, my answer was a frustrated "I don't *know*!" I wanted to grow up, I wanted to escape from Omaha, I wanted to travel and live in an amazing apartment in a big city with someone brilliant and talented. Well, I had all of that now. But I was still frustrated and unhappy. What *did* I want? I felt like a witch had cursed me at birth and said, "No matter what you achieve, it will never be enough."

Chapter 8

In mid-October Mark enrolled in a class in small engine mechanics in Providence, Rhode Island, that met Monday nights for ten weeks. He was comfortable and competent riding his motorcycle, and the distance was just fifty miles. He needed the course to obtain his captain's license, and it was the first action he had taken independently that suggested he might find a way to be in Boston with me and develop a life of his own as well.

My moodiness continued. Still distressed over the incident at the dinner party, I decided to see my former psychotherapist, Lee Richards. Lee was a few years older than I, tall and heavy-set, with an imposing voice and appealing reserve. Prior to Lee, all my therapists had been female, and it had been a leap of faith to trust a man with my vulnerability, particularly a straight man. But there was something about his solidness, his lack of people-pleasing, that had slowly allowed me to move toward him. As much as I had looked forward to seeing him again, I was filled with anxiety when I arrived in his office.

Spreading his hands wide, he said, "What brings you back?"

"I feel like a gnat on a hot griddle," I replied. "There is so much to say and I don't even know where to start." From there I unloaded: Mark moving to Boston, his court case, the new apartment, how crowded and trapped I felt. Out of the blue I remembered the night the boy fell from the roof and I started crying uncontrollably. Lee sat quietly, never taking his eyes from my face.

"There was this kid," I said. "Students were having a party on the roof, and he had his back to the edge and stepped off." I stopped to steady my voice. "We heard him cry out and saw him dead on the steps just below our front window. And later there was so much blood on the stairs. It broke my heart." I cried hard for another minute, then the intensity of what had broken through began to abate. I kept looking at Lee, how calm and steady he seemed, and gradually I could feel his support, the support of the chair I was in, and the familiarity of the office.

"It's curious," I said. "I was not aware of having held all this in."

"That's the nature of trauma, isn't it?" he replied. "We need to feel safe to feel something like this so deeply. Did you and Mark deal with the shock of this event together?"

I thought about the question. "We talked about it, have referred back to it several times. But this is the first time I've cried. It's a relief to feel the impact of it in my body."

"Why didn't you and Mark cry together?"

I laughed, then caught myself and felt embarrassed. "Mark doesn't cry, Lee, and he hates when I cry. It's messy. He doesn't do messy."

Lee lifted his eyebrows. "I'm thinking about what you said at the beginning of the session, 'feeling like a gnat on a hot griddle.' In this instance, you seem pretty swamped by unexpressed feelings."

I remembered the dizzying months when Mark and I fell in love, how swept up I was. "I actually don't think I've felt completely grounded since I fell in love with Mark. This whole last year has felt like a free fall."

"Like stepping backward off a roof?" I knew the question was genuine.

"Pretty close," I replied.

"But you have lived to tell the tale."

"I have indeed." For the first time in months I felt shaky but clear. I thought of all the packing and unpacking, the stress of settling into the new space, my fears of Mark not being able to show up in the relationship. "Lee, I really need help," I said. "I need to learn to let things take their course. I'm trying so hard to manage everything in my life, and it's not working."

He smiled and reached for his appointment book. "How is nine a.m. on Monday?" he said.

*

In addition to therapy, I decided to study meditation, using Lawrence LeShan's *How to Meditate*. I began sitting for fifteen minutes every morning, simply doing breath counting, one to four. My mind was like a flock of wild parrots, but LeShan said, "The goal is not to reach four, but to learn to lead the mind back to one, over and over." I considered my practice a success if I could keep myself in the chair for fifteen minutes, whatever else happened.

Meanwhile Mark settled into the curriculum of engine repair, studying his manuals and going to the marina in Providence to get hands-on practice. He frequently went to New York for a day or two before his class, wanting to move the lawsuit along as best he could. There was little drama, which was a relief.

The following weekend we were to meet at Mark's friend's house in Bellport, where we had spent the most romantic of weekends the previous fall. He was taking the train out from New York and I would drive from Boston. I had been excited for many days about the trip, but by midafternoon Thursday I was exhausted and regretted having agreed to leave right after work. Traffic was sluggish getting out of the city, and I was extremely tense about arriving in New London, Connecticut, in time to make my ferry reservation. I arrived in time but the ferry was running late, so we didn't dock in Orient Point until well after dark. I had never driven in the area and got lost three times trying to find the road to Bellport. Blinded by headlights and feeling hopelessly enraged, I started screaming at the top of my voice, "Goddamn you, Michael Ward! Goddamn you!" I wanted to run the car into a tree. When I finally arrived in the driveway of the house, trembling, I sat and counted my breaths, one to four, one to four, until I got my heart rate down to normal. I said nothing about the experience to Mark.

Mark's little sailboat, a Sunfish, was stored in the garage at Bellport, and we sailed in the Great South Bay both days, gliding past the homes on the shore of Fire Island, cutting back across to Sayville and up to Bellport. It was deeply relaxing. Much of the time we were quiet, in a companionable way rather than the tense silence that had become too familiar in Boston. Sitting naked by the pool with the water gurgling and the lush foliage protecting us from the eyes of the neighbors, I wished that I felt the wild and crazy love for him that I had felt a year earlier. The sex was still good, but I missed the emotional merging that early love brings. I watched him as he dozed, stretched out beside me, and felt a little ache in my heart. We were in a different place, and I needed to find a way to love him as he was now, and to love our relationship for what it was as well.

The weeks passed quickly, both of us busy. I kept up a punishing schedule of running and exercise, sometimes wondering whether I was running away from something or running toward it. Mark began seeing more of Arnie Kruger and spent several days helping him install a new stove in his apartment. Having done so many of the renovations in the McIntyre Building himself, Mark was adept at simple plumbing and electrical work. I continued to resent Arnie for many reasons, mostly because it seemed to me that he called Mark only when he wanted help with something. Mark made friends with a violinist named Robert Smith, who came to the house one morning a week for several months to play duets. It was pleasurable to sit in the bay window at the table, writing in my journal before leaving for work and listening to Mark practice.

Our friend Kirk visited briefly in mid-November and brought his sensibility for decorating and style to the space, moving pictures around, rearranging the furniture. The apartment finally felt complete, especially what Mark liked to call "the public rooms," including the sleeping alcove, where our bed was always neatly made. We kept fresh flowers on the table in the window, tall gladioli or alstroemeria, and I felt a rush of pleasure every day getting off the elevator and seeing the beautiful living room open out into the view of the river and Cambridge. This had been my dream. The room called Hell, however, remained a challenge. Mark said, "Most kitchens have a junk drawer. We have a junk room!"

I tried to be amused but kept the mismatched doors closed as much as possible. I longed for perfect order.

*

Mark and I were joining friends in Puerto Rico for the long Thanksgiving weekend. On the plane flight I was quiet and Mark asked me if I was angry with him.

"No," I said, "I just feel flat. I want to have a good time this weekend and be close with you, but I don't feel like we're connected."

"Oh no, not again!" he said irritably. "You said that in September! We can't go through this every two months."

I wanted to hit him. It felt crazy-making to me that he saw talking about feelings as being something he couldn't manage even every two months.

"I'm sorry this upsets you," I said. "But I can't be in a relationship long-term that isn't emotionally connected. We've been doing better lately, but to me it's merely pleasant, not engaged. This vacation is an opportunity to be closer." I rested my hand on his arm. "Is that such a bad thing?"

Once he thought about it, he settled down. We talked for an hour, what had been happening for him, how painful it was to feel stranded in Boston when the world of sailing that he loved was happening 1,500 miles to the south. He said, "I'm afraid to talk to you about these feelings because you'll be mad at me for not being happy. Or I'll be burdening you."

I felt surprised at what he'd said and thought for a moment. "I don't think that's true, sweetheart. Maybe that was your mother. My problem is when you *don't* talk to me about what you feel. I just want to know what's happening internally. When I lose the emotional connection with you, I'm adrift."

"A lot of the time I don't know what I'm feeling, or what I'm supposed to feel," he said.

I sat with that for a moment. "That has never occurred to me before. I mistakenly assume we're all feeling something most of the time. I need to remember what you said. We're so different."

We also acknowledged that moving into 27 Bay State Road, while financially sensible, had been a mistake. It was simply too small, and we couldn't get away from each other. We made a pact to do our best to enjoy what we loved about it and to tolerate the rest, just for one year.

The trip gave us four warm days and cool nights. Boston had been surprisingly mild in October and November, but nothing compared with island breezes. We were back at the Beach House, with Rae at the helm and a bevy of Latin boys to flirt with. We rented a car and went to Luquillo Beach one day, spent the morning in the water and then drove to the El Yunque rainforest. We were in bliss with all the native flowers, orchids of all colors and brilliantly colored birds. We had dinners in Old San Juan and were outdoors whenever possible. The heat was erotic and delightful. When we got back to our room we fell into bed and made love. After a particularly athletic encounter, he asked impishly, "Am I feeling enough?"

At dinner one night we told our friends about Mark's brief but intense bout with fever on our prior visit to Puerto Rico. We never had figured out what caused it. This trip was mostly benign, however. I read more of *How to Meditate* and sat each day with my back against a palm tree, watching my thoughts, absorbed in the sounds of the surf crashing on the shore. Mark read *Middlemarch* and studied his engine manuals. It was a peaceful time, and hopeful.

*

All of a sudden it was early December and everything seemed to shift into fourth gear. Mark was in New York nearly every week meeting with his partners and their attorney. Twice he went down to the city thinking his case would be called, only to hear upon arrival that the date had been postponed. His moods rose and fell like the tides, but he resolutely believed that he would be vindicated and that his tenant would have to pay him two years of escrowed back rent. "The light at the end of the tunnel," he declared. I was anxious about the resolution, holding less certainty about the outcome than he did, but I kept that to myself.

We spent a few days together in New York after Christmas, planning to drive out to Betts and Gerry's house on Long Island to celebrate New Year's Eve. Mark got a phone call saying yet another court date had been set, this time for December 30, so I drove out to Syosset by myself the day before. Mark called me the following morning from the city, sounding excited, to say they were on their way to court. Barring something unforeseen, he would meet me at the train station on Long Island on the 5:45 commuter.

I had a stomachache all day. I tried to be optimistic, rehearsed different greetings of congratulation, imagined him arriving with a big bouquet of flowers and a bigger grin. Maybe we would sing "Happy Days Are Here Again." What I did not imagine was him getting off the train looking like Willy Loman, his body slumped, face ashen and dejected.

"Want to talk about it?" I asked.

"We got a bad judge. Housing court in New York is historically biased toward occupants, not owners. The Secretary of State's office, invoking a provision of co-op law, gave our tenants the same rights as those with rent stabilization. I not only lost the case, but I have to pay my tenant's court costs, which are thousands of dollars."

I hadn't a clue what to say. I realized I was furious, not at the court but at Mark. Why hadn't he considered the possibility of losing? Why hadn't he thought about a single alternative plan? I felt completely exhausted from the months of dealing with this colossal drain of energy and resources. But he looked so defeated that my anger fizzled. This wasn't a time to be angry. I pulled myself together and walked to his side. Putting my arm around his shoulders, I gave him a squeeze and said, "Let's go to Betts and Gerry's and have a drink."

Chapter 9

On our second New Year's Eve together, held in the loving embrace of our friends, we tried to come to grips with losing the court case.

"You'll appeal," Gerry said. "You'll get a different judge. Everyone knows housing court judges hate landlords. You'll get a different lawyer."

Betts took a different approach, drawing Mark into the kitchen to help her with our New Year's Eve dinner, a feast that would include rack of lamb, Mark's favorite. He gamely went along, making *vichyssoise* to start, and the two of them then concocted something with strawberries, dark chocolate, and *crème fraîche* for dessert. But when she and I were setting the table in the dining room, she said to me in a low voice, "He's sleepwalking." I was having difficulty recovering from seeing Mark at the train station and felt mostly numb, a smile at the ready but my mind a million miles away. *What were we going to do?*

Gerry and I drove to a fancy liquor store and he bought two bottles of expensive champagne, which he said were guaranteed to put life back into the dead. I said they would need to.

"Mike, you have to be kind to him. He's devastated."

"I feel trapped, Gerry. He's like my dad, a bright guy who couldn't get it together."

"He's a good man, and he's worth the effort. Help him figure out what to do." The late afternoon sunlight was weak, reinforcing my bleak outlook.

"I'll do my best, but I'm telling you, I want to jump a freight train."

Before dinner the four of us took a break to shower and change, and we all emerged refreshed. It was, after all, New Year's Eve. The evening turned out to be much more enjoyable than we might have imagined. Dinner was splendid from start to finish, the table gleaming with Betts's best china, crystal, and silver. Conversation became lively as champagne flowed.

Gerry and Mark both fell asleep on the sofa in front of the fireplace about 11:00 as Betts and I cleared the dishes, talking quietly in the manner of old friends. I felt safe, the feeling of impending doom pushed to the far horizon. She poured each of us a little cognac. In his sleep Mark had found safe harbor, resting his head against Gerry's shoulder. Betts and I sat in wingback chairs pulled close by the fire and continued our talk.

"Girlfriend," I asked, "why do you think Mark has so little ambition?"

"Oh, he has ambition," she said. "He has big dreams."

"I know the dreams," I replied. "A sailboat of his own, an income from his properties in New York, plying the warm waters of the Caribbean. But it looks to me like a very long road from what he has to what he wants."

She smiled. "I think he has to put forth some practical effort to save the dreams right now. It's called going back to work."

"I tell him that all the time. He's like a kid who believes if he hopes hard enough for something, that wish will come true. This dream of his has become a nightmare for me."

"What about your ambitions, Mike? Do you have what you want in Boston?"

I stirred and stretched in my chair, fighting off the effects of alcohol and fatigue. "Good question. I think I've become so preoccupied with Mark's situation that I've lost track of my own. I know that I want to continue to become a better therapist, and I've had some success in Boston. I think sometimes about writing." I looked at my cognac snifter and said, "Booze doesn't help to develop any of these ambitions, I might add."

We rose when we heard bells and whistles, then fireworks going off. As we moved toward the window, Gerry began to snore. We looked at our men and laughed softly.

"Midnight!" Betts said. "Let's toast to all of us then, our families and friends included. To 1983, healthy, wealthy, and wise." We clinked our glasses, kissed, and tossed down the rest of our cognac.

*

On the way back to Boston in the car the next day, I told Mark about my conversation with Betts and asked, "What *do* you have ambition for?"

Without hesitating, he said flatly, "Nothing. I bet everything on the investment in the McIntyre Building, and I still believe it will pay off in the long run."

He's still stuck, I thought, and tried a different tack. "Do you have no wish to be really good at something?"

"I worked hard at the piano," he said, looking out the window at the passing landscape of Connecticut. "But I wasn't quite good enough to think about Juilliard, and I knew Mom and Dad wanted me to teach. Then I worked hard to get my Ph.D., until I realized I didn't want to be a college academic, nor did I want a career in translation. My parents pushed and pushed, to no avail."

"And you dug in."

"Yes, I did." His smile held no humor. "Didn't your parents push you?"

"Sure, but it was different. Your parents only had you and Bert. There were eight of us, and all I ever heard from my parents was 'go to college, get an education, have a better life than we've had.' My greatest aspiration was to be a high school English teacher, a goal post I ran past in my early twenties. First college teaching, then educational testing, and then I became a shrink. I don't know what's next. But for better or worse, I always feel the pull of the future."

Mark put his hand on my knee and squeezed, keeping his eyes on the road. "Good for you. For me, my only aspiration is to sail."

I watched him, his hands resting on the wheel and eyes intently gazing forward, and wondered what it would take to move him out of his entrenched position with his parents. If he'd let himself teach, even part time, and earn some decent income, he'd feel so much relief. But then they would have won. He had to cling to the dream of sailing, even if he lost everything else in the process.

*

January in New England, another winter. The reality of Mark's loss hit us hard. Mark looked as if he were walking underwater, expressionless, voice without affect. My initial feeling of fury at the train station in Syosset had dissipated, and I worked to be supportive and hopeful. I encouraged Mark to talk to his partners and sort out what, if anything, to do about an appeal. He set off for New York on the train a few days later and I breathed a sigh of relief. It was my first time alone in many weeks. I began meditating again and sank into the stillness of winter.

Mark returned from New York in somewhat better spirits, though with a minor medical problem: oral thrush. I had never heard of it. He'd seen his dentist, who diagnosed a small white patch on the back of his tongue, and said if it got worse, he should see a doctor. I asked what caused it and he said, in his case, he thought stress. When Mark tried to show me the patch, it was hard to make out, and we thought it might already be clearing up.

It was a delight to sit facing each other on the long blue sofa with our legs entangled, catching up. His partners had decided to try for an appeal, based on elements of the law that they felt the judge had not adequately considered. I had no intention of getting emotionally invested in another legal battle. He said, "I felt so much better being back in New York, Mike. I know it's the same winter there as it is here, but I feel so much more alive in Manhattan. Betts and I had lunch, and she asked if we ever talk about moving to the city."

I almost threw my hands in the air. "Not now, Mark, please."

"No, I don't mean now. But look. You have good friends down there. We have people we see up here, but our closest couple friends are there, and you still have friends from training there. Even after a year and a half, I feel like a fish out of water in Boston."

I began plucking at a loose piece of yarn in the afghan my mother had sent for Christmas. Truth be told, I had been fantasizing again about living in New York, or San Francisco. My choice of Boston had been shaped by my flight from Princeton and a few connections I had for developing a psychotherapy practice. Maybe a bigger, less uptight city would be more fulfilling.

He said, "I know you're intimidated by the prospect of starting over four years after moving here. But you're not yet forty. And I know you love the city. Do you have any secret dreams?"

Against my better judgment, I began to relent. "I'd like to create a therapeutic program of some kind for gay men. Stopping smoking, for example, or 'Learning to Love the Body You Have.' There is so much body dysmorphia in our community, and so many unhealthy behaviors. Or I could develop a program for how to meet men."

"What for?"

"Dating groups. Get a group of twenty or thirty men together and do exercises: how to meet someone, how to put him and yourself at ease, how to stay present. For decades gay men have met by having sex first. This is 1983: Why can't we date like other people?"

"These are things you could do as easily in New York as Boston, right?"

"Yes, but Mark, we also have to have money to pay rent and bills."

"I know. At least we have this possibility on the table, which makes me breathe easier. And I promise I'll work harder to bring in money from sailing jobs."

"Deal," I said. And we shook on it.

Our discussion brought some immediate results for Mark. He made phone calls to people he knew in Florida and lined up two jobs, one moving a sailboat from Fort Lauderdale to St. Thomas, the other crewing on a large yacht. Neither paid a lot of money, but he would get some salary and accumulate more hours of experience for his license. These were not long-term solutions, but there was movement in the right direction. I began to feel cautiously optimistic.

*

In late January I went to Mexico for a weeklong professional conference and spent a substantial amount of time with a close friend and colleague, Rosanne Lawson. We had trained together to be therapists in Manhattan, in the same group as Betts, and the three of us had been fast friends. Rosanne and I both lived in New Jersey while we were in training, and she moved to San Francisco about the time I moved to Boston.

While in New Jersey we had co-led "marathon weekends" with clients, doing group therapy with a dozen or so people. At the conference we explored the possibility of working together again a few times a year, her traveling to Boston and me to San Francisco. I shared with Rosanne my plans with Mark to explore moving, and soon we were talking about the possibility of Mark and me moving to the Bay Area and my setting up a practice there. When I returned home, Mark's response to exploring possibilities in San Francisco was positive. He wasn't giving up on New York City, but he was happy to add another option to our list of possible futures away from Boston.

Midweek, Mark and I had drinks with Arnie Kruger, not something I ever looked forward to. I never knew when I would say something that he'd bristle at, and he invariably set my teeth on edge. Mark was still wrestling with depression after losing the case, and his first sailing gig was a couple of weeks away. I thought drinks with Arnie might lift his spirits, if not mine.

"Darling!" Arnie said to Mark as we sat down at Fritz in the South End. "How *are* you?"

"I'm looking forward to Florida, Arnie. This weather!" Mark made a face.

"And you, dear," Arnie said, turning to me with his Cheshire Cat smile. "How are *you*?"

"Couldn't be better, Arnie. I'm just back from a conference in Mexico, so I'm not as oppressed by the cold as my boyfriend is." Though it had been many months since the fateful dinner party, I thought it circumspect not to ask about Max.

The conversation drifted into talk about Arnie's editing work ("tedious") and the winter ("endless"). Mark brought up the possibility of our moving, visibly brightening when he mentioned New York.

"But darling," Arnie said, "where would you live? And on what? At least Mike has work here." He grimaced theatrically.

I jumped in. "That's what we're exploring, Arnie. We're daydreaming in a way, but with purpose." Mark was looking stricken. With enthusiasm I said brightly, "We're also looking at San Francisco as an option."

Arnie gasped and swallowed the rest of his martini. "You can't be serious."

"Why not?"

"San Francisco? Dreadful city! Full of Midwesterners who didn't have the talent or guts to make it on the East Coast. Truth be told, one can only really make it in New York."

Dead silence on our end. Finally I asked, "Another martini, Arnie?"

*

Boston was in its bipolar mode, winter into spring, freezing one day, warm the next. Mark came home from his first trip sunburned and refreshed. We made love almost immediately, something familiar and safe when so little else seemed dependable. We were together only three nights before he had to leave again for nearly a month, and I would be traveling as well. Good news on the work front: he was making money, and his self-esteem seemed stronger.

He sat me down in the living room before he headed to the airport and said, "We need to talk." Then he laughed awkwardly.

"What's so funny?"

"It just sounds dramatic: 'We need to talk.' But it's time that I initiate one of these conversations. You've been doing the heavy lifting in this department."

"Fire away," I said.

"I believe in us. I believe in this relationship. And I want to do whatever needs to be done to make it work. I can't believe I'm the one saying this, but I think we need to see somebody. Professionally." This was about the last thing I would have imagined he'd say, and I was stunned.

"Mark, I think there are a lot of things that an objective third party could help us see," I said. "But you're leaving now for nearly a month, and much of the time you'll be out of touch by phone. I'm traveling to San Francisco as well, to work with Rosanne. It's going to be hard to stay connected."

"Well, we could start counseling when I come back." He hesitated for a moment, then said, "I've also been thinking about where we'll live. What about splitting time between New York and Boston? If I have a place down there, we could have a larger life. We just have to build a bigger frame to hold us."

Does he ever think about where money would come from for these big moves? I wondered. "You realize we would need even more income for two places to live than we need now."

"I know that, Mike. But things will get settled in court soon and I'm convinced that this time my partners and I will prevail. Our attorney is very optimistic."

"I wish I were so sanguine," I replied. I wanted to be more supportive, but I felt too much doubt.

Chapter 10

Mark left Boston to begin the second sailing gig, and the first night he was gone I had a dream.

I was visiting Mom and Dad in Omaha when they told me that my childhood friend (and fellow sexual explorer) Vito Caniglia had moved back to Omaha and was living in their basement. As we were talking about him, Vito came into the room. I was electrified. He was gorgeous and bizarre simultaneously, both butch and flamboyant. He was beautifully muscled and full of sexual tension and energy as he paced about. He had what I thought were scars—shiny scar tissue—in four or five places on his upper body. But in better light I could see that they were recent tattoos, and the flesh was still healing, hence shiny and puffy. We went downtown to a gay bar, and I kept trying to think of someplace we could go to have sex, like a parking lot or a park. At the same time I felt terrified to be seen with him because he was so outrageously, defiantly gay, and I feared for my own safety.

The next day, still feeling disturbed by the dream, I went to my therapy session with Lee. After hearing a bit of the dream, he said, "Let's use a Gestalt therapy technique. I'd like you to take each character in the dream and speak from the first person. Is it OK with you if I videotape the session for my psychodrama class?"

"Sure," I replied. I had attended his psychodrama training program the previous year and knew the ropes. Remaining seated, I spoke from my parents' perspectives first, how strange it was for them to see Vito after all these years, how much he had changed. Mom and Dad seemed very neutral to me, guarded. Then Lee suggested I "inhabit" the character of Vito.

"I'm Vito Caniglia!" Suddenly I leapt onto a nearby sofa, flexed my biceps, then jumped to the floor and strutted up and down the room. "I'm sexy and powerful and energetic. I'm hot!" I put my face right in front of Lee's: "And I don't take shit from anybody." I pulled my shirt off and threw it to the floor. "See these scars and tattoos? One is of the Eiffel Tower, and this one's a lavender fist. *I want to be noticed!*"

Lee asked Vito what he thought of Mike.

"Oh, he's really cute. He's pretty quiet, but I like him. I'm going to jazz up his life. He's nervous about that, huh?" He barked a laugh, sounding a little crazy.

Lee directed me to be Mike in the dream. I put my shirt on and moved to the far corner of the room, my hands covering my face, then peeked out from between my fingers.

"I'm horrified! Vito makes me so nervous! I'm wildly attracted to him, but I'm afraid he'll make a mess of my life. I want to take him downtown to go dancing, but I'm afraid to be seen with him, he's so outrageous. He's sure to cause trouble."

Lee asked if there was more. I shook my head, flopping down onto the sofa. "Would you like to see some of the video?" When I nodded, he played back just the last few minutes of Vito's monologue. I was amazed at how alive I looked as Vito, eyes bright, hyper-alert.

"When we were about six," I said, "Vito and I were playing at my house after school and decided to show each other our penises. I tried to figure out a place where we would not be seen and chose my bedroom. I had to leave the door open or Mom would know something was going on, so we went behind the open door, figuring she wouldn't come in. We were breathless and giggling, taking our pants down and looking, then touching. All of a sudden Mom's voice was shockingly close: 'Boys? What are you doing?'

Frozen, I squeaked out, 'Nothing, Mama. Just playing.' We desperately started pulling up our underpants, which had become entangled around our ankles. Mom's voice was inches away, on the other side of the open door.

"'Where are you?'

"'Right here, Mama.' I knew I couldn't get my pants up in time and I started to cry. She stepped into the small room and loomed above us. When she saw what we were doing, she started screaming and hitting me on the head.

"'Shame on you, Michael Ward. Shame on you, you dirty little snot!' She slapped me with each shouted word. Vito slipped behind her and was out the door in a flash, leaving me hunched down on the floor, trying to protect my head with my arms, still trapped in my tangled underwear."

As the story wound down, I was aware of tears on my face, but I felt cold and hard inside. Lee asked, "What happened then?"

"I don't remember."

"Did that put an end to exploring?"

"Don't kid yourself. It put an end to being careless. I never got caught again."

*

Mark called me from Miami on March 15, a Tuesday morning. He'd only been gone two days, and I was surprised and pleased. Maybe he was missing me.

"Aren't you busy provisioning your boat?" I asked.

"Yes, we'll finish up today and head out in the next day or two."

"What are the people like?"

"The owners are nice. It's a good-sized boat, nearly sixty feet, and plenty of crew. It should be fun." But his voice was flat.

"Is something wrong, sweetheart?"

"Kirk called me last night from New York. Have you heard about the article in yesterday's *New York Native*?" The *Native* was a popular gay newspaper that had been reporting more and more news about gay men getting sick. Wrapped up in my own world in Boston, I thought of this illness as something that was happening in New York.

"Tell me," I said.

"It's called '1,112 and Counting.' Larry Kramer wrote it." I knew Larry Kramer only through his novel *Faggots*, which I had found both fascinating and distasteful, more sexually explicit than anything I had read before about gay sex and promiscuity. "It looks like this AIDS thing is a much bigger deal than we thought."

"I'll pick up a copy later today."

"You remember David," he said, "the guy who died around the same time Boyd Morrow did? He's on Larry Kramer's list of people who have died from this."

I began to feel uneasy. *Why is he bringing this up now? It doesn't have anything to do with us.* "I'm really sorry, honey. I wish I were there with you. I can hear that you're upset." I paused for a moment and then added, "No one knows what Boyd died of, right? You don't know that he died of—" I couldn't make myself say "AIDS" and finally said, "this new thing."

He sighed audibly. "No, I guess you're right. But this news is still upsetting. I'm so glad you were home. I started to feel concerned about going out to sea and not being connected to you for so long."

"The time will go by quickly," I replied, sounding more casual than I felt. "Remember, I'll be in San Francisco when you get back, assuming you're only out three weeks. But we'll be together soon after that."

"Thanks," he said. "I'm really fine. I just wanted you to know this."

When I hung up the phone I found myself sitting on the harpsichord bench. *AIDS. What a weird name for a disease,* I thought. *It's too creepy.* I wasn't even sure what the letters stood for. I ran my index finger up the keys, the sound comforting and familiar. I loved listening to Mark practice and realized that I hadn't heard him play in a long time. Suddenly he felt very far away.

*

At the gym later that week I was jumping rope, the rope slapping the floor, *pocketa pocketa pocketa*. A handsome young man stood nearer to me than I was comfortable with, watching me, and finally I stopped and glared at him.

He burst out laughing, suddenly looking young and mischievous. "What?" he said.

"What do you mean, 'What?' You're staring at me."

"No, I'm admiring you. That is to say, I am admiring your skillfulness in jumping rope."

I couldn't help but smile. "It's hard to concentrate with you watching so closely."

"I apologize then," he said with a little bow. "Maybe when you're not so busy we could say hello?"

I was charmed. He was tall and slim, had short black hair and green eyes and a slight but discernible accent. The gym was crowded and I went about my routine, our eyes meeting occasionally. When I needed to shower and get to the office, I told him I would be back on Friday morning if he wanted to "say hello" then.

Though the flirtation had been modest, he was on my mind when I drove into the parking lot on Friday. I was pleasantly surprised when I found him working with weights as I came out onto the floor. When he saw me and smiled, I thought to myself, *I could get in serious trouble with this one*. His green eyes were so unusual, and they crinkled when he smiled. We did a few of the machines and weights together but mostly stayed to our own routines, then met at the coffee bar near the lobby.

"My name is Cesar Tejada. It's not *see-zer*, it's *say-sar*." I shook his hand and told him my name.

"Are you in a relationship?" he asked as we settled onto seats at the counter.

"Are you always this forward?" I responded. "Yes, I'm in a relationship. At the moment it's rocky, but it's definitely a relationship."

"I should say I'm sorry that it's rocky," he said. "I like how you jump rope. Other things too."

"Don't tell me those. Tell me where you're from, where you got that cute accent."

"Panama. But I came to Boston College for my BSN and then went to Northeastern to become a nurse practitioner. Now I work for a lovely gay doctor who has a private practice. I am *not* in a relationship. I like your eyes."

I said, "Your English is very good."

"My mother went to college in Boston and then returned to Panama. Do you speak Spanish?"

"Very little."

"How about French? I also speak French."

"Not in any form you would recognize," I replied.

Our conversation drifted into a comfortable patter about families, schools, his childhood in Panama. He was twenty-eight but seemed more mature. He had an attractive combination of formality and playfulness. When coffee was over, I said, "I don't want to be presumptuous, but I really am in a relationship, so I'm not available in any serious way."

"I understand, but I hope we can continue to talk."

And talk we did. I saw him at the gym again the following Monday and agreed to meet him after work for dinner on Wednesday. He was an intelligent and charming dinner companion, and I enjoyed telling him about my exploits in Spain when I was teaching school overseas. He had had several boyfriends since coming to the States but was aware of wanting to "build a nest" with someone.

"I'm ready for something more than disco, drugs, and sex."

"What else is there?" I teased.

"You know. Like what you and Mark have."

"I'm not sure what we have right now. I think I imagined him to be someone that he's not."

"Do you love him?" Cesar asked.

"Yes," I said without hesitation. "I love him a lot. But love by itself is not enough. There need to be common goals and values, and all kinds of things that create the structure of a relationship. I don't know if we have that."

When Cesar dropped me off on Bay State Road after dinner, he asked if he could kiss me goodnight. This encounter was definitely within the boundaries of my contract with Mark, but suddenly I felt like a high school boy on a date, awkward but excited. He leaned in and kissed me gently. As I rode up in the elevator to our apartment, I could still feel the warmth of his kiss on my mouth.

*

I finally got a copy of the *New York Native* article that had so upset Mark. I had subscribed to the *Advocate*, a gay news monthly out of Los Angeles, for at least a decade, and I viewed the *Native* as a much less dependable resource for national news since it mostly focused on life in the city. When I read Larry Kramer's article, it struck me as hysterical and melodramatic, filled with incendiary accusations and histrionic language. The *Advocate* had also printed several news stories about "the gay disease" in recent months, but what they pointed out repeatedly was that there was no real data to go on. Kramer's use of 1,112 cases, the number itself, was shocking. But there were hundreds of thousands of gay men in New York. And this was the United States. We had the best health care in the world. I heard Kramer's alarm but refused to take it in. Yes, I'd had multiple partners, but over twenty years. And the only time I'd been to the baths was when my partner Frank threw my thirty-third birthday party at Man's Country in Manhattan, and we'd made a joke of the whole scene, both titillated and repelled by the sexual acts we witnessed. Frank had brought in a cake from the erotic bakery in the shape of a penis, with one candle artfully placed on the erect member, and our party drank champagne and wandered through the hallways. It was fun, but the action was not our style. A friend later described the event as "a group of New Jersey housewives out for a lark." When I reflected on my history, I didn't see how AIDS related to me at all.

On his sailing trip Mark was unable to make phone contact, and I felt increasingly distant from him. I was shutting down, something I experienced when there was too much happening at once. I was drinking more and I hadn't meditated in weeks. I kept pushing away the feeling that there was a dark cloud hovering over us. I didn't want any part of it.

*

Cesar had planned a trip to the Russian River, north of San Francisco, just before I was scheduled to meet Rosanne to do a therapy weekend in Marin County. We would overlap in the Bay Area for one afternoon and evening. I arrived to chaos at Rosanne's place, half of a two-family house in the Upper Haight. She had recently separated from her second husband and was very unsettled. Her seven-year-old son was furious that she was leaving for the weekend and sending him to a babysitter. And we had yet to plan the work of the weekend. An hour after I arrived at her house, Cesar showed up. My understanding had been that "we would connect if we could" that evening; his was that we were going to spend the evening and night together. Rosanne pointed out that giving Cesar her address showed a strong indication that I planned to see him, and she was understandably annoyed. She was lovely to him, however. I was wired, happy to see Rosanne, happy to see Cesar, and completely confused about what to do. In short order we decided that Cesar and I would spend a couple of hours hanging out together while Rosanne got her son settled and her packing done, then she and I would have a late dinner and do our planning.

On impulse, I suggested to Cesar that we soak in the hot tub on the deck behind Rosanne's house and then go out for a drink. Despite having seen each other in various states of undress at the gym, there was some momentary self-consciousness for both of us at getting naked together, but the discomfort was both pleasurable and tantalizing. We smoked a joint and began catching up. He'd had an enjoyable vacation at "the River" and told several funny stories, one about a man coming into his cabin after he'd fallen asleep.

"I was startled awake by his breathing, heavy breathing. He was standing in the doorway, I can see his . . ." He searched for the word. "Outline?"

"Silhouette?"

"Yes, silhouette. And I screamed, 'There's a bear, a bear is in my house!' People came running from all around and the man ran naked into the woods!"

The marijuana made his accent much more pronounced, and I was hooked. After a while we dried off, dressed, kissed for a moment, and wandered around the neighborhood, finally stopping for coffee and pastry in a café on Haight Street. Surrounded by gay men, I remembered the *New York Native* article. "Cesar, you're a nurse practitioner with gay patients. Did you see any evidence of AIDS in the men at Russian River?"

"No. I think to see the illness, you'd have to be here for a while. It's like New York. The numbers are small, and there are tens of thousands of gay men in both cities."

"But is it serious?"

"Yes. It is serious. But no one is certain about transmission. The men who are sick tend to be very sexually active, the baths, alcohol and drugs, multiple partners. Gay men need to cut down on numbers of contacts."

"Not a problem for me." I smiled at him.

He laid his hand on mine and gently squeezed it. "Are we ever going to sleep together? I thought tonight . . ."

"Maybe yes to the first question, definitely no to the second."

His green eyes were soft. "I really like you, Mike. I really would like to see if something can happen for us."

I wanted to discourage him, but I couldn't make myself look away. "I don't know what's going to happen with Mark and me. That's all I can tell you, Cesar. You know I like you. But I have to sort things out with Mark first."

*

The therapy weekend, located in a private home north of the city, went extremely well. Rosanne and I had always enjoyed working together, and her clients were eager to experience being with two therapists at once. On the ride home we had our first opportunity since Mexico to share deeply. She talked about her separation, how it felt both painful and liberating, and asked about Mark and me.

I said, "He says I want to change him, that I don't accept who he is. Maybe that's true. I can't figure out what we're *doing* together. I still love him."

"But?"

"But where is it going? When we're together, I go to work and come home to him cooking or reading. I can't afford to support him. I want a partnership." I sighed. "We're considering going into couples therapy."

"You and I are much alike, my dear. We're ambitious, we want to do something in the world, to make a difference. Mark is a wonderful man, but his happiness seems mostly to arise from hanging out on boats. There's nothing wrong with that, it just may not be enough for you."

I had some time to explore the Castro after our return, jammed as usual with gay men looking for casual sex, then one more evening with Rosanne before flying to Boston on Wednesday. Mark had left a message from Miami on her answering machine saying they'd been delayed in getting back and he probably wouldn't be returning to Boston before Friday. When could we talk? He was staying at John Batson's but working at the marina many hours a day, cleaning the boat and restocking it for the owner's next trip. I left a message at John's: "I'll be back in Boston tomorrow. If I can't reach you at John's, I'll see you on Friday."

I then called Cesar and asked him to pick me up at Logan. We went directly from the airport to his apartment in the South End. It was beautifully furnished, and in the course of our conversation Cesar revealed that his father was currently the ambassador from Panama to a country in Central America. No wonder Cesar was so accomplished. I spent the night. It unfolded simply, very little conversation about staying, no need for negotiation. It felt wonderful to be touched, and his desire for me was welcome. We undressed each other slowly in silence and kissed for a long time. I didn't think until later that I hadn't been kissed like that since Mark had developed thrush in January. I slept soundly for the first time in days, returning to my apartment early the next morning very relaxed, only to find a cheery telephone message from Mark. "Happy Thursday! I finished my work and got an earlier flight. I'll be home by noon."

I panicked, feeling short of breath. *What was I thinking?* My whole body was trembling. I hadn't had a moment to think about or integrate what had just happened with Cesar. I thought, *Stop this. Act as if things are normal.* But what *was* normal at this point? Clean the house. Take a shower. Start the laundry. Buy some groceries. Gradually my anxiety subsided as I got busy and I decided I could figure out this new complication in my life once I had some time alone. When Mark got home, I greeted him warmly and chatted as if it had been three days rather than nearly a month since we'd even spoken to each other. He was exhausted and mostly wanted to cuddle rather than talk. Several of his crewmates had been Spanish. When I blurted out that I had met a young man at the gym who spoke both Spanish and French, he asked, "Will I get to meet him?" and without thinking I said, "Of course."

After relating nothing more important than highlights of our travels, we fell into bed and into a deep sleep late in the afternoon. I realized when I woke up at 7:00 that he might not get up until morning. He was finally in his own bed and was not responsible for sailing, provisioning, or otherwise caretaking. His breath was deep and regular as I paced and stared out the window at the river, which seemed to be moving swiftly downstream toward the harbor. I drank rum on the rocks. I could easily have started smoking but didn't have any cigarettes. I thought over and over, *What was I thinking?*

We sleepwalked through the next few days. There was much to do, especially for Mark, who had been out of touch for some time. He had long conversations by telephone with his attorney and his partners in New York. They were pressing their appeal and needed more money from him. I had no idea where money came from when he needed it, whether there was just enough from his other tenants to squeak by or whether he borrowed money from his parents. I also was not privy to what he earned working on boats. He steadfastly kept his finances private, but he did continue to pay for the utilities on our apartment. On the Monday following our reunion in Boston, we received a letter from our landlord, a reminder that, from April 1, we had sixty days to either renew our lease for another year or give our notice to move out on August 31.

"I'm not prepared to deal with this now," he said, pacing from the window to the sofa and back.

"We have sixty days to decide."

"I won't commit to staying in Boston."

"Is that a definite decision?"

After a moment's hesitation, he said, "Yes."

Days of confusion and fatigue overwhelmed me, and I suddenly felt enraged. "Do you want to split up?" I asked coldly.

"What? No, I don't want to split up!" he snapped. "But I can't commit to living here for another year. I have to see how the appeal comes out. If we win, it will relieve some pressure on me."

I sat in the wingback chair and watched him. I wanted to feel compassion, to be tender and understanding. I felt neither of those things, however. I felt cold fury. "If you do win the appeal, do you want to renew the lease?"

He looked taken aback and sat down at the table, about as far from me as he could get and still be in the room. "No. I don't want to live in Boston. But we have other options. Or may have, if I win the appeal."

"Mark, do you have any idea what it's like for me to listen to this? You want a home, which I'm mostly paying for. You don't have a place to live in New York. You are once again caught up in a court case that has no visible end. You have no job and are constantly worried about money." My voice rose, louder and louder. "Assuming that *I* don't want to split up, what am I supposed to do? Let go of this apartment? Give up my practice? Put my stuff in storage and wander around with you, dragging a worn canvas duffel bag?"

He put up his hand. "Don't let's fight," he said.

"Why not? Isn't there something worth fighting for here?"

He looked out the window, his shoulders sagging. "I guess it probably wasn't realistic for me to expect you to see me through another financial crisis."

"I've said this before: I can't do this relationship by myself."

"Now I feel seduced and abandoned," he said. "You wanted me to move up here, you wanted to make a life together."

"I didn't know that would include partnership with someone who seems to have given up on adult life."

We were quiet then. I struggled to calm down, sick with anger and confusion. Finally he asked, "Do you have the name of a couples therapist we could see?"

"Yes."

"If you leave me the name and number, I'll make the call for an appointment."

Chapter 11

Just before Memorial Day my parents came to Boston for a few days before venturing north on a tour of New England. They didn't come east very often and I wanted their stay to go well. Mark and I had quieted down a bit after he scheduled an appointment for us with Roger Burlingame, a psychologist who had been recommended to us by a colleague at my office. But our connection was tenuous, and I was concerned that Mom and Dad would pick up on our tension.

When I was growing up, it was not unusual for my friends or those of my siblings to come to our house after school and end up staying for dinner. There was a general rowdiness and sense of fun in the house. Mom was in perpetual motion, cooking, cleaning, doing laundry and ironing, baking bread and cake and cookies, and managing a big vegetable garden in the summer. And talking, always talking, a cup of coffee within reach and a Chesterfield in her hand. She was whip-thin. Dad was quieter and more easy-going than Mom, who had a quick temper and a sharp tongue.

Dad was also a binge drinker. He would be sober for months at a time and there was relative peace in the house. Mom was barely out of high school when they married, and she told me once that she didn't realize Dad was an alcoholic until she was pregnant with Tom, her third baby in three years. She spoke to her mother, who said, "You made your bed, Anna Mary. Don't complain to me." His periods of drinking always felt to me like darkness: I would come into the house after school as a little boy and look to see the expression on my mother's face. If he was drinking, her lips would be compressed and her expression tight. We never knew what precipitated a binge or why it ended, though sometimes the police ended it for him. Otherwise he was generally a nice guy and never physically hurt me. But he was like Teflon, hard to connect with, hard to get any sort of emotional response from. When he was fifty-four, Dad managed to "put down the drink," as the Irish say, and never picked it up again.

Prior to this visit, the only time Mark had spent with my parents was during our brief stopover in Omaha on the way to Colorado the previous summer. I had no idea what their impact would be on Mark, but I need not have worried. They were more at ease and emotionally open than I had ever seen them. Dad had retired a few years earlier, and I was moved during the three days they visited by how affectionate they were with each other. Their favorite thing about our apartment was the view, and they would sit hand in hand in the bay window and watch the sailboats on the river, never bored, grateful to Mark and me for taking such good care of them. Mark found them bright and entertaining and, like his parents, well read and thoughtful. They liked him in turn, were a little intimidated by his reserve but relaxed when they found they could make him laugh. We went to a Red Sox game, walked the Freedom Trail, visited the Museum of Fine Arts, and ate in the North End. The few days went swiftly, and their happiness in being together brought a measure of peace and closeness to Mark and me. After they left, the image of them sitting in the window holding hands lingered. I thought of the years when their relationship felt like a battleground and it gave me hope for my dilemma with Mark.

*

And there was still what I thought of as the problem with Cesar. Since Mark had come home, Cesar had backed off a little, but when we talked at the gym, he always asked for more: lunch, dinner, time alone. My attraction to him never abated, but the anxiety attack I had experienced after going from Cesar's bed to Mark's had been lesson enough. I could not juggle two relationships, no matter how hip I wished to be. Mark asked again about "the guy at the gym who speaks Spanish and French." I was suspicious of the question until I realized he was always looking for people with whom he could converse in French or Arabic.

With almost no forethought, I asked Cesar if he would like to come to dinner and meet Mark. From one perspective it seemed insane, but my fondest hope was that it would defuse the situation for me.

Cesar looked at me speculatively. "Why would you want me to meet Mark?"

"I wish I could tell you, but I'm not clear. I've mentioned you to him, only as a new friend at the gym, and he's always interested in knowing people from other cultures."

"Does he know that we've slept together?"

"No."

He continued to examine my face. "You don't want a three-way, do you?"

I felt shocked at the suggestion, then laughed at my primness. "No, Cesar. The invitation is to dinner only."

"OK, then. Why not?" He was shaking his head as he walked away.

We set the date for the following weekend and Mark suggested I invite Fern Ganley as a fourth. Originally from Chicago, Fern was a single woman in her mid-forties, silver-haired, slim, and reserved. We had been fellow patients in a therapy group several years earlier and from the very beginning I felt like a brother to her. Mark was also fond of Fern, who, though heterosexual, had many gay friends and was "socially graceful."

On the day of the dinner, Mark was busy in the kitchen preparing salmon, and I was cleaning the house and obsessing. I had no idea what I wanted to happen, only that my conflicted feelings for both men would get resolved in some way. Fern arrived first, carrying a bunch of white peonies from her garden. She looked lovely, summery in a light blue dress, and her presence immediately anchored me. I had told her nothing about Cesar other than that he was a friend from the gym. He arrived a few minutes later with irises, and Fern put the flowers in vases while I showed Cesar the apartment.

The evening unfolded easily. The others all seemed completely relaxed, and several times Fern and I got into conversation in English while Mark and Cesar chatted in French. After one glass of wine in the living area, we moved to the table in the bay window and enjoyed Mark's wonderful meal. Twice I caught Cesar looking at me, but his expression was so neutral that I could only guess at what he was thinking. I remembered that he had grown up in a house of diplomats and had probably learned early how to wear a mask. He told funny stories of his childhood as an "ambassador's brat," and I felt a small ache in my heart at his sweetness. I knew I needed to let him go.

After dessert, a strawberry-rhubarb tart that elicited groans of pleasure from our guests and a wide smile from Mark, we gathered by the elevator to say our goodbyes. Cesar said he would walk Fern to her car, so there was no need for Mark and me to go downstairs with them. Fern and I hugged and chatted for a minute while Mark and Cesar spoke rapidly in French, looking serious. I felt a prickle of paranoia. But in another moment they were shaking hands and smiling. Cesar gave me a quick hug and thanked us both, saying it had been an interesting and enjoyable evening. Fern gave a little wave of her hand, and the elevator doors closed behind them.

It was still relatively early. Mark poured each of us a half-glass of wine and said, "Let's sit down for a minute before we clean up." I briefly thought of the dinner party when Max and I had gone to the roof and felt grateful to be feeling quite sober, having had only two glasses of wine. Mark said, "Cesar's a sweetheart. So bright! I envy him his youth."

"He's a good man," I said. I was uncertain where the conversation was going, and what Mark said next was totally unexpected.

"I remembered you said he was a nurse practitioner, and I asked him if it would be possible to see him professionally about my thrush. It hasn't gotten any better in these past two months. In fact, I think it's worse." He took a sip of wine.

"How worried are you?" I felt confused. How had Cesar gotten involved in Mark's health care?

"Not terribly. It's just that it should have cleared up by now with the meds my doctor in New York prescribed. I think it's worth having someone else look at it." His voice was steady, no indication of anxiety. "So I'm going to call his office on Monday and go in to have a culture taken."

I stood up and began to clear the dessert dishes. "OK. Why don't you sit down with the *Times* and I'll do the clean up?" My mind was racing. I felt stupid to have brought them together. Suddenly Cesar was more involved in my relationship than I could have imagined. *And why wasn't the thrush gone?*

*

Roger Burlingame's office was less than a mile from our apartment, so we walked to our first therapy session. We were both nervous. I was aware of longing for help and had rehearsed various things to say, but they all fled my mind as we entered his room.

Roger was a big man, over six feet tall and probably twenty pounds heavier than I was. He was wearing khakis and a maroon Lacoste pullover. I was relieved that he wasn't a jacket-and-tie guy. His manner was genial, but there was an underlying no-bullshit directness that was both attractive and a little intimidating. After a brief discussion about insurance coverage and co-pays, Roger asked, "Who'd like to begin?"

When Mark said, "I will," I tried not to look surprised. I'd spent a year and a half trying to get him to express his feelings, and all of a sudden he was ready to talk. He laid out his perspective on our dilemma: our meeting and falling in love, his moving to Boston the previous September, his lack of income. "I've had some problems with cash flow this last year, so Mike has had to shoulder more than his share of the financial burden," he said. "But I'm hoping that those problems will be resolved shortly."

When he paused, Roger asked, "Are the problems you're dealing with as a couple primarily financial?"

I jumped in. "It's more complicated than that, Roger. We'll be together two years in September. When I met him, Mark was a sailor in Florida. He moved up here to be with me but he hasn't been able to create a life for himself, or a means of support. I've been questioning the viability of the relationship. He doesn't want to live in Boston, and I don't want to leave my practice here unless there's some certainty of making a living somewhere else."

"Tell me how you met," he said.

And so we began, telling the story of falling in love. Mark said with gravity, "I had given up on love until I met Mike." I reached over and took his hand. It felt good to remember happier days, and I could feel some of my defense against being open to Mark begin to soften. Roger interrupted to ask questions, to redirect or clarify. We talked briefly about our exploration of moving to another city together, then Mark said to me, "We have to talk about the lease."

I said, "We have a deadline to deal with. Our lease expires at the end of August. If Mark is not going to stay in Boston, I should find a less expensive place to live. We were supposed to give our landlord ninety days' notice of our plans last week, but he's given us an extension until July 1."

Mark moved forward in his chair and caught Roger's attention. His voice was tense. "I can't stay here unless I can find a way to continue sailing and complete the requirements for my captain's license. I'm starting to make some contacts here and went to a meeting last week of gay men who are interested in sailing. But I don't feel like I can commit to being here and paying rent for another year."

I wanted to say, "You haven't *been* paying rent!" but bit my tongue. All of a sudden the session turned for me. I felt furious and stuck, and the time was nearly over. Mark and I both leaned forward, poised for Roger to offer something, any kind of solution.

Roger looked at us and smiled. "Well, I'm beginning to see where the work is here. Would you like to schedule a second session?" There was a moment of confusion and then we laughed, the tension breaking. Walking back home, we agreed that Roger seemed like a good fit.

I went to work and Mark had a coffee date with a man from the sailing enthusiasts' group. At dinner that evening, Mark was excited. His meeting with Ted White had gone well. Ted, who was thirty-eight, had just purchased a large sailboat and had too little experience to sail it alone. Mark said they'd talked about taking a two-week sail to Maine in August to break in the boat, which was named the *Delphic Oracle*. He wanted to know if I would go with him and Ted, and probably a fourth person, to be determined. I liked the idea of it, but said I wanted to meet Ted first.

"Of course. We'll be taking some day sails to get to know the boat together. You can come on some of those with me."

"At least one," I promised. Then, with a jolt, I remembered the lease. I blurted, "Assuming we're still together. You've already declared you don't want to stay in Boston."

There was a long silence. I could see the happiness and excitement drain from Mark's face. He said tentatively, "We've never talked explicitly about the possibility of breaking up. What do you think you would do?"

Looking at him, I was hit by a wave of hopelessness. There were too many complications to manage. "I don't know, Mark. I know that I love you, but that's not enough. Our problems feel insurmountable."

"I'm sorry that I'm not enough for you." He sounded bitter.

"That's not fair. You know that's not what I'm saying."

"No, Mike, I don't. I feel like I always come up short for you. Once I felt that you loved me unconditionally." He laughed humorlessly. "You told me that you'd waited all your life for me."

Stung, I said, "I feel like you just slapped me."

He watched me for a moment, then said, "So how do we solve these problems?" He was smirking. "You're the professional."

"I'm not our therapist, Mark."

"Why not?" he said. "It's your business. You deal with this stuff all the time. Feelings." He spit out the last word.

"I'm ready to start breaking dishes. I feel like you'll never understand what I need." I left the table and went into the bathroom to splash water on my face. I felt tired and old. When we went to bed, I clung to the edge on my side, not wanting to touch or be touched.

*

The telephone rang a few days later. It was a sunny morning in early June. The emotional storm had passed, for the moment anyway. Mark was at the harpsichord, and I walked into the kitchen and answered the wall phone. It was Cesar. Though we sometimes talked when I was at the office, I was surprised that he would call me at home, then I remembered that Mark had been to his office to have a culture taken.

"Cesar? What's up, my friend?"

"Mike, we got the tests back on Mark's fungal culture. Is he there?"

I was standing in the kitchen doorway, watching Mark practicing a difficult passage from Haydn. "Yes." I don't know why, probably a response to the anxiety in his voice, but I didn't say, "Shall I give him the phone?" I waited for Cesar to continue.

"Mike, I'm concerned. His thrush is deeply entrenched. We're going to try a much stronger antifungal medication. I can't say for sure what this means, but it's not good."

I continued to watch Mark play. He was totally absorbed and had not looked up at me. "That's . . . very interesting, Cesar. I'll try to see that movie. Did you call to talk to Mark?"

"Oh. I'm sorry. I shouldn't even be telling you this, but Mike, I care about you so much."

"Thanks, Cesar. I'll put him on." I walked into the living room, stretching the long cord to where Mark sat on the bench. "It's for you, sweetheart." I walked back into the kitchen and stared vacantly at the sink. *What the fuck was he saying? And why tell me?*

Mark came around the corner to hang up the phone and I jumped. "Daydreaming?" he asked, sounding amused.

"Oh, yes, I was thinking about the movie Cesar saw last night."

"What was it?"

I said the first thing that came to mind. "The new *Star Wars* movie."

"He liked it, I take it."

I couldn't believe he was so calm. I turned to rinse my coffee cup in the sink and, without looking at his face, said, "What did Cesar want?"

"Oh, my test came back. I need to go on a new antifungal medication. This damned thrush is a tough one. I told him about living in Tunisia for three years and traveling all over Africa. I know I have amoebas in my gut from those days. Maybe that's causing the problem."

He returned to the harpsichord and repeated the challenging passage until it was perfect.

Chapter 12

Several days later, Mark made a quick trip to New York for business and arrived back in Boston after I was already in bed. I'd done eight individual sessions that day and I was exhausted. He, on the other hand, was practically turning cartwheels.

"I won the appeal! The notice came in the mail at the building. My lawyer has been out of town so he didn't know it until I called him in Miami."

"What does it mean?" I asked, struggling to be fully awake.

"It means," he said with uncharacteristic drama, "that a lot of my troubles are over. Not all of them by any means, but at least the tenant's escrowed rent will be released to me. He has to pay his own legal fees, and we'll negotiate a new lease that will likely give me more income than I would have gotten before."

"Congratulations," I said, getting up and going to hug him. "Really. This is wonderful news." I sat back down on the edge of the bed.

"Mike, this is going to make a real difference to us. I was doing the math on the ride home. I'll have to pay my lawyer a good chunk of the money, but I can catch up on some of the other debts and be less under the gun than I've been since I've known you."

I asked, "What does that mean about you staying in Boston?"

He hesitated. "We'll have to talk more." He sat down next to me. "Look, honey, I can at least pay something toward the rent now. This really is a good first step. I'm helping Ted on his boat and making more connections, so I might be able to get jobs up here where I'll earn money and get more hours toward my license. I got my certificate from my engine mechanics course last week. My original plan to get my captain's license is finally coming together. Please be happy for me."

I put my arms around him and hugged him. "I'm thrilled for you. You've had a lot of grief to deal with over this and I'm happy that there's positive movement." Something relaxed in me, a defense that had been there for months. Maybe this relationship could work out.

*

Once again we found ourselves in Roger's office. We had only been seeing him for a month, but some ways in which we related to each other had already changed. We were listening to each other better. I had turned over the therapist's role to Roger and could just be part of the couple. He was sometimes gruff and made me squirm, but his directness felt more like being seen than being caught.

"What's up with the lease?" Roger asked.

"We have to tell the landlord this Friday," I replied. "We're down to the wire."

He looked at each of us. "So?"

There was a long pause. "I'm uncertain where Mark is, but now I'm ambivalent. I don't want to move, but at this point I'm not sure I'm ready to commit to another year together either."

Roger looked at Mark. "And you?"

"I don't want to break up." He looked at me and paused. "And I do want to be committed to our being together for another year, wherever we are."

"Even if Boston is my only option?" I asked, surprised, and he nodded.

Roger looked amused. "The ball is back in your court, Mike. The two of you seem to be reversing positions."

I thought for a moment. "I can commit to being together through September. I know I've been in a flap about the lease, but the worst that can happen is that, if we break up, I could stay on in the apartment, or we could pay the penalty and break the lease." I turned to look at Mark. "I'm sorry, but I often feel so disconnected from you."

"What do you think, Mark?" Roger asked.

"I'm sorry Mike has pulled back so far." He looked forlorn. "However, we've got the rest of the summer to work on this."

Walking home, he asked, "How long do we have to be in therapy?"

"As long as it takes," I replied. "Change takes time."

"I always knew it was a lifetime commitment," he said, then punched me lightly on the biceps. I laughed, once again aware that there was much about him that I loved.

*

We did a weekend sailing trip with Mark's new friend, Ted, joined by a couple of Ted's gay business associates. The *Delphic Oracle* had been refitted since I'd first seen her, and the interior was beautiful. Ted was justifiably proud and pointed out the quality of the cabinetry and the comfort of the six berths below. We were blessed with sunny weather, and Mark took the boat out of Plymouth Harbor and down the coast to Provincetown while Ted visited with his friends. After anchoring, we had lunch on the deck, which I prepared in the galley. Mark and I were in a peculiar social position; technically, we were not there as friends, nor were we there as staff. Ted paid for the food, alcohol, and all boat expenses; Mark brought his expertise as a sailor; and I took on the responsibility of the galley, which helped me to feel useful and also gave me a place to hide when I wanted to. Ted and his friends were all graduates of prep schools, Ivy League colleges, and business schools. Ted's forebears had practically come to America on the *Mayflower,* and he had an effortless sense of privilege that I both envied and despised. On this first sailing trip, the conversation at lunch turned to where we'd all gone to school. Even though Mark had not been to an Ivy League college, his graduate work at the University of Michigan carried status. When he said he had majored in Arabic Studies, the guys were impressed. Before someone asked, I said, "I went to the University of Nebraska," followed by a self-deprecating laugh. There was the briefest of pauses, then one of Ted's friends said, "They have a hell of a football team, don't they? The Cornhuskers." I nodded and nudged the conversation along, neglecting to say that I'd attended the Omaha campus and had barely visited the main campus in Lincoln.

After lunch we took the dinghy into Provincetown and tied up on the pier. It was early in the summer and the crowds were spirited. We walked companionably, enjoying the carnival atmosphere that characterizes this tiny town in the summer months, then went back to the boat for the return trip. Ted took the wheel with Mark at his side, and the *Oracle* headed east around the tip of the peninsula, past Herring Cove and Race Point. With a strong tailwind we followed the coast west until we reached the Cape Cod Canal. The day remained fine and there were pleasant moments of lazing in the sunshine and intermittent conversation. I cleaned up the galley before we got back to Plymouth shortly before sunset. We said cordial goodbyes to our companions, declining a drink at the marina bar.

On the drive home, Mark asked if I'd enjoyed the day.

"Ted's nice. He's well mannered and interesting, though I find all the business talk a little boring."

"Well, that's how those guys know each other. It's only natural."

"Yeah," I replied, "but there's a fair amount of weenie wagging going on about whose company is growing faster and what car they just bought."

"It's just what they talk about, honey. It doesn't mean anything."

"My own insecurity, I'm sure. Not to worry. I'm glad you found Ted, and I'll support this friendship in any way I can."

He rested his hand on my knee as he drove, a simple and welcome connection.

Our schedule was in summer mode. I worked three long days in the middle of the week so that I could take both Friday and Monday to travel if I wished. Mark had committed one weekend to celebrating his parents' forty-fifth wedding anniversary in New York. Ida's extended family would be there, as well as Mark's brother Bert and his second wife and two sons. Mark was not looking forward to it but felt obligated to participate. He said, "I don't think you would enjoy it," and I assumed I had not been invited. My not going let me avoid the potential problem of discerning how I would be introduced to the family at large, and I looked forward to a few days alone.

I thought of the long weekend without Mark as a retreat and decided not to fill it with people and events. It was a rare opportunity to deepen my meditation practice and to accomplish some things both at home and the office. The Friday Mark left was gratifying, a sunny day spent mostly sorting and filing a mountain of paperwork. I fell into bed early, feeling virtuous.

On Saturday morning I awoke to leaden skies and temperatures in the low fifties. I meditated and had breakfast, realizing that my energy had shifted with the weather. The day stretched out before me, empty. I felt restless and irritable. At noon I walked down into the Back Bay in a light mist and moved through the crowds on Newbury Street, at loose ends. A chilly fog blew in from the harbor. I ended up at Chaps, one of fifteen or so men sitting at the two bars drinking beer. A very drunk guy in his fifties sat down next to me and put his hand on my knee. I got up silently and moved to a different stool. The bartender asked what the weather was like and I said, "Pea soup."

"Ugh," he said, setting down my Budweiser. "This kind of weather always reminds me of slasher movies."

"Thanks," I replied. "You've succeeded in making my bad mood worse." We both laughed, but the cigarette smoke and dimness indoors were depressing, so I wandered home, finally admitting to myself that I was missing Mark. I was usually so busy when we were apart that I was aware only of his absence, not of missing his presence. And today would have been the kind of day to hang out in the house, do projects, read and cuddle and nap.

However, I awoke Sunday morning surprisingly rested. I meditated, looked out the window at the rainclouds lumbering across the sky, and wrote many pages in my journal. My relationship with Mark still felt rocky, and my life full of uncertainty. But taking the time to write about it brought relief, and when the sun finally emerged in the afternoon, I took a long walk along the river, watching the cormorants dive for food. By the time Mark called me in the evening, I was open and affectionate on the phone. He was headed back into Manhattan from Queens, had an appointment Monday morning, and then would be home late in the afternoon. I promised to save the *Times* crossword so that we could do it together upon his return.

*

Back in Boston, Mark told me his doctor had diagnosed him with shingles. I didn't know he was going to the doctor. Nor did I know what shingles was.

"Don't old people get shingles?" I asked.

93

"Shingles is stress-related. And I've had plenty of stress to deal with. But I feel better now that the Prednisone is knocking it out. And the thrush is a little better from the new meds. The doctor did say that we probably shouldn't kiss right now. You can't catch shingles from me, but it's better if I'm not exposed to anything you might carry while this is healing."

"I can live with that," I said. But I felt troubled. "Are you sure you're OK? Should I be worried?"

"Let's not make a mountain out of a molehill," he chided. Then he told me some tales of the family anniversary celebration and Eddie managing to knock back three Manhattans before Ida caught him.

*

At the end of June, Mark and I were in good spirits when we made the long drive to catch the ferry to Cherry Grove, looking forward to ten days off. Money pressures had lessened, and we both felt that the therapy sessions were beneficial. The weather was flawless, hot and dry, and I was excited to once again be in a community that was almost entirely gay. There was some buzz, more like an undercurrent, of conversation about AIDS. We still knew no one in Boston who had been diagnosed, though Cesar had told me at the gym that his boss, Dr. Mazzullo, had some patients now. I had also heard that a man named Larry Kessler had formed something called the AIDS Action Committee in Boston. Three of Mark's friends in New York had died, and another was sick. These deaths arrived like lightning bolts: men got sick, then really sick, then died, all in the space of a few months. The *New York Native* wrote consistently about Gay Men's Health Crisis in Manhattan, with Larry Kramer's rhetoric at a fever pitch. But my friends and I felt insulated from "the plague." As Arnie Kruger said to Mark, "I'm too vanilla to get AIDS!" Most of the people I knew in Boston felt the same way.

We spent the week going to the beach, walking, cooking on the grill on the tiny patio of our friends' studio apartment, and reading. I continued to muse about the direction of my life and to write in my journal. Rosanne and I had led two therapy weekends together by this time and had several more scheduled for the fall. I was developing a model for working with the concept of self-image: how do we see ourselves, how do we see our bodies, what needs to change in order to become the person we want to be? Affirmations were popular, and I said to myself over and over, "I do enough, I have enough, I am enough." I wanted badly to believe these words and to drop more fully into my life with Mark. In Cherry Grove I felt close to him and simply enjoyed our time together, day by day.

On July 1, my thirty-ninth birthday, we celebrated our last evening on the island at the Monster: sirloin steak, a bottle of good wine, and Death by Chocolate cake with a sparkler in it. Dozens of other patrons joined in to sing "Happy

Birthday." From there we walked with friends to the Ice Palace and danced until the wee hours. Mark, who frequently declined to dance, never left the floor that night.

*

Mark took frequent sailing forays with Ted in preparation for a longer trip planned for the end of August, and he celebrated his forty-first birthday on the *Oracle* on a midweek day trip, when I was at the office. He did not want a party, so we had dinner out the next night, a romantic encounter that ended pleasurably at home. Over these weeks Mark and I continued to talk about our options, feeling increasingly allied as we did more work with Roger. I wondered if what I had characterized in him as emotionally withholding might be a defense that was dissolving over time. Our sex life revived. We were unable to kiss, but it was gratifying all the same.

With Mark sailing more often, I saw Cesar one night for dinner and experienced again what had attracted me to him in the first place, his provocative humor and lovely green eyes. He asked about Mark and I gave him the update regarding shingles. He was somewhat guarded in his response and finally said, "I want to apologize for how I talked to you on the phone about his thrush. It was unprofessional. I've felt bad about it ever since."

"I wondered what that was about. I was really upset by it, not the thrush but how worried you sounded."

"I shouldn't have said anything to you. The thrush and the shingles may both simply be caused by extreme stress. I lost my professional judgment. Maybe I was still hoping something would work out for us."

"I hope it will work out to be a friendship, Cesar. Under other circumstances, I would have gone deeper, but . . ."

"*No estaba en las estrellas.*"

"Please, translate for me."

"It was not in the stars."

Chapter 13

At the end of August, what Mark continually referred to as "the main event" was upon us: two weeks aboard the *Delphic Oracle*, sailing up the coast of Maine to Bar Harbor. Mark had been provisioning the boat for weeks, preparing food ahead as he had done for our sail on the *Dancing Bear*. We had our usual agreement, Ted paying expenses and Mark and me helping. By this time it was clear that we were in fact, if not in name, "staff." It wasn't that Ted wasn't polite to us. But I felt the distance, the difference between how he related to his friends and how he related to us. With his friends he had conversations; with me he gave directions like "You might want to neaten up the galley." Mark said it was all in my head, but I didn't believe that for a minute.

My role was more complex on this trip. In addition to being the galley slave, not that I ever said that out loud, I was also to be second mate and would stand three-hour watches at the helm at night when we were motoring up the coast. I had had time at the wheel on other trips during the day but couldn't imagine myself alone on the deck ever, let alone at night. The trip began with just the three of us, in good weather, and I managed to deal with my two watches without panicking. The first night I was very anxious, however, alone on the dark ocean in a big sailboat, responsible for two lives in addition to my own, with only the Loran navigation system to guide me. Ted stayed with me for the beginning of my first evening watch and Mark came up a little early for the second. In between I managed my anxiety by counting my breaths and admiring the stars. The next morning I was exhausted but felt quite the sailor.

Four days into the trip we picked up a friend of Ted's in Rockland, Maine, who continued on with us to Mount Desert Island. Paul was twenty-three, in business school, and Ted had advised him on a project for a class. It was clear to me within five minutes that there was a potential problem, as I watched Ted watch Paul. Mark and I exchanged a private glance, Mark raising and lowering his eyebrows like Groucho Marx. Paul was very cute and full of energy. He also seemed oblivious to Ted's clear romantic interest. Mark and I withdrew into the anonymity of our roles and really only related to them at dinner, when we all drank too much and then Mark and I turned in early. We anchored each night in the harbor of another coastal village, beautiful towns with lobster boats in the harbor and perfect little cottages like Monopoly houses. We ate fine meals that Mark had prepared or bought lobster off the boats and grilled it on the deck. I had plenty of private time to write in my journal and read.

Initially the days were idyllic, and I was happy to be aboard. But as time passed, I felt isolated. Ted was totally infatuated with Paul and spoke to me only to suggest tasks. "The storage locker needs some straightening out." Or a cheery "The aft deck could use a good scrubbing!" Mark spent progressively more time when we were anchored each day working on the engine, which was in a tiny crawl space behind the aft cabin. There was something wrong with the firing mechanism, and twice he went into the harbormaster for help, then spent more hours tinkering. He could keep the motor going, but he wanted it running smoothly. He had a reaction to continued exposure to the fumes in the hold, an irritated throat-clearing that progressed into a deep cough. He was completely absorbed in the problem with the motor, as well as his roles as co-captain, first mate, and chef. I gradually shut down and became quiet, a smile frozen on my face.

We celebrated our second anniversary on September 2 in Castine Bay. Mark gave me a card that read,

Dearest Mike,

How to tell you how my new life, begun two years ago, feels—and that you mean so much to me—comfort, companionship, solace, pleasure—all of what I'd hoped love was, and found it to be with you.

Many more years for us.

Yours, and your

Mark

I felt vile and heartless. I had given him an anniversary card on which I'd written something superficial about "this new adventure" and "hope that things are easier for us in the coming year." We were on different planets. All the sweet closeness I'd experienced with him on Fire Island had dissolved into resentment. I felt trapped and wished only to be off the boat and away from Ted's condescension.

I made two telephone calls on the trip, one to Rosanne from a pay phone in Castine, the other to Betts and Gerry from a bar in Southwest Harbor. I was desperate for emotional contact and felt more grounded after the conversations. I talked to Mark about my feeling isolated on the boat and he felt criticized, couldn't understand why I wasn't happy, let alone that there was something I needed from him. He said, "Don't I have enough to do on this trip without dealing with your feelings?"

I wanted to push him overboard. "I'm sorry my feelings are such a burden, Mark."

"C'mon, Mike, don't be like that. I feel like a servant of two masters."

"I feel like a servant, period. And our king is lovesick and more imperious by the day."

"It will be easier when Paul leaves the boat tomorrow. Ted isn't good at not getting what he wants."

"I'm sorry. I just thought this trip was going to be more fun than it's turned out to be."

"We might have been happier on a smaller sailboat with less wealthy companions."

"Like we were with John and Kirk," I said, beginning to regain my sense of humor. "Thank you for acknowledging my feelings." The tension began to dissolve. Almost as an afterthought, I added, "I'm worried about your cough. Are you sleeping?"

"Enough," he said, moving to get up. "We'll be in Somes Sound tomorrow and should be able to get off the boat for a nice walk." He headed back to his engine.

Somes Sound, the only fjord on the East Coast, turned out to be extraordinary, so large it almost split the island in two. We anchored in Boothbay Harbor and the four of us took the dinghy into shore, Paul carrying his rucksack, looking like the college kid he was. We left them to walk into town, where Paul would head to the bus station to get a ride back to Boston. Mark and I had a long walk along the road in the opposite direction, admiring the lush green of the shrubbery and the abundance of birds. We passed a lone grave set back from the road with a little fence around it. Mark wondered aloud who had been buried in such a lovely and private place, and we wandered over to admire the worn gravestone.

We spent a quiet evening on the *Oracle*. Ted turned in early, and Mark and I lay on the deck after dinner for the first time on the trip, cuddling against the chill. Despite his cough and fatigue, he was in good humor. The engine was finally purring to his satisfaction. The stars were brilliantly clear and distinct in the night sky. Mark told me about the North Star, "the sailor's favorite guide," explaining that it stays in a fixed position relative to everything else in our solar system, moving approximately every 25,000 years. I understood for the first time how the earth both rotates and orbits, Mark holding up an imaginary earth in his left hand and moving it through space. For a split second I felt the thrill and terror of my utter insignificance in the big picture. Mark ended by saying, "Not even the North Star will endure. In time another star will take its place." He kissed me on the forehead and we headed to our berths.

We spent four more days getting back to Boston in beautiful sailing weather, again staying overnight in harbors and eating freshly caught lobster. Mark kept the engine working well and had a clear sense of triumph, telling me, "All that driving to Providence on Mondays paid off." His cough persisted, however, and he looked forward to getting home as much as I did.

*

Back in our apartment at last, we unpacked, did laundry, and slept for much of Sunday. Walking up to Roger's on Monday morning, Mark suggested we talk about "the nice things on the trip." I made a snide comment about Ted, and we were off and running. By the time we got into Roger's office I unleashed my worst self, hostile and persecuting. I complained about Ted's elitism, being treated like a servant, and then launched into Mark's failings, ending with, "If you can't make some contact with your feelings, we might as well break the fucking lease right now."

Mark was silent, looking somewhere at the blank wall between Roger and the door.

Roger finally said, "Mark, I hate to see you eat shit. When you won't stand up to Mike, as far as I'm concerned, you're eating shit."

The room was very still. I could feel my face grow hot. Roger looked at me. "If I were Mark," he said, "I'd want to kick you in the teeth."

I wanted to stand up and say, "You're not a therapist, Roger Burlingame, you're a bully!" But I had a sickening realization that I was the bully in the room. I felt flooded with shame. I stammered out, "I don't want to hear that from you, Roger. I want him to push back."

Roger looked at Mark, who said, "I can't talk like that, Mike. It's not in my nature."

"Mark, I'm asking you. Push back, however that shows up. Don't collapse."

"I'm afraid I'll say something that will damage the relationship so badly, it can't be repaired." He started coughing again.

I said, "For me, our lack of emotional contact is much more damaging."

"I thought we were learning to fight a few months ago. Haven't I gotten any better?" he asked.

I had to admit he had. "But you seem remote so much of the time. It makes me crazy!"

Roger said quietly, "Mike, can you love him just as he is?"

I shrugged my shoulders, feeling helpless. "I'll try. I'm sorry. I feel so stuck."

As the intensity abated, Mark reached out and took my hand. We agreed to deal with issues as they came up and not to save up resentments. By the end of the session, my shame and despair began to lift.

Coming out into the bright sunlight, we were quiet walking home. The weather was mild, but the trees were beginning to change. Mark broke the silence.

"There will be piles of leaves on the ground before we know it."

"How do you feel about fall coming?"

"Assuming I ever feel better, I look forward to moving the *Skua* down to Florida. After that, who knows?"

In the apartment I made sandwiches for us. By unstated agreement we sat at the table in the window and read Sunday's *New York Times*, then stretched out on the bed and fell asleep. When I woke up he was curled against me and I could feel that he was aroused. We hadn't made love since before the sailing trip. We took our time undressing and touching, but because of the continued presence of the thrush, we were still unable to kiss on the lips. Without the shield of my anger and disappointment I felt tenderness, and we were quiet afterward for long minutes.

"Do you wonder why we don't fuck anymore?" he asked.

Surprised, I said, "I've assumed it felt too intimate to you."

"My venereal warts are back, and the treatment that has cured them before is not working." We were both quiet again, and then he said, "I worry about AIDS." It was the first time he had ever used that word in relation to himself. I could hardly breathe. *We can't be having this conversation*, I thought.

We were lying naked facing each other, and I held his gaze, pushing my panic down. "From what I've read, if you had it, you'd know it. None of your symptoms are extraordinary."

"I know, but this cough isn't going away. My breathing is affected. Maybe it's time to see a specialist. I'm going to call Cesar at his office this afternoon and ask him to get me a referral." Throughout his narration Mark's voice was without emotion, whether for his own sake or mine, I didn't know.

"Good idea. Maybe he'll reassure you. I just don't think your symptoms are bad enough." But the black cloud that I'd felt hovering before felt terribly close. We still didn't know anyone personally in Boston with AIDS, but we knew from friends that there had to be fifty or sixty men already diagnosed.

The next morning, running too fast along the dirt path on the Cambridge side of the river, I stumbled and nearly fell. I sat down in the grass, panting like a dog. *He's not afraid he's going to get AIDS, Mike. He's afraid he already has it.* I was soaked with sweat. *Oh, dear God, what if he really is sick?* I had tried to avoid reading the *New York Native* articles, believing that they really didn't have anything to do with me. Could I really have been blind all these months? Feeling unsteady, I got up and slowly walked back home.

Cesar referred Mark to his boss, Dr. John Mazzullo, at New England Medical Center. John was an internist who saw many gay men in his practice, and we had several friends in common. He was willing to see Mark immediately and the appointment calmed Mark down somewhat. Initially John treated him for a virus, which seemed to have no discernible effect. After several days Mark made a second visit, and John treated him for bacterial pneumonia. I was unable to attend either appointment because of my work schedule. Mark remained calm, said John had told him to "think positive and rest a lot," which he did. But his breathing continued to be effortful, and he reported that he could not get a full breath when he lay on his right side. When it became clear that Mark was not responding to the second treatment, John said it was time for him to see Dr. Jerome Groopman, an oncologist and infectious disease specialist at Beth Israel Deaconess Hospital. Mark was asked to bring his partner, if he had one, and his most recent X-rays.

We had to wait until Friday, four days away. We were gentle with each other but didn't talk much. What was there to say? My mind, however, was never quiet, imagining one dire scenario after another. I felt fortunate to be working, absorbed in my clients' issues, at least for the duration of the sessions. While Mark slept deeply, I hardly slept at all, and I fantasized he had lung cancer. At this point that seemed like a more hopeful diagnosis than AIDS.

Friday morning found us sitting in Dr. Groopman's office. He was quite tall, taller that I, and thin. He looked to be in his mid-thirties. He told us he had just moved his family from L.A. to Boston and that his wife was an endocrinologist. Both his smile and manner were friendly, but I was so anxious I could barely hear his comments. I felt like I was observing him through the wrong end of a telescope. He took Mark's medical history and asked about our relationship and our sexual histories. His matter-of-factness made the sharing of intimate information relatively easy. Had we gone to the baths? What about multiple partners? Did we use condoms? Were we monogamous? He took notes throughout the interview, then a long look at the X-rays.

"Mark, I assume you know that having either an opportunistic infection such as Kaposi's sarcoma (KS), which is a type of cancer, or *Pneumocystis* pneumonia (PCP), constitutes an AIDS diagnosis. Your symptoms are not necessarily AIDS-related, but we need to do more tests. You have a very healthy history and we could make a case for other diagnoses. But let's get the tests done first." The word *AIDS* was finally in the room. He scheduled Mark for a bronchoscopy the following week. "You'll need to stay in for a night or two after the procedure," he said. "We'll be taking biopsies from many sites. In the meantime, please get your blood work done." We shook hands with him and both left feeling marginally better. Hadn't the doctor been optimistic? On the way home we thought of another possibility: maybe Mark was ill but not with AIDS. We decided not to tell many people about the upcoming procedure, particularly his parents. We clung to the hope that his test would be negative.

The bronchoscopy was scheduled for the following Thursday. Much to my dismay, Mark insisted on going to New York on Sunday, promising he would return as soon as possible. I put up resistance to no avail. There was legal work he had to take care of. I spent Monday cleaning the apartment, taking things out of cupboards to wash, shaking out rugs and blankets on the roof, not giving myself a moment to think. I spoke to Mark briefly that evening. He said he'd met with his attorney, had "dealt with a few issues," and would come home in the morning. After saying goodnight, I drank rum on the rocks in bed and tried to read the *Globe*, but my mind was running full tilt, images of KS lesions from a *Native* article I'd inadvertently seen penetrating my denial. I finally fell asleep with the light on.

*

On his return from New York, Mark had blood tests and an intake with the pulmonologist, Dr. Janice Murphy. He reported that he could now lie on his right side and still breathe. The night before the bronchoscopy, I told him I was sorry that things between us had been so stressful over the summer. He said, "Mike, we had a lot of good times, Fire Island and your birthday party. The sailing was great for me. And at least we have some practice in fighting now." He smiled. But that seemed like a small victory, considering how stressful these months had been.

Wednesday afternoon I took Mark to the Deaconess Hospital for admission. He filled out reams of paperwork in the office with the help of a volunteer who managed to be both warm and brisk simultaneously. Once again I was moved by how dignified Mark was, serious but in no way dramatizing the situation. He was admitted to the Farr Building, Room 1104. Dr. Murphy visited him in his room, telling us that the procedure was tentatively scheduled for 10:00 the next morning. When she left, Mark said, "Can I make a last request?"

My heart nearly stopped in my chest. Had he really said those words? "Anything."

"Will you go to Chef Chang's and get me some eggplant with garlic sauce and hot and spicy beef?"

It took me several seconds to understand what he'd asked, and then I started laughing. "You order on the hospital phone," I said, "and I'll go pick up the food." I was shaking my head as I went out the door.

The procedure was not performed until just after noon. When Mark was returned to his room, he slept for two hours, his mouth making little convulsive movements and his hands weakly grasping the sheet covering him. He had a cannula attached to his nostrils that was delivering oxygen. The doctors had taken six different biopsies from his lungs, plus cell scrapings for "washing." His breathing was shallow and I wondered if his lungs hurt. When he awoke he was briefly foggy, then struggled to speak. "What did they find?" His voice was a whisper.

"Nothing yet, sweetheart. The lab tests won't be back until Monday."

"My throat feels like a tank drove through it."

"Do you want a little water or ice chips?"

"Yes. And I'm hungry." When I looked surprised, he said, "I haven't eaten since last night."

"I know. It just seems incongruous that you are in a hospital bed right after invasive surgery and the first thing you want is food." I grinned at him. "You are truly amazing."

He closed his eyes for a moment, then opened them and smiled. "Maybe some ice cream?"

I checked with the nurse and then fed him small bites of vanilla ice cream. After a few minutes he said, "I feel so foolish, being fed."

"I'm happy to be able to do something. I feel pretty helpless."

"Well, I'll be out of here soon enough," he replied.

"Do you want me to call your folks?"

His parents knew he had been sick but did not know about the hospitalization. "Let's wait until we know what's wrong with me."

*

Mark had recovered enough by Saturday that the staff released him in the afternoon. While his throat was quite sore, he much preferred to wait for the test results at home. We spent most of the time on the sofa or in bed, did the *Times* puzzle on Sunday morning, and ate take-out. We said little about the situation, just drifted from hour to hour. Our mutual anxiety seemed to have been replaced by a low-level dread. Mark had no desire to talk about the situation with anyone. I had a few hurried conversations with my close women friends but worked to keep the lid on what was happening. As always, I kept busy, preferring action to the recurring scenarios of doom that ran through my mind.

Dr. Groopman called on Monday afternoon. I answered the phone and could tell from his voice that the news was not good. He said without preamble, "Mike, I'm sorry, I really didn't expect *Pneumocystis*. You'll have to bring him right over." I handed the phone to Mark and watched his face lose expression as he listened.

"OK, thank you for calling. I'll get my things together." He handed me back the phone and we looked at each other. Neither of us spoke, then Mark closed his eyes for a moment. I wanted desperately to say or do something helpful, but my anxiety was paralyzing.

Finally I said, "I'll make us a cup of tea first, then we'll pack your bag." He nodded and I went out to the kitchen, put the kettle on the stove, and got out our favorite mugs, his with a sailboat and mine with the Boston skyline. Suddenly I sat down hard on a chair. Inhale, exhale, one to four. The house was absolutely still. When the kettle whistled I jumped, then prepared the tea and joined Mark on the sofa. His voice was steady despite the labored breathing.

"At least we know for sure what we're dealing with," he said. I wanted to cry in the worst way but knew it was the last thing he would want to deal with. I picked up his little suitcase for the hospital and we went down to the car in silence.

Mark's check-in at the hospital was expedited and he was put into a room immediately. Within fifteen minutes he was in a hospital gown and had a cannula hooked to his nostrils. I could tell he was struggling to breathe, and I asked him if he needed more air. "No," he said, "I need less anxiety." Dr. Groopman showed up soon after that. He had become a positive force for us in such a short time. Mark brightened when he saw him, relaxing even more when the doctor said, "It's fine to call me Jerry."

He said, "We're going to start you on a course of antibiotics, Bactrim first, to deal with the virus. It's worked with some other patients and I'm confident we can arrest it." Mark nodded but did not speak. "If Bactrim doesn't work, we'll go to Pentamadine." He briefly laid his hand on Mark's shoulder. "We just need you to rest and let the medicine do its job."

I asked, "Do you have any idea how long he'll be hospitalized? I should call his parents."

"It's hard to predict. Let's see how he responds to the Bactrim."

When the doctor left I lay down on the bed next to Mark and tucked myself against his side, careful not to jostle the line to the oxygen tank and putting no pressure on his chest. We were quiet for what seemed like a long time. Finally I remembered his toast on our first anniversary. "Shoulder to shoulder," I said.

Barely audible, he murmured, "Yes," then dozed until a nurse came into the room.

*

Early in the evening I had a painful conversation with Eddie and Ida from the pay phone in the empty visitor's lounge. They knew he had been hospitalized for tests but did not yet know the results. When I told them that the diagnosis was PCP, Ida's anxiety went sky high, and Eddie hurried her through the rest of the conversation. They agreed to await my next call before scheduling a visit.

As I returned to Mark's room from the visitor's lounge, I wondered how I would explain to them the presence of the large red stickers on the door to Mark's room: PRECAUTIONARY ISOLATION. There was also a list in large print with elaborate directions for how those who entered should wear gowns, gloves, surgical caps, and masks. *Abandon hope, all ye who enter here.* I felt grief-stricken putting on all the paraphernalia, and disloyal. I'd been sharing a bed and a life with Mark for more than two years. From what could they protect me now? I asked a nurse if it was required, and she said yes. The first time I gowned up and entered the room, I could see from Mark's expression that he didn't immediately recognize me, and I pulled the mask away from my face.

"I feel like a leper," he said.

"This is too *Twilight Zone*, sweetheart. I'm really sorry. The nurse said I had to wear the whole *megillah*. They're just being careful."

"They're frightened of me. That's what's upsetting," he said defiantly. "Every time they come in, it looks like aliens are invading my room. I feel like I've awakened in a horror movie."

Struggling to sound hopeful, I said, "They'll have the Bactrim ready to administer soon, and we'll be on the way to bringing you back home."

"Let's hope so," he replied without conviction.

I rarely wore the mask after that, though I kept it around my neck in case anyone made a fuss. I hated how separate it made me feel from Mark.

On that first night in the hospital, we pinned our hopes on Bactrim, though we were warned that 60 to 70 percent of all patients were allergic to it. Mark had an IV in his right arm that pumped in first Bactrim and then dextrose. He watched every move each medical person made and asked questions about every procedure. He forced himself to stay alert when anything was being administered. During that first evening I sat on the side of the bed, holding his hand and talking quietly about a favorite fantasy we shared: visiting Tunisia, where he had taught for three years, and what it might be like to travel up the mountain to Sidi Bou Said, where the school he had worked at was located. At first I yanked my hand away from his every time someone came into the room, fearing they'd be homophobic. But after a while I thought, *We're here for the long haul. We might as well be real and see what happens.* Sometimes the aides and support staff seemed nervous to be in the room, but the doctors and nurses were unfailingly attentive and caring. Mark was only the 100th person in Massachusetts to be diagnosed with AIDS, and the few other AIDS patients in the Deaconess were much sicker than he was.

Within a few days it became apparent that Mark was having an allergic reaction to the Bactrim. He developed a prickly red rash all over his body. Jerry Groopman switched his treatment to Pentamadine after Mark signed a release form acknowledging all the potential side effects: kidney damage, bone marrow depletion, the development of abscesses at the site of his injections, and so forth. The drug was experimental and potentially toxic. But we had no alternative. Another few days and Mark's struggle with breathing finally began to ease up. Gradually he became less reliant on his cannula for support.

Mark spoke briefly to his parents several times on the phone and finally felt strong enough after a week to invite them to come to Boston. They arrived on Friday and said they'd already rented a motel room and would stay "as long as you need us." Standing awkwardly in gowns and masks, they began by talking about the traffic coming up and how much Aunt Pearl wished she could be with them. I moved to the corner of the room, a silent witness, as they seated themselves near the bed. Eddie said, "So how are you, Junior? Are you going to be all right?"

"The doctors are doing the best they can, Dad. This second medication seems to be effective." No one mentioned the word *AIDS*. His mother said they had told their friends he had pneumonia and would be home soon. "Close enough," Mark said, shooting me a look across the room. When the conversation moved to neighborhood and family news, I excused myself and went to the cafeteria for lunch.

In the hubbub of the cafeteria, I found a quiet spot in the corner and felt relieved to be alone, despite the presence of at least sixty other people. I had little experience being hospitalized myself, the last time having been at age ten when I had my appendix out. The stimulation, the noise and bright lights, exhausted me. And now that I knew Mark's diagnosis, I had to confront the reality of a whole new world opening up, one that was extremely terrifying. As I toyed with my salad, I thought again what had passed through my mind in the visitor's lounge when Mark was diagnosed: *Nothing will ever be the same.* I was devastated on a very deep level and could imagine a nightmare scenario of illness, culminating in Mark's death. But I was optimistic by nature, and little was known about this disease. Surely researchers would find a cure before long. Sitting at my little table in the basement of the hospital, I could see the bare outline of a battle plan: *we just have to keep him alive long enough to find a cure.* I felt heartened by that thought. The number of patients seemed high for an unknown illness, but we had to fight. Neither of us were quitters.

Later in the afternoon Jerry Groopman popped in. Ida was beside herself with pleasure to meet him, thanking him repeatedly and saying how grateful they were that he was taking such good care of their boy. "I'm sorry I'm such a mess, Doctor," she said, patting her hair. "It took us nearly five hours to get here. The traffic!" Jerry was all smiles, gracious and gentle, and Mark was more relaxed in that moment than I'd seen him be in a week. After Jerry left, Ida looked at Mark. "He is Jewish, isn't he?"

"Would it make a difference?"

"Of course not. But I know he's Jewish. He's so intelligent!"

"Mom, please!" Mark said, trying not to laugh.

Eddie and Ida stayed until dinnertime on Friday and returned on Saturday morning, announcing that they thought they would drive back home that afternoon if Mark didn't need them to be there. He said, "I'll be fine, Mike will be here with me." My presence seemed to be taken for granted. Before they left that afternoon, Ida cornered me in the little kitchen off the visitor's lounge to "have a talk."

"Darling, I just want to tell you how grateful we are that Mark has you." She began to cry. "I have to tell you, I'm afraid I was a bad mother. I've always been afraid I ruined his ability to love." She grasped my hand so hard it hurt. "You know what he told me? He told me he loved you, and that his home is with you." She wiped her eyes with a tissue and said, "Mike, everyone needs someone in life, to have meals with, to read with. I'm so glad he has you."

Then she shook my hand. My heart opened completely to her, and I squeezed her hand with both of mine. "Thank you, Ida. That means the world to me."

*

For the next week I went to the hospital at 7:00 a.m., then to the office around noon, returning to the hospital by 7:00 p.m. to spend an hour or two before bedtime. I was tired but felt purposeful. Mark was clearly improving. He was off IVs on Tuesday, then off oxygen on Wednesday. I read an article in the *New York Native* about an AIDS conference held near the NIH the previous week. Scientists reported that patients with KS lived an average of seventeen months, patients with PCP for seven months. It was hard to reconcile that information with the image of Mark on the Exercycle in his hospital room on Thursday morning, pedaling for fifteen minutes and working up a sweat. He grinned as he dismounted the bike and held up his fingers in a victory sign. He was told he would be discharged on Friday. He'd been in for two weeks. He was afraid to leave the security of the hospital, but I was ready for him to come home.

Larry Kessler had contacted us from the AIDS Action Committee. He came by the hospital to introduce himself and sent Mark flowers with a note that said, "We are with you all the way." Our closest friends, who had known why Mark had been hospitalized, mobilized to help. Whatever fears they held about catching the disease they kept to themselves. Fern Ganley and my friend Steven Holt began organizing, making lists of which of our friends could spend time with Mark if he needed someone at home when I was at work. Deborah Haynor helped me figure out how much to tell my clients and took referrals that I didn't have time to respond to. She arranged with Mark to bring lunch to the apartment on Fridays and spend her lunch hour with him. I found it much easier to feel my feelings openly with them, tearing up, talking about my fears of the future, and they were patient and present with me, solidly supportive in such a difficult time.

I was sleeping badly, often woke up crying, but on a deep level I was resolute. Whether I was ready or not, this was my fight as well as his, as long as he was alive. Friends asked me, "Do you think you have it?" And I would say, "I'm obviously at risk. But what do I know? There's no test for it yet." I wasn't sure I even wanted to know. Apprehension filled my heart whenever the thought crossed my mind.

The night before Mark was discharged I had a dream in which I was standing on the street with Rosanne. We were arguing about suicide. Vito Caniglia, my childhood friend, drove up in an old car and said, "I just heard." I said to him, "I have five months to live." He said, "I know."

I thought about the dream when I woke up. I didn't need Freud to interpret it. I made coffee and sat at the table where we'd had so many wonderful dinners. I wrote in my journal, "If I have AIDS, I'll kill myself if he dies. I can't go through this with him and then deal with it alone." I felt stronger for having made the decision.

PART THREE

Chapter 14

When Mark returned home from the Deaconess, he was tense and quiet. He saw germs lurking everywhere. I found him in the kitchen one morning wiping all the surfaces with Windex. When I raised my eyebrows, he scowled at me and said, "We have to do something about this place."

"What about this place?" I asked.

"It has to be really clean. My immune system is nonexistent. I could get any opportunistic infection."

"You've been reading scary stories in the *New York Native*, haven't you?" I said.

"It doesn't mean that what I'm saying isn't true," he snapped.

"OK, OK. I'm just suggesting that opportunistic infections are probably not running amok in our kitchen on Bay State Road. And we don't have pets, so you don't have to deal with whatever they might be carrying. *And* we've asked friends who visit not to come if they have colds or feel sick. There are limits to what we can do, Mark."

He sat down on the edge of a kitchen chair, leaving his scrubbing cloth and the Windex on the counter. "I just feel paranoid."

"Of course you do. I think we need to make some contact with other people who are dealing with AIDS in Boston. Want me to check around?"

"Yes," he said, and then pretended to read an open cookbook that was sitting on the table. He hadn't cooked for many weeks.

Later that afternoon I visited Peter Lombardi, who was the coordinator of the AIDS Action Committee "buddy program." He had not yet met Mark but said that he had several possibilities available when Mark was ready to accept a buddy. I told him that what we really needed was to meet with other couples affected by AIDS.

"At the moment there are only two 'intact' couples in Boston, Mike, and the partners with AIDS are very sick. Two other couples are breaking up and the well partners are moving out." When I did a double take, he said, "People are afraid of getting infected."

"But wouldn't they already be infected?"

"We know little about transmission and even less about the incubation period." I mulled that over for a moment. It had never occurred to me to leave Mark. Yes, I was afraid. But how could I leave him when he was sick? Peter continued. "Larry Kessler and I are putting together a support group for people with AIDS, a 'PWA group.' Do you think Mark would be interested?"

"Maybe. He's not much of a joiner, but he needs more stimulation. He's afraid to go out of the house."

"I'll give him a call," he said.

Much to my surprise, Mark took to the idea immediately. He talked to Peter the next day and found out there were five other men who were ready to join. "It will be a relief to be with people who understand me," he said. I felt excluded from that group but understood what he meant.

October became November. Ever so slowly we created a new normal. Mark and I began going to a noontime meditation class once a week in Cambridge. The class was taught by a quiet, thoughtful man named Harrison Hoblitzelle, who was called Hob. I committed to sitting daily for twenty minutes. Mark enjoyed the class and found the practice useful in quieting his mind. Hob said, "Meditation reminds us that we are always home. It is not a method to get someplace, but rather to be more fully where we are." Mark asked in class one day, "What if we don't want to be where we are?" Hob said, "In reality, where else could we be?"

For the first time since our return from the sailing trip, we had an appointment to see Roger Burlingame. It had been six or seven weeks but it felt like a lifetime. His sturdy presence and empathy were nourishing.

"How are you managing?" he asked.

"Barely," Mark said with a rueful laugh. "It's bizarre to think how much our life has changed since we were here last. Mike has been taking good care of me. I can't get over being tired all the time."

Roger turned to me. "Mike?"

"Just sitting here with you, remembering being furious with Mark about the sailing trip, seems so distant. I keep hoping it's a bad dream and we'll wake up."

"But how are you *managing*?"

I thought for a moment. My world, our world, looked entirely different from how it had looked the last time we were at Roger's. But we had pulled together and were creating a routine that worked well enough. "Actually, we're managing pretty well. We're going to a meditation class together. Mark is getting involved with the AIDS Action Committee. And we're both starting to sleep better again. All those things help."

Little by little we began to relate the trauma of the last two months, the shock of the diagnosis and fear that Mark might not survive his bout of PCP. Mark talked about how bizarre it had been to have people coming in and out of his room completely gowned and masked. "Then my parents came in and I wanted to laugh," he said. "They're both so small, they looked like gnomes dressed up for a Halloween party." His voice trembled, but he would not let himself cry.

"What are you feeling now, Mark?" Roger asked.

"Unclean, physically and morally. It's like telling people you have syphilis, only worse. In the hospital, I told Mike I felt like a leper."

Roger nodded, his gaze steady and sympathetic. There was a moment of quiet in the room. Finally Mark asked, "Can I come to see you by myself sometimes?"

"Of course," he replied.

As Mark and I headed back down Beacon Street, snow began falling, an early beginning to winter.

*

Most of the time my life felt like a treadmill set on high. My private practice remained full, and I believed I needed to keep earning as much money as possible, given that Mark had had to give up his boat-moving jobs and put the pursuit of his captain's license on hold. My colleagues at the office, Warren Brewer and Mariel Kinsey, were supportive and loving. I could unload all of my feelings with them without filtering: fear, anger, grief. Many of my clients wanted to know more than I thought was appropriate. Over and over I said, "Let's keep the focus on your work." But unspoken questions floated in the air: Are *you* sick, Mike? Are you going to leave me? And I would remember Jerry Groopman saying, "Of course, partners are in the high-risk group."

New people came into our lives. The first was Mitch Katz, a young man assigned to Mark from the AAC's buddy program. Barely twenty-three, Mitch was a second-year medical student at Harvard. I never saw them together that I didn't think of my mother's phrase "thick as thieves." They shared so much, both of them Jewish New Yorkers, well educated, bookish, and introverted. They developed an immediate connection, and Mark told me after his second visit from Mitch, "It's like I've known him all my life."

Then we were introduced to Richard Piper and Patrick Roll. We had become friends with John Mazzullo, the physician who had first treated Mark after the sailing trip, and told him that we wished we knew another couple in our situation. John had met Richard when he was diagnosed with Kaposi's sarcoma, and he invited the two couples and Larry Kessler to brunch at his condo on Marlborough Street. It was a beautiful Sunday morning. Mark and I walked the five blocks in the sunshine, both nervous and excited. Larry, big and slow-moving, always reminded me of a fatherly bear, and I sat next to him at first and simply enjoyed the light streaming in the tall windows and the buzz of conversation. Then I remembered why we were there. I watched John, gregarious and socially adept, weave a web of comfort and safety around his guests.

Richard was in his late twenties, Patrick in his early thirties, and they'd been partnered only a year. Richard had completed medical school and his internship in June. He was scheduled to return to San Francisco to begin a residency in ophthalmology and then was diagnosed with KS. They were both handsome and youthful, but where Richard was extroverted and impish, Patrick was serious and reflective. Mark and Richard sat beside each other for most of the morning, immediately connecting the way Mark had with Mitch. This was new behavior for him. Patrick was quiet much of the time, so I helped John with the food and tried to stay out of the way.

Mark attended his first PWA group, which met every Tuesday night for two hours at the offices of the AAC. My greatest worry was that it would be a downer for Mark, having heard that some of the men were more debilitated than he was at this point. But he came home from his first meeting bubbling.

"Great guys, all of them. There are five others. I'm the oldest, most are in their thirties, one or maybe two in their twenties. Very diverse group. Some are chatty, some are quiet. All of us are freaking out. That was the best part."

"I don't understand."

"We're all in the same boat. It was amazing to hear other men say the exact things I've been feeling. Richard was there, of course, and David, Edward, Pedro and Louie." He paused for breath and sat down. I watched his face and felt a smile emerge on my own. It was lovely to feel a moment of happiness.

"It's wonderful to see you excited," I said.

"I feel alive again, Mike. Not like I used to feel, but in my head I've been putting myself in a casket ever since my diagnosis. We talked tonight in the group about possible cures. One guy heard that vitamin C in large doses might strengthen your immune system. We just have to keep ourselves alive until they find a cure." Seeing him like this, bubbling with excitement, brought me a huge sense of relief.

"That's your job now, Mark, to keep yourself alive and reasonably well until they find a cure. Jerry says that they're working on that night and day." I felt hopeful in the moment and wanted to support his hopefulness as well.

Much of November was spent waiting for a treatment program. Would it be Alpha Interferon? Might they let the patients sign waivers and be guinea pigs for Gamma Interferon? What about the trials for Interleukin II? Mark and the men in his PWA group grew close, and I saw yet another side of his character emerge, a kind of older brother, caretaking and reassuring with the other men. Because Mark was the oldest in the group, as well as intelligent and articulate, he said the younger men looked up to him. He and Richard, also bright and verbal, formed a tight bond, despite the fourteen-year age difference. I was grateful that he was forming close relationships, since both Arnie Kruger and Ted White had dropped out of sight as soon as Mark was diagnosed. To me it was a small loss, but for him I was grateful that we were connecting in such meaningful ways with other men directly affected by AIDS. Meanwhile I was busy at work and doing most of the housework, grocery shopping, and cooking. Alcohol and marijuana became my daily friends. Mark was never critical of my drinking or smoking and seemed relatively unaware of my state.

When I first called my parents to say Mark had been diagnosed with AIDS, I had kept my voice as neutral as possible. I shaped the delivery with optimistic phrases like "labs working on promising drugs" and "doctors all over the world investigating cures." What amazed me, after I got off the phone with my mother, was that she didn't ask me if I was also infected. Nor did she in her letters. Our conversations were few and far between for a couple of months. But in late November I was feeling tired and frazzled, and I called to ask how their Thanksgiving had been. We chatted for a few minutes and then she asked how Mark was.

I said, "Up and down."

"I guess that's to be expected, honey. There doesn't seem to be much the doctors know, at least from what little I read in the paper."

"Well, we try to remain hopeful." The conversation felt hollow. I decided to take a leap and say what was actually going on. "I'm feeling swamped, Mom. It's hard to juggle everything that needs attention, and I'm tired all the time. Mark can't really do much, and I'm always on the run."

"Why isn't he helping, honey? Isn't he home all day now?"

"Yes, but he's depleted much of the time, and worried, and depressed."

"Well, it doesn't sound like he's doing you much good."

I could feel my jaw set. "Mom, you make it sound like he's malingering. He's exhausted!"

"Well, so are you, Mike. Maybe you need to do a little less and let him do more. I'm worried about *your* health, getting so run down." She paused to choose her words carefully. "I wonder if maybe he might get better medical care in New York. He could be with his parents then."

It dawned on me that she was hoping there was an escape hatch. Did she honestly imagine I'd leave him? Without missing a beat I said, "I'm here for the duration, Mom. In sickness and in health."

To her credit, she said, "That's what I was afraid you'd say." We were silent for a moment and my anger fizzled. She said, "I'm sorry, honey. This is a terrible time for you." It was the first thing she had said that I experienced as sympathetic. I felt hot tears and my voice caught.

"Thanks, Mom. Sometimes I just get overwhelmed and I—"

"Oh, honey," she interrupted, "don't get worked up on the phone. Things will get better, you'll see."

My throat closed around my unfinished sentence. I asked how Dad was doing and went numb for the remainder of the conversation.

*

We spent more time with Richard and Patrick, who were generally upbeat. Richard was a tonic for Mark, who was always in a better space after seeing him or talking on the phone. In the buddies group, the six men connected more and more deeply. When one got sicker, the other five rallied behind him. I was aware as we moved toward Christmas that our lives had changed in ways I had not anticipated. Mark depended on me for all things practical but took much of his psychological and emotional support from his group and from Mitch. He rarely had any of them over to the house when I was home. I felt excluded until Deborah reminded me that Mark needed to be with people who were also sick. There was a barrier between us: he was diagnosed, I was not. There was still no diagnostic test for the virus, though scientists around the world were scrambling to find one.

We constantly searched for information. Newspapers like the *New York Times* occasionally reported statistics from the CDC or events related to AIDS in the non-gay population: first hemophiliacs, then Haitians. The *New York Native* was our primary source for news, and much of what they reported was hearsay. Rumors were rampant. *There is a conspiracy from deep in the government to spread the virus among gay men in order to rid the population of homosexuals. There are going to be internment camps set up for anyone diagnosed with HIV.* Month after month the numbers of the sick increased, the suffering became more widespread across the country, and the federal government refused to act in a meaningful way, despite cries from the CDC for increased funding. President Reagan said nothing publicly about the existence of what had become an escalating crisis. There had been more than 3,500 AIDS-related deaths in the U.S. by the end of December 1983. The absence of government involvement and intervention was enraging. Protests began to be held in major cities, and gay activists in New York put the heat on Mayor Koch, to no avail.

In Boston, Jerry Groopman and his staff were investigating every possible resource, and they belonged to an informal network of providers around the country who were doing on-the-ground research. Mark and his cohorts had frequent appointments in Harris Hall at the Deaconess, where their blood was drawn and studied. They increasingly dealt with diagnoses of other diseases that resulted from immune suppression: cryptosporidium, cytomegalovirus, toxoplasmosis. Mark carried parasites in his gut from his years in Africa and developed *Giardia*, which caused bouts of painful diarrhea. Patrick and I and other "seemingly healthy" partners were also studied, though what we waited for was a diagnosis of our own. We continued our siege mentality: just hold out until they find a cure.

*

At Christmas we had invitations for holiday festivities but, given Mark's general level of fatigue, we opted to see a few people at a time at home. Unlike previous years, I cooked dinner on New Year's Eve. Nothing fancy—salad, pork chops, and corn bread. Mark made the gravy, which was delicious. I opened a bottle of white wine while I cooked and continued to drink it at the table. I had a slight buzz on as we finished dinner.

"Let's sit on the couch for dessert. It's just ice cream." I put another log on the fire and took the dishes out to the kitchen. When I returned with sundaes, his eyes lit up. He still loved sweets.

"Wonderful dinner, honey. I should have been sharing the cooking with you all this time."

"Pooh," I said. "You're comparing Julia Child to Fannie Farmer." I brought my wine and his water to the sofa and handed him his glass. "Let's toast to a happier and healthier new year, and wish for a cure to AIDS and a resumption of what we used to call normal life."

"I'll drink to that," he said.

It was only about 8:30, but we had no intention of staying up until midnight. I said, "I've been thinking about Hell. The one in our apartment, not in the afterlife. How about if we get a used sofa bed for out there? Something that would at least get our guests off the floor." We'd been using an old futon mattress when people stayed overnight.

"I don't know," he said, yawning. "Do we really want to invest money in furniture?"

"I'm not thinking elaborate, just something that would suggest more than a college student's crash pad." I took another sip of wine.

He grinned. "I'm thinking of something bigger, actually. I've been doing some research in the newspapers. I'm hoping that 1984 might be the Year of the Condo."

I was stopped in my tracks, thinking maybe he was kidding. "How?"

"I know you hate this phrase, but it's still true: the market is very favorable, especially for first-time buyers. I believe I'm going to get better, and I know you're not going to leave Boston anytime soon. It just seems crazy to me that we're spending so much money on rent."

"But our life is full of uncertainty right now."

"We don't have to buy it today, Mike. We can see how things go. But do me a favor. Trust me on this. Let's just look at some places together, maybe beginning in February. You need to have a stable investment, and I'll figure out a way to help."

"Can we buy it together?"

He paused, drank a little water, then looked me right in the eye. "I promise. I will invest with you."

He had never purchased a stick of furniture or even a lamp for our apartment. I had once said in anger, "If we broke up, there would be no fight over personal property because we own nothing jointly."

"Let's drink to that," I said, and raised my glass. "To 1984 and the Year of the Condo!" No mention was made of the possibility of him dying. I had a sneaking suspicion that he was watching out for my future, whether he lived or died.

Chapter 15

New Year's Day brought bitterly cold weather. We watched the Charles River begin to ice up from our perch above Storrow Drive and talked animatedly about our new project.

"Here," he said, spreading open pages from the Real Estate section of the Sunday *Globe* on the dining room table. He had already circled a dozen ads for units in Back Bay, Brookline, and Cambridge while I was cooking breakfast. "These will give you an idea of what we might look for."

I had never been good with money. Like many kids from blue-collar families, I tended to do what my father had done, live from paycheck to paycheck. Although I earned significantly more money than Dad, I had a nice apartment, a car, and a lifestyle that required a substantial amount of upkeep. I also had credit card debt.

"How will we ever get a mortgage?" I asked.

"We'll have to figure out how *you* will get a mortgage. I have too much debt in New York to be considered a good credit risk. And I'm unemployed."

"Can I get one on my own?"

"Let's assume so for now. You have to be optimistic." He was clearly enjoying himself and I appreciated his enthusiasm. The only property I had ever owned was with Frank in New Jersey, and he had done most of the financial planning to make that happen.

We brought our excitement to Roger a few days later. After we laid out our plans for a condo, we asked him what he thought.

"Why now?" he asked.

I was disappointed that he didn't seem excited. "Why not now?"

Mark jumped in before Roger could respond. "I'm the one driving the bus here. I've wanted Mike to have an investment in real estate ever since we met. He's spent a fortune on rent in Boston in the last five years, money that could have gone into equity. I want him to be secure."

When Roger remained quiet, I said, "Do you think it's a bad idea?"

"I'm just curious about the timing, guys. You have a lot on your plates right now. Mark, has your new treatment protocol begun yet?"

"No," Mark responded. "I know where you're going with this, Roger. What if I get worse rather than better? What if I die suddenly? Mike still needs an investment and a place to live. And if I can help make that happen, all the better."

"Can't argue with that," he said. But his tone was neutral.

*

I stopped drinking on January 10. I'd been drinking or smoking pot nearly every night for several months, conscious of waiting for the "ahhh" that slowed the hamster wheel running continuously in my head. My plan was to stop for ten weeks and see if I could learn to relax without substances. I meditated every morning, even on weekends. Mark and I signed up for a second series of Vipassana meditation classes with Hob in Cambridge, and this time Richard enrolled as well. I joined a new gym. Fitness had gotten little of my attention since Mark's diagnosis, and I rediscovered the pleasure of working out until I was physically exhausted.

Meanwhile Mark was holding his ground, meeting frequently with his buddy Mitch and with the men from his PWA group. Jerry Groopman asked him to speak to the students at Harvard Medical School, which he enjoyed, and he was appointed to the Mayor's Council on AIDS as a representative of his PWA group. Under the most unexpected circumstances, Mark had finally found a community in Boston.

The number of men in Massachusetts with AIDS had grown significantly, and all were on tenterhooks waiting for a new experimental medication to try. They'd waited all of December for Alpha Interferon and for Interleukin II, to no avail. Mark and Richard finally tried mega-doses of vitamin C, dissolving the powder in water and drinking so much of it that they had to pee constantly. Eventually their skin took on an orange tinge. They were disappointed in the results but found the skin color hilarious. Richard's KS was gradually spreading, and he had many lesions on his legs. They reminded me of leeches, or what I imagined leeches looked like. Richard was grateful that none of his lesions were visible if he wore long pants and long sleeves. Mark developed a light rash on his face, *molluscum contagiosum*, tiny white warts high on his cheeks that made him self-conscious. They argued good-naturedly about whose symptoms were grossest, sharing the kind of cynical humor that soldiers in battle develop. Through all this uncertainty their friendship deepened, with a sweetness I had not seen Mark show to anyone before.

In early February a group called Gay and Lesbian Physicians of New England (GALPONE) hosted a Sunday brunch. It was held at the home of Dr. Peter Page, a specialist in transfusion medicine who worked for the American Red Cross. John Mazzullo and Ken Mayer, both MDs working with AIDS patients in Boston, had asked Peter to bring together the GALPONE members, who numbered in the dozens, with the staff of the AIDS Action Committee and the men from the PWA group. Many gay physicians were closeted and had no medical contact with patients with AIDS. John and Ken hoped to create an opportunity for informal dialogue between the two groups.

Richard and Patrick and Mark and I arrived at the brunch together. All of us had seen beautiful homes before, but Peter's brownstone in the Back Bay was in a class of its own: an open, airy space with a foyer that contained a full-sized birch tree whose branches reached toward the skylight three stories above. I tried not to gawk.

Richard, on the other hand, was irreverent. "Kid!" he said to Mark. "Here's the condo you and Mike have been looking for. It has just the right amount of gasp quality."

"No, dear," Mark replied. "Only you doctors can afford digs like this. What do you think, Pat? Could you live here?"

"Too big," he smiled, shrugging out of his jacket. "I like cozy." Richard moved into the small group already assembled and began greeting people by name. He was the only person in the room, to my knowledge, who was a member of both groups.

Peter welcomed us warmly. He had heard that Mark had spoken to the first-year students at the medical school and they began a lively conversation as they drifted toward the buffet table across the living room, leaving Patrick and me still standing with our coats in hand. I said, "Hey, we've been stranded!"

"A familiar feeling for me in groups of doctors," Pat replied. "Let's get something to eat."

After half an hour of socializing, Ken Mayer called the group to order. He spoke about the rapid spread of the disease and the efforts being made to get Washington to respond effectively. He also said the medical community was hopeful that Gamma Interferon trials would begin soon. Larry Kessler talked about AIDS-related complex (ARC), a term just coming into use for a constellation of symptoms that often began with lymphadenopathy. ARC typically preceded an AIDS diagnosis. He said, "We can expect a big backlash nationwide when the country at large realizes how many tens of thousands of men have this. Dentists in New York are already refusing to treat gay men for fear of infection. How soon will this happen in Boston?"

Joe Interante, a gay man whose partner, Paul, had died after a seven-month illness, spoke very movingly about their life together and ended by saying, "History will judge us as a movement for how we take care of our own in this crisis." I felt proud to be a man like Joe, committed to staying with Mark.

I was standing in a corner of the room with John Mazzullo and was struck by the fact that I knew most of the people there. I saw only a handful of men, presumably physicians, whom I did not know. "John," I whispered, "how many doctors actually turned out from GALPONE?"

"Aside from the hosts, four or five," he replied. "I'm heartsick. Many of our members are closeted and they're afraid to be publicly associated with AIDS. We're mostly preaching to the choir here."

*

When Jerry Groopman announced that a clinical trial for Gamma Interferon, the first of many experimental drugs to be studied in Boston, would begin on February 21, not everyone was chosen for the protocol. T-cells had to be low enough to demonstrate a positive immune response to the drug. Those who were chosen, Mark and Richard among them, were ecstatic, then felt guilty. "Why couldn't all of us try it?" Mark asked, knowing the answer already.

The six men in Phase One of the trial group met at the Deaconess Hospital every Tuesday for eight weeks. Because the side effects of Gamma Interferon were not well understood, it was administered in dilute form, and each infusion lasted for several hours. After the first session, Mark got copies of the script for Harvey Fierstein's *Torch Song Trilogy* to help the guys pass the time and assigned roles to each man. They read the play aloud over the course of three sessions. I stopped into the hospital one morning to bring Mark something he'd forgotten and was struck by the bizarreness of the scene: six gay men attached to IV bags on poles, sitting in a semi-circle with playbooks in their laps. Some were reading seriously, some goofing on the lines. Richard called out, "Don't we look like a group of middle-aged women sitting in a beauty parlor? All we need are conical hair dryers and curlers!"

*

Rosanne came from San Francisco to co-lead a therapy weekend on the Cape. It was a joy to share my work with someone I trusted deeply, and it shifted my focus, if only briefly, from Mark's illness. We returned home Sunday afternoon tired but revitalized. Meanwhile Mark had overdone his activities and was like a weak battery drained of energy. He was under the covers on the bed in the alcove looking wan, and began listing the failing health of one friend after another. I could feel myself sinking. When Rosanne and I went out to pick up Chinese food, I said, "I hate this fucking illness! I get slammed with bad news whenever I drop my guard. Bam!"

"You're in a tough spot. Mark's the patient, so his needs come first."

I snapped at her. "I would like, just once, to say, 'What about my feelings?' I'm not a saint."

"Mike, we all hate the illness, but don't take your frustration out on Mark." She moved to hug me, which I grudgingly responded to.

I was still feeling irritable when the three of us sat down to dinner. I watched Rosanne sip her white wine and thought, *I would kill for a glass of rum on the rocks right now.* I had been sober for seven weeks and felt ready to chuck the final three out the window. Conversation was desultory until Mark said, "I looked through the condos for sale in the *Globe* today. The spring market is finally picking up." We had looked at a few places in February. I figured I could manage $70,000. But it was clear as we began the search that I would likely be priced out of the market in the three neighborhoods we had targeted.

Mark and Rosanne traded stories about deals they had done in real estate. I sulked, still out of sorts and very tired. When Mark persisted in saying "*we're* looking," "*we're* buying," I interrupted.

"But your name won't be on the mortgage or on the deed, and you don't know how much money you can put in for the down payment."

"True. What are you upset about?"

I waited a long moment, then my words tumbled out. "I thought when you said that we were going to buy a condo that we were making an investment together. But it feels to me like I'm the one who's behind the eight ball: I get the mortgage, I get the condo fee, I get the responsibility."

"Mike, I don't need the investment. You do." He was clearly making an effort to be patient. "I'll contribute what I can to the down payment and I'll pay you rent, which you'll apply to the mortgage. What's wrong with that?"

"I wanted us to own this together. I wanted to be *invested* together. I keep hitting my head against a brick wall on this." I had gone back to an old hurt, but it still felt fresh.

Rosanne kicked me under the table and stood up. "I'm going to clear these dishes. Mike, will you see if there's any ice cream?" She glared at me in the kitchen and mouthed the words, "Back off!" I felt like a two-year-old who had acted up at the supper table.

We limped through dessert, Rosanne describing some recent antics of her son at school as Mark and I pretended to listen. Her life sounded so normal to me, far outside the war zone I lived in. She retired to Hell and Mark and I brushed our teeth, not making eye contact in the bathroom mirror. In bed, Mark said, "I felt humiliated by your behavior at dinner."

I was mortified. "If there's any comfort in it, I wanted to cut my tongue out. I didn't take into account how tired I am. And I really wanted a drink! I feel overwhelmed at the prospect of buying a condo alone." I refused to add, "I'm afraid you'll die," as if his having money invested in it would make him stay alive.

"I'm supporting you as much as I can, sweetheart. Do you want to shelve the project?"

"I need to get information on mortgages, see if it's even possible to get one on my own. Maybe I'll have to wait until next year."

He moved closer on the bed and gently pulled my arm around his neck. "OK, I'll back off a bit. I don't want to create even more stress in your life than I already have." He kissed me and switched off the light, and we curled up together in the semi-darkness. He fell asleep almost immediately as I watched the headlights of cars on the road below reflected on the ceiling. My mind wouldn't stop spinning: the evening, the condo, his illness, my exhaustion. I wondered how long I could live with this stress without crashing.

*

Not long after Rosanne returned to San Francisco, I came down with a virulent case of the flu. My temperature slightly exceeded 101 degrees for about three days and I had to remain in bed. Mark looked so worried that I finally said to him, "People still get the flu, honey. It's not an AIDS marker." But I'd not had a cold, nor canceled a therapy session for reasons of health, since I'd moved to Boston five years earlier.

"Do you want some tea now?" Mark asked. "You really should eat something. How about toast?" I felt fragile and achy. Even my teeth hurt. Mark fed me Tylenol and read to me as I drifted in and out of fragmented dreams. He took my temperature several times each night, wanting to be sure my fever wasn't climbing. Fern came over on the third day with groceries and made lunch. I listened from my bed in the alcove, drifting in and out of consciousness. Fern had had a lump in her breast and I heard Mark saying how relieved he was that it turned out to be benign.

On the fourth day the fever lifted, leaving me weak but alert. Mark asked, "How does it feel to be the patient for a change?"

"Completely alien," I replied. "Definitely not 'me.' But I've appreciated how caring and generous you've been. Did you worry about catching my bug?"

"I asked Mitch what to do, and he said I'd already been exposed, so just to take good care of myself and sleep on the sofa." He was sitting on the edge of the bed holding my hand. "It feels good to be the caretaker for a change."

"It's weird for me to be in this position. I'm reminded of that fever you got on our first trip to Puerto Rico." I became aware of how relaxed he seemed, lacking the pinched expression he had worn for months. He actually looked relatively healthy. "Are you feeling as good as you look?"

"Yes. I think the Gamma is definitely helping. I know my energy is better. Jerry's staff is ready to do the immunologic studies on the results of the first four weeks. I'm afraid to feel optimistic, but I do."

"It's nice to see you have some color again. And even after 24/7 nursing duty, you don't look depleted." I took his hand and gave it a squeeze. I felt some optimism as well.

"Now we need to get *you* back in shape," he replied.

*

Mark's results on Gamma Interferon did show a positive immune response. We were elated until we found out Richard's numbers had not increased and he was being dropped from the study, which would continue another four weeks. Mark and Richard spent hours together searching the *Native* for more experimental treatments, to no avail. I, who had scorned the paper's rhetoric, now read every issue. It was the best and only resource for a broad range of information about the epidemic.

Early April was filled with warm days as the fruit trees along the Charles popped into bloom. My episode with the flu was several weeks in the past, but I still occasionally woke up at night sweating, and a small area in my left armpit had begun to ache. It was uncomfortable rather than painful. Despite these minor nuisances, the opportunity to run along the Charles was irresistible, and I traded the gym for the river at least every other day. I would go out the basement door of the building and up the alley to the pedestrian walkway over Storrow Drive to begin my run, then west along the river toward Watertown, over the BU Bridge to Cambridge, and east down Memorial Drive to the Museum of Science. Crossing the Longfellow Bridge, I'd loop back around and come up along the Esplanade, slow to a walk, and sit on a park bench to gaze at the river until my breathing returned to normal. The distance was about nine miles.

One morning in mid-April, on a park bench at the end of my run, I found myself ruminating again over how I'd manage if I did get diagnosed with AIDS. Absentmindedly the fingers of my right hand were massaging what now felt like a lump in my left armpit. I felt a chill creep up the back of my neck and into my sweat-soaked hair. A lump. What was I thinking, not taking this seriously? I'd had the lump for days.

The sailboats from Community Boating were just beginning to appear that spring, the sails startlingly white against the blue river. On the Longfellow Bridge, construction workers in harnesses were suspended on ropes as they sandblasted columns. I watched the men move across the scaffolding, minuscule against the backdrop of the bridge and the skyline of downtown Boston. Lost in thought, I'd been holding my breath and exhaled.

Mark was reading when I got home, and after a quick greeting I slipped into the bathroom and showered. I thought if I could get dressed and go to the office, work mode would kick in and the anxiety would pass. But as soon as he saw my face he said, "What's wrong? Did you see a ghost on your run?"

"The curse of being Irish. Whatever I feel is apparent to the world." I meant it to be a joke but he didn't smile. We sat facing each other on the sofa and entangled our legs. I steadied my breath and told him the cascade of thoughts I'd just had.

"Let's call Jerry's office right now and find out when he can see you," he said.

"Mark, please, let's not overreact. We can wait a couple of days."

"No. Even if it turns out to be a series of unrelated symptoms, you're not going to sleep until you hear that from Jerry. Neither will I, for that matter."

We were in the doctor's office two days later, and I laid out five symptoms: the unusual flu, some night sweats, intermittent diarrhea, a recurring sore throat, and the pain in my armpit. Jerry said, "I'm so glad you came in," and I felt immediately better. He gave me a thorough physical exam and discovered a node about two centimeters wide on the lymph gland in my armpit, another smaller one on a gland in the left side of my throat, and some red spots under my tongue. The larger node was a concern as a possible precursor of ARC and would need to be biopsied. "I believe people know their own bodies," he said, "and if you feel there's something going on in your body, we need to address that." I felt like throwing up. Surely I couldn't be getting sick now when Mark seemed to be getting better.

Mark took me down to the lab for what Jerry termed "simple blood work." I handed the form I'd been given to the technician and she asked what the tests were for. When I looked confused, she said, "What are your symptoms?" I said, "Lymphadenopathy," and she typed that into the computer. Mark was out of his seat in a heartbeat and took the paper Jerry had given me off the desk.

"Dr. Groopman wrote *diarrhea* here as the symptom. That's what should go on the record."

The young woman looked at him. "The patient indicated that—"

Before she could go any further, he placed the paper in front of her on the desk. "Dr. Groopman wrote down *diarrhea*. That is the symptom that should go on the record." His voice was shaking.

"Sir," she said irritably, "the patient—"

"We want to see your supervisor immediately. Mike, don't give her any more information!" He went to a wall phone in the hallway and called Jerry's office manager. I could hear his voice raised and I was shocked. I had never seen him like this. The tech's face had lost all color. Her supervisor came in and the crisis was over in thirty seconds. "His symptom is diarrhea, Susan," she said. And to me, "I'm sorry if this has upset you."

On the way back to the car, Mark said that the last thing I would want on my insurance record was lymphadenopathy. "Hundreds of men are being screwed out of their insurance, or denied insurance, as a result of mistakes like that. You have to really pay attention. And you cannot allow people to fuck with you." This was a new Mark Halberstadt, exhibiting a level of assertive behavior I had never witnessed before. I felt sorry for the technician but grateful for his protectiveness.

In a few days the simple blood tests came back normal. I wanted to get the biopsy done on my lymph gland, but I had very limited health insurance. I was feeling well again and feared that maybe I'd exaggerated the whole thing.

Our friend Gerry Ente called from Long Island to find out the results of the tests. He was very direct. "The blood work and even the biopsy can come back normal, but this still could be an early stage of ARC. It's a progressive deterioration in the system, slow moving, in which the glands begin to change. You need to be followed closely, Mike. Please take this seriously. If it's more prudent to get the biopsy done away from Boston, come down to Long Island. We'll get the procedure done anonymously, and without insurance."

*

Mark continued his relentless campaign to get me into a condo, and looking at units was the most pleasant distraction we had. He bugged me about "staying on point." I met with several mortgage lenders who said that it was unlikely that I could get a mortgage on my own. My income was good but I had limited savings and too much credit card debt. Exploring with brokers was addictive, however, and one morning we found a beautiful unit on Beacon Street just past Park Drive, a fourth-floor walkup in a brownstone. We bit our tongues until the broker left us alone inside and then jumped up and down. It was advertised as a "Back Bay–style condo," only a thousand square feet, but it had three skylights, two bedrooms, and two baths, and the potential for securing roof rights. The only bad news: they were asking $110,000. We went to a French bakery across the street for coffee and croissants to talk it over.

"It's just like a New York neighborhood," Mark said. "Look, there's a grocery, a liquor store, a dry cleaners, three restaurants, a Greek diner. It's perfect!"

"It's too expensive, Mark. I was worried about bumping up to $80,000. This is out of the ballpark."

"Remember my mantra," he said, pulling out a little note pad and pencil. "Always buy up, because you'll grow into the payment." He began working the numbers, figuring mortgage payments, taxes, condo fees, then listing what cash we could pull together between us. "We're only short about $10,000!"

I started laughing. "Wow! Only $10,000."

"I'm serious. To you that's a lot of money. To others, it's chicken feed."

"Then there is the ever-present issue of the mortgage. I can't get it alone."

"So who has $10,000 to loan and would cosign the note?"

"I must admit I've been thinking for a while about talking to my brother Joe. He's the only person I can imagine asking. But it's a lot of money, and he has his own mortgage to deal with."

"He and his wife also have good jobs. What do you have to lose by asking?"

"We prize self-reliance in my family. I shouldn't need to ask for financial help at my age."

But I was closest to Joe of any of my brothers, and I finally screwed up my courage and called him. He asked me to give him a few days to think about it and talk it over with his wife, but he called back the next day and said yes. "Both Pat and I agree with Mark on all points: you need an investment and you'll grow into the mortgage payment. Welcome to adult life!"

Mark wangled the asking price down to $103,000, and we were in business. Mark and I went out to dinner to celebrate and, for the first time in ten weeks, I drank several glasses of wine at dinner. I was surprised that the effect was to make me more preoccupied than relaxed, and the inner critic started up: *Why did you start drinking now? Aren't things difficult enough already? Why can't you just deal with what you're feeling?*

*

Jerry Groopman left a message with my service to call him, saying he had news. I was afraid he was going to ask if I'd had the node biopsied, and since I had not yet been approved for new health insurance, I had not. But it was news of a different sort. "Robert Gallo at the NIH has developed what he hopes will be a test to detect the virus for AIDS. At the moment it's being called HTLV-3. Soon he's going to be collecting blood samples from gay men in New York, San Francisco, and Boston and will do a study to determine the accuracy of his test. You can be in the first cohort to be tested if you're willing."

"Yes," I said. "My Grandfather Murray used to say, 'The devil you know is better than the devil you don't know.' If the devil is in my blood, I guess it's better to know." Despite the lighthearted sound of my response, I felt sobered. I had my blood drawn for the study in mid-May.

The Gamma Interferon group Mark had been part of had finished in mid-April without producing statistically significant results, though he obviously had benefitted from the drug. He and Richard were on to new vitamins and whey protein in large doses. As he said ironically, "Desperate men require desperate measures." When I told him I had enrolled in Dr. Gallo's trial for HTLV-3, he didn't say much but asked every few days if I'd heard anything. I reassured him that when I did, he would be the first to know. I did a substantial amount of obsessing while I ran: *Do I have the virus? Do I have antibodies? If I'm sick, how will I manage knowing and still continue to take care of Mark?* All six of the original members of Mark's group were still alive, but others that I'd only heard about had joined the group and died within a few months. And there was a progression in symptoms among all of them. The face of AIDS was drawing nearer to me personally. No matter what the results of Dr. Gallo's test were, I knew the information would change me and change us. If I were healthy, I feared it would further separate me from Mark, making me "the well partner" rather than "the apparently well partner." If I were sick, I'd be joining him in his illness.

*

In early June we hit a hard patch. Mark was tiring more easily again without the Gamma. I drove him down to New York City on a Friday to stay for two nights with close friends and to meet with his attorney. He perked up when we crossed over the Triborough Bridge into Manhattan, clearly looking forward to being away from the gloom of Boston. I dropped him off at the attorney's office and then drove out to Fire Island for a couple of nights by myself. Knowing that he was with people who loved him relieved me briefly of my hypervigilance. We had one short phone check-in on Saturday morning and he sounded fine. I spent the two days walking the long stretch of beach between Cherry Grove and the Pines, crisscrossing the boardwalks we had walked, passing the house where we'd had our first night together. By this time two more of the six roommates with whom he had shared that house were sick. AIDS was inescapable. I was reminded of Mark at every turn. In the late afternoons I sat at the bar in the Monster drinking beer, simply trying to allow my central nervous system to calm down. It was a relief to be alone and to zone out. I felt like a soldier on furlough from the front.

When Mark arrived in Cherry Grove on Sunday, he was ashen and short of breath. As near as I could put together, he was responding to what had happened in Boston in the few days we'd been gone. His friends in the PWA group were under siege: Pedro Martinez had died the day we left, David Tiffany remained in a coma, and Richard was convinced he would be next, "to make three."

It took hours for Mark to settle down, and I believed that our being separated had been a bad idea. He was used to a more protected environment at home. While he'd gotten done what he needed to do in the city, the stimulation and pace had rattled him. He said repeatedly, "I shouldn't have left Boston, I shouldn't have left the guys." I knew it was fruitless to suggest that his presence would have changed nothing. We spent the whole evening cuddling on the sofa, and talking, me rubbing his back, and the rigidity in his body gradually diminished. We left for Boston the next day.

A week later, in the late afternoon of Monday, June 11, I got a message from my answering service to call Jerry Groopman. I had two clients left to see before going from Cambridge to Brookline for David Tiffany's memorial service. He had died a few days after we returned to Boston. I debated postponing the call until the next morning but found myself dialing the number from memory. When I identified myself to the office manager, she put me through to Jerry immediately. There was no small talk.

"You tested positive for the HTLV-3 virus, Mike. Don't jump to conclusions about this. These are the very first clinical trials. What we know is that everyone who has AIDS has HTLV-3, but there are many men in these trials who have it but seem otherwise healthy. Some may never develop full-blown AIDS." Listening to him, I had my first experience of going into shock. *Did he just say I do have the virus?* I sat down, afraid I was going to pass out.

I was silent long enough that he said, "Are you there?'"

"Yes, Jerry. I'm sorry. I'm at work and have to see a client now." I heard my voice, completely toneless, but felt powerless to respond otherwise. "Thank you for calling."

He said, "Don't panic. At this point we believe the incubation period is two to five years. We're learning so much now. It might just mean that you're a carrier."

Right. And it might just mean that I'm dead in the water.

I stared blankly out the window for a few moments and, still in shock, met with my clients, one after the other. I felt grateful that the professional habit of listening closely kept me present to their work, though later I couldn't remember a word I had said.

David's memorial service was held in the garden of a mansion in Brookline. It was a hot but beautiful early summer evening, and dozens of people were scattered across the lawn. Guests had been asked to wear white instead of black, and at first sight they looked like wraiths or angels. I tried to relax and appear normal, smiling, greeting friends, heartache arising as I remembered that this was the third memorial service in two months for people from Mark's original group. These losses were happening so quickly now. I was also worried about the impact of my diagnosis on Mark. I knew he would be devastated, and I tried futilely to figure out a way to soften the news. But how do you soften a potential death sentence?

The service was structured as a Quaker meeting: people shared when and if they felt moved to, with long silences between speakers. Finally we stood in a large circle, hand in hand, while a man played "Blowing in the Wind" on a harpsichord that had been placed in a gazebo. The only time I cried was when Mark spoke about his friendship with David, how much he would miss being able to count on his courage and sense of humor. Wine and soft drinks were then available and people milled around.

I got Richard and Patrick alone for a few minutes and told them about the test results. Richard hugged me and asked, "Does Mark know?"

"I'll tell him when we get home, or maybe tomorrow."

"No," Richard said firmly, "let him know tonight. He's done nothing but worry about it for weeks."

I could see Mark working his way toward us through the small crowd and said, "Let's just talk about David's service for now."

Later, when I told Mark, he was silent for long moments. We were sitting in the bay window looking west down the river toward the remnants of the sunset, and he reached over and took my hand. I had spoken calmly and repeated all the reassuring things Jerry had said to me. Finally he said, "I wonder if we need to change our game plan."

"What's our game plan?" I asked.

"Despite the threat of you having ARC, we've been operating for many months as if I'm the patient here. But if you become sick, we'll need to think about how to take care of you as well."

I felt a rush of love for him, so grave and worn out from these last difficult weeks. We carried so much grief, the losses of our friends, the pressures of these long months, and the false promise of Mark regaining his health.

"I think we stay with the game plan we have, sweetheart. I feel fine physically, other than being tired and scared. Let's go on the assumption that I'm a carrier until proven otherwise. Who knows, someday one of the drugs or treatments they come up with may work, and you'll get better. We'll all get better."

He said, "I'm sorry that Pedro and David won't have the chance to get better."

"Me too."

Chapter 16

Our week-long rental on Lieutenant Island had seemed like a great idea in February, when the winter was bitter and Mark was not so sick. But by the middle of June his breathing was becoming effortful. All the same, he wanted badly to have this time together, and I was determined to make it happen. I packed up sheets and towels and books and music, optimistically putting in swimsuits and beach chairs. It reminded me of preparing to go to Fire Island in previous summers, except this time the bags included medications, vitamins, supplements of all kinds, a large outdoor umbrella, and a big straw hat to protect Mark's skin from the sun. The upper half of his face was now covered with a bright red rash and still peppered with tiny white warts. He was acutely self-conscious about how he looked, and the condition was made worse by direct sunlight. After a childhood of summer camps and then rentals on Fire Island, with Mark running bareheaded on beaches, the sun was no longer his friend.

We left Boston at 7:00 on Saturday morning to avoid the traffic that builds up for miles before the bridge onto Cape Cod. It was a beautiful day and we were in high spirits, listening to the music from Sondheim's *Follies* and relishing the week ahead: no medical appointments, no support group meetings, no stuffy apartment boxing us in. We held the fragile belief that freedom lay ahead.

Despite the early hour, we hit a two-mile backup at the Sagamore Rotary, inching along as the sun bore down on my car, an old white VW Rabbit named Grace Slick. June is often a beautiful, temperate month on Cape Cod, but that summer it was like the Gobi Desert, hot and airless. Mark sweated copiously in the meager output of the car's air conditioner, drinking water from a half-gallon plastic jug. Our sing-along with Yvonne DeCarlo on "I'm Still Here" petered out into silence. I clicked off the cassette. Mark dozed. My neck ached from the tension of driving. We began the crawl around the rotary and up the on-ramp to the bridge. As I crossed into the right lane, Mark startled awake and looked up the Cape Cod Canal toward the bay.

"Do you remember where we were ten months ago?" he asked.

"Tell me," I said.

"Passing beneath this bridge, on the *Delphic Oracle*."

I had a vivid memory of standing in the bow of Ted's boat and being filled with excitement, a great adventure ahead. I glanced over at Mark as the traffic began to ease up and saw he was lost in thought, sailing, I was sure, in happier times.

It took another hour and a half to reach our turn off, and we were fried. But as we crossed the little tidal bridge onto Lieutenant Island, we shouted with glee. Such beauty! Great open spaces, acres of dune grass, the hilly island dotted with houses large and small. We read our directions carefully and finally found the sandy drive leading through scrub pines to our rental. A perfect Cape cottage, clapboard siding weathered silver-gray, somewhat ramshackle in appearance but totally charming. I found the key under an old ceramic jug, as instructed, and let us into the house. It had mismatched but comfortable furniture, a small kitchen with a wooden table and chairs, and a single bedroom with a double bed. The prize, however, was the living room, as funky as the rest but with glass sliders onto a wooden deck and a view that seemed to go on forever. We could see across the tidal marsh all the way to Provincetown, the Pilgrim Monument, and Long Point Lighthouse at the very tip of the Cape. We grinned at each other: home for a week. I unpacked the car and we ate yogurt and fruit before falling asleep on the couch, lulled by the sound of distant waves.

At sunset, feeling more rested, we drank iced tea and began what became a daily ritual: sitting on the sofa in the living room, looking out the sliders over the hillock of marsh grass to our own little beach on the bay. We had a pirated cassette tape of Louise Hay, the first recording she ever made, called "AIDS, a Positive Approach." We listened to it so often that Mark joked that she should be sharing the cost of the rent with us. Her voice was deep and resonant, trance inducing, and she talked about fear being the problem, fear hovering like a black cloud. "But that cloud has a string connected to it, and the string is in your hand. Let it go now, let it drift away and disappear." For those moments that we listened, we were with her, letting the cloud go, the sky opening to serenity and deep blue peace. Otherwise, for me at least, fear was a constant if low-grade presence, a stone in my gut.

On Sunday, Mark seemed more energetic. Jerry Groopman had given him a spirometer, a small plastic cylinder with a mouthpiece on it. He would take a deep breath and blow into the device, trying to raise the little plastic ball in the cylinder up to the top. This morning he was able to move the ball three quarters of the way, which gave him a sense of success. We took a short walk, and I made bacon and eggs and toast. He had some appetite and his humor was good. He talked about Paris, meeting Noël Coward and several famous actors in the year he studied at the Sorbonne.

"They would have parties, exquisite food and wine, and invite the pretty young students from the university to provide *divertissement*." He laughed. "Of course the parties became orgies. It was Paris. I felt like the towel bearer to the gods." I had heard this story before but now his lightheartedness made it more poignant. It was easy to see him at nineteen when he laughed, open and happy, the memories reviving his sense of a life before his illness.

We took a nap in the early afternoon heat. There was a cool breeze coming off the marsh and we lay naked on the sheets, reminiscing about our meeting on Fire Island, how vulnerable we felt as we fell in love. We were curled together like spoons and I realized I was aroused. Uncertain that Mark would respond, I started to move back and he said, "Please . . . stay." Just moving against him, I came, then gave him a backrub. I don't think he ever got aroused, but our connection was strong and sweet. Sex had been a powerful force in our relationship from the beginning, but after his diagnosis, the constant stress made it difficult to open up sexually. As he said ironically, "It's not easy to get hard when you're confronting your mortality."

Later in the day we went out onto the deck. He chilled easily, so I wrapped him in a comforter and took his picture peeking out of the opening at the top like an Eskimo. He started doing Charles Ludlam as Camille:

"Nanine, I'm cold. Throw another fagot on the fire."

"But there are no fagots in the house, Madame."

Archly: "What? No fagots in the house?"

I couldn't help but laugh, how ridiculous he looked, how sweet the camping, and I took another photo.

He said, "Caption that picture, 'Mark starts having the chills.'"

My smile faded and I put the camera in its case, the moment of happiness evaporating.

Mitch, Mark's buddy from the AAC, came by Monday after lunch on his way back to Boston from Provincetown. Mark's breath had become labored again. I made iced tea and went outside to an adirondack chair so they could talk alone. After an hour or so Mitch came out and asked if I wanted to go for a run, so we took off down the beach, deserted in late afternoon. I asked, "What's the prognosis, Doctor?" regretting my levity when his expression didn't change. He hadn't seen Mark for a week. Without breaking stride, I said, "He's worse, isn't he?"

"Yes, he's worse. He's so depleted, Mike. I think he's been expending an enormous amount of energy trying to keep up the facade of doing well the last nine months, and he just doesn't have the reserves."

Even through my denial I could see, day after day, that Mark's life was shrinking, I could hear the rasp in his breath. I wouldn't let myself cry, afraid to allow any crack in my armor for fear I wouldn't be able to reassemble it. We continued to run along the edge of the surf. After a moment, I asked Mitch directly, "Is he dying?"

Still looking ahead, he said, "If it's PCP, it depends on medication. He can't keep this up much longer without some kind of medical intervention."

We walked back in silence. Before Mitch went in to tell Mark goodbye, I asked if he thought Mark knew. He gave me a small smile and a hug before saying, "Hard to tell. He doesn't talk about dying, at least not to me." I didn't tell him that Mark didn't talk about dying with anyone that I was aware of.

After Mitch left I called Jerry Groopman's office and asked that he phone Mark as soon as possible. He returned the call within twenty minutes, talked to Mark about what was happening, and suggested that he come back to Boston for a bronchoscopy. We decided it would be less wearing to have him fly up from Provincetown in the morning and fly back in the afternoon, with Mitch providing transportation between Logan and the Deaconess Hospital. Everything moved quickly. We both slept poorly Monday night, Mark propped on pillows. I woke up off and on, listening to the shallowness of his breath, then lay against him and dozed off again. It felt timeless, and my mind was relatively quiet in the dark night.

Early Tuesday morning we made the short drive to Provincetown Airport and Mark boarded a Cape Air commuter plane to Boston. I returned to the cottage, made a pot of coffee, and rolled a joint. I felt disoriented and suddenly very vulnerable. I took my coffee into the living room, aware of being alone. The view was not the same without him by my side. I started to cry, at first just tears running down my face, finally curling up where Mark usually sat and howling. I had never felt so adrift or frightened. All of my energies, our energies, had been focused on keeping him alive, on "getting him better," and I knew he was slipping away from me. I had been anxious for months but now felt something more like panic: *I can't do this anymore, I can't keep up the pretense that he's going to get better.* I rocked on the sofa as I had rocked in childhood, pulling myself into a ball, and finally dropped into a troubled sleep.

Several hours later I was awakened by the ringing of the telephone: Mark was leaving Logan for Provincetown and would arrive thirty-five minutes later. I was horrified by my reflection in the mirror, hair flattened from perspiration and eyes swollen. "You look like a train wreck," I muttered as I splashed water on my face and headed out the door to the airport.

Mark looked exhausted. He dozed in the car on the ride back to Lieutenant Island and then revived a little with food and iced tea. His only comment about the trip to the hospital was that Jerry was concerned. Mark had declined his suggestion that he remain in Boston until the test results were back on Thursday, saying that the time at the beach house was important to both of us.

To further complicate what was already a complicated week, I received a phone call that I had to return to Boston on Thursday to close on our condo. The closing had been postponed repeatedly, and I was ready to back out of the deal, but Mark insisted we go forward.

We waited then, through Tuesday evening and into the next morning. The surreal quality persisted, though everything appeared the same: the cottage, the sunshine, the bay. We talked very little, eating when we were hungry but not in an organized or thoughtful way. Marking time. In the evening we again listened to Louise, sitting side by side on the sofa, our hands barely touching.

Wednesday turned out to be our last day alone, though we didn't know it at the time. Once more we slept into the morning. I awoke first and made coffee, aware that the weeping the day before had gotten something out of my system, a knot of dread that had been in my belly since Mark's diagnosis. Since I was not symptomatic, I could push my own diagnosis into the background. It would have to be dealt with at some time, but not today. In this moment I simply felt empty. Mark came out and settled sleepily onto the old daybed on the deck, lying back on the cushions. I rested the backs of my fingers against his cheek. He felt slightly feverish to me but wanted no part of the thermometer or the spirometer, waving them off like annoying insects. He said, "There's nothing they can tell us now that will change anything. Let's wait to see what the test says." I had brought out berries and toasted a bagel, but neither of us had much of an appetite. He put a pillow on my lap and rested his head there, watching the interplay of sun and clouds.

"I feel so repulsive, skinny and clammy—and with this horrid rash on my face. When you touched me the other day and got turned on, I felt, just for a moment, like myself, like someone who was sexual and desirable." He paused to steady his breath. "Thank you for that. You're taking such good care of me, honey. I abhor being a burden." He paused again and I bit my tongue, knowing that space to express his feelings, not reassurance, was what he needed.

It was a timeless state, the whole day, sitting and watching the beautiful view, the shifting gold and green of the dune grass, how the colors changed in the breeze as the sun moved across the marsh. I didn't go for a walk because I wanted to be there when the doctor called. We again listened to the tape. I told him I could listen to it all day, it was the only time I completely let go, and he said that was true for him too, he felt safe then and when we cuddled in bed at night.

Jerry Groopman called about 7:30 to see how Mark was doing and said they would have the results of the bronchoscopy in the morning. He wanted Mark to be there so they could look at them together. We sat in the living room in the twilight, watching the sun sink into a dark bank of clouds that lay across the horizon behind Provincetown. Then we slept, deeply this time, nestled together like babies in a crib, and awoke early to make the drive to Boston. The traffic was not as bad as it should have been at rush hour, and I dropped Mark off at the Deaconess to meet Jerry and went on to the lawyer's office, arriving in plenty of time for the closing.

Chapter 17

At the Deaconess, I headed for Jerry's office in Harris Hall, only to be told by his receptionist that Mark had been admitted. I arrived in Room 901 to find him sitting on the edge of the bed. Jerry came in right behind me.

"I'm glad to get the two of you together," Jerry said. "The results of the bronchoscopy confirm the presence of *Pneumocystis*." He added, "And your performance on the spirometer shows a twenty percent loss of breathing function from the test we did when you were in on Tuesday." I felt shocked, though the evidence of the decline was apparent.

Mark said, "The last few days have been really tough."

"Well, you're here now, in good hands, and I want you to relax. That will help the most." Jerry glanced out the window at the view of the Riverway, the park lush with a dozen shades of green. "Take in the view." He smiled. "I'll make sure you get VIP treatment."

I stood up, realized I didn't know why or where I thought I was going, and sat back down. "What happens now?"

"We'll get Mark into a gown, get some oxygen in here, and begin to make life easier for him. I'm going back to consult with the team and we'll decide how best to treat the PCP." Jerry headed out the door.

I was surprised by Mark's apparent calm as he changed into a johnny and climbed under the covers. A nurse came in to take his vitals and a technician arrived with the oxygen equipment, swiftly and efficiently hooking up a cannula to Mark's nostrils and looping it around his ears. Less than fifteen minutes had passed since I'd entered the hospital, but the brief feeling of lightness after the condo closing had faded. However, Mark was clearly feeling more secure. Soon Mitch showed up, as well as Richard and Patrick, and the buzz of conversation made life seem closer to normal. I made a list of what Mark needed from home and bid them all goodbye, thinking, *All men to their battle stations.* I felt purposeful.

My first phone call from the apartment was to his parents, who wanted to come up immediately. No amount of pleading would convince them to stay in New

York. That afternoon the Halberstadts climbed into their ancient Oldsmobile and drove the five hours to Boston, arriving just about dinnertime. There was a small storm of fussing and kissing when they came into his room, but Mark remained quiet and steady, reassuring them that, despite the seriousness of the diagnosis, the doctor seemed confident that they could treat the infection. Though I didn't see her often, I'd grown very fond of Ida, and I appreciated knowing someone who loved Mark at least as much as I did. Her incessant talking didn't bother me the way it did him. She wasn't my mother.

After some brief conversation about the traffic on the drive up and how Aunt Pearl was getting along, Ida peppered Mark with questions about his health. He faded fast, responding but giving very little information. Finally I suggested to the senior Halberstadts that we go to the cafeteria for a bite to eat and let Mark rest.

"So?" Ida said as soon as we sat down with our trays. The cafeteria was crowded and noisy. I seated myself near Eddie, whose hearing was marginal at best.

"I can only tell you what the doctor told us," I said. "I don't know the long-term prognosis. I do know that Mark's very sick, that he has the same virus he had last September, and Dr. Groopman has several drugs that he hopes can knock it out."

"How long will it take for him to get better?" she asked. When I hesitated, she said, "Please, tell us the truth."

"There's no guarantee that any of the drugs will work."

Eddie was eating his meatloaf, potatoes, and gravy with great concentration. Sitting at my side, he looked up and said, "Could this kill him?"

"I know a couple of people who have had two bouts of PCP and are still alive. But Mark is very worn down. You can see that from looking at him."

Ida had not touched her food. She took out a tissue and wiped her eyes, then made a little production of cleaning her glasses. There was nothing left to say. We made our way back to Mark's room and found him sleeping, so we slipped out and said our goodnights. They returned to New York the next day after spending the morning with him.

My second phone call from the apartment had been to Fern, who agreed to meet me at 9:00 that evening to drive back to Lieutenant Island and clear our belongings out of the cottage. Though we knew it was a long shot, Mark and I had hoped to return and have two more days in the rental house.

Fern and I arrived in Wellfleet about 11:00. The house, so welcoming before, felt strange now, cluttered and disorganized. She went to sleep right away and I sat out on the deck for a while, no moon to illuminate the bay but the lights of Provincetown bright in the distance. I imagined men dancing at the Boatslip and cruising in the bars and clubs, all the intensity of gay life percolating. That world now felt alien to me. Eventually my fatigue won the battle with my overstimulated mind and I went to bed. At dawn I awoke to the sound of birds singing, and in short order we packed up the car and headed home.

Fern said, "I want to talk to you about something but I'm afraid my timing may be off."

"Talk away."

"How worried are you about having tested positive for HTLV-3? I ask because you haven't seemed very present since you found out. Not that there aren't plenty of other good reasons to want to be somewhere else, but I keep noticing it."

Traffic was picking up and I wished we were already back in Boston. I hated being separated from Mark. I had the irrational belief that nothing could happen to him if I were there, despite the very clear evidence to the contrary. "I do think about it," I said. "I feel anxious when I imagine the bugs or whatever they are swimming around in my blood. But I don't feel sick. So it's more like a theory. The longer I live with the diagnosis and no symptoms, the less real it feels."

"I know you're taking the best care of yourself that you can right now, but I really want you to look at how much you're drinking and smoking pot." She put her hand on my arm before I could reply and said, "I'm not criticizing, I'm just saying that if you're positive, your immune system is already compromised. You need to be taking really good care of yourself."

I knew Fern was trying to be helpful, but I felt a wave of despair. I was doing the best I could. We were both quiet, the traffic increasingly dense as we neared the Southeast Expressway, then she said, "I can't stand the idea of you going through what's happening with Mark." She squeezed my arm. "Don't forget you can talk to me anytime."

At the hospital we found that Jerry had managed to get DFMO, a promising experimental drug, flown up from Atlanta during the night. The treatment had begun and hopes were high. People were in and out constantly: nurses, technicians, phlebotomists, aides. During a quiet moment in the afternoon we listened to Louise's tape, taking refuge in the flow of the meditation. "You are always in charge, and you are always safe." The hypnotic power of her words held us.

*

The following day was my fortieth birthday. There had been plans for a party at the cottage with a small group of friends. Now my wish was to ignore the event, but Mark and Fern wouldn't hear of it. On that Sunday morning, Mark's room was pleasantly quiet. I suggested we read the *Times* in his bed, but he was restless and said he'd been bothered by dreams.

"Want to tell me about them?" I asked.

"Nothing very clear. I dream about Boyd all the time. Not about him being gone, just seeing him on the street or at the McIntyre Building. He doesn't see me, though. He's been dead almost two years."

"I remember we were on Fire Island when you found out."

Hoping to lighten his mood, I looked around the room and spied a small, beautifully wrapped package on the window ledge. "Did someone bring you a present?" I asked.

"Oh my God!" he said, laughing. "Happy birthday! I completely forgot. You're turning forty today and I'm feeling sorry for myself."

"I would hardly call being on oxygen with an IV of DFMO pouring into your veins feeling sorry for yourself."

"Let's save the package for later and get down to the real business of Sunday morning," he said, and we settled side by side and began to work on the crossword puzzle.

At lunchtime I was surprised by a small group of friends, who arrived with balloons, a cake, and a pile of presents. There were insulting birthday cards about turning forty and gag gifts of all sorts. The irony of even having a birthday, let alone celebrating it, did not escape me. Mark gave me the small package last. In it I discovered a simple gold band. Having a commitment ceremony had been a topic we had visited theoretically a few times before he got sick: I was invariably for, he against, saying it was "a parody of a heterosexist institution." Once he was diagnosed, the subject dropped entirely from conversation. I was speechless, lost in a jumble of conflicting feelings.

The room got quiet and he said, "Hey, this is supposed to make you happy. Here's the proof that I'm invested."

"I *am* happy," I said, fighting back tears. "Just caught off guard."

He reached for the ring and said, "Let me do the honors," slipping it onto my finger. It fit perfectly. When it was time for cake, Deborah, Steven, Richard and Patrick, Fern, and Mark all sang lustily as I mimed blowing out the chunky 4 and 0 candles.

The Fourth of July was stifling. Mark had been on DFMO for five days, with modest results. Up until then I had arranged my schedule so that I could go to the Deaconess and be with Mark when the doctors came in around 8:30 a.m., then go to my office in Cambridge and still be back in time to eat dinner with him in his room. Seeing my colleagues and clients was a relief from my constant hyper-vigilance at the hospital. But time was chronically short. So was my temper. I had not managed to find an air conditioner that would significantly cool the apartment. Looming in the distance was our move to the condo, but I negotiated keeping our current space an extra month and decided I'd worry about moving at a later date. I wished I'd gotten a T-shirt for my birthday that said "Tired and Cranky." It dawned on me as I walked to the hospital that holiday morning that I'd been too busy and fatigued to cry for several days. No wonder I felt so backed up.

Mark improved a little more in the next two days, enough so that the doctors decided to remove the cannula to see if he could breathe on his own. We were briefly relieved, declaring it a move in the right direction. We were also excited that Jerry had managed to get Biogen Pharmaceuticals to release more Gamma Interferon for Mark, so now he was getting two promising drugs. He was "huffing and puffing" without the supplemental oxygen, but there was still a chance he might win another round. His two primary-care nurses, Jeff and Marcia, were supportive and optimistic. They made a point of coming in when their shifts were over to say goodbye and to tell Mark when they would return. Mark said repeatedly that the care at the hospital was amazing, especially since we had heard that staff in some hospitals in other cities would not even bring food trays into the rooms of AIDS patients for fear of being infected.

Two more days slipped past. Larry Kessler from the AAC visited often. Richard and Patrick, Mitch, and Fern all moved in and out seamlessly, bringing food that he rarely ate, good humor, and devoted companionship. Mark's brother, Bert, came to visit for the first time. I had never understood their relationship, how there could be only the two of them, a few years apart, with no apparent emotional connection. Mark said their mother had favored him in all things. Bert's first wife had also deeply offended Mark when she found out he was gay and told Bert she didn't want their two sons to be "exposed" to him. I was not in the room during the conversation between Mark and Bert, but both seemed the better for having talked. Mark later said he was "tying up loose ends."

"Are you feeling any optimism?" I asked.

"I guess so. But I'm really tired." He closed his eyes. "How long have I been in the hospital this time?"

"Nearly two weeks."

He asked, "How are you holding up?"

"Fine," I said quickly, and we both laughed at the absurdity of the response. "Very tired. And scared almost all the time. I miss the privacy of our days on Lieutenant Island."

"Me too. There's certainly no privacy here. I long to cuddle with you." He was quiet for a few minutes and I thought he'd fallen asleep. I pulled my chair over next to the bed and took his hand. He said, "I'm going to have to ask for the oxygen mask back. It's too much effort to breathe."

"Are you sure?"

He opened his eyes and squeezed my hand. "I'm not giving up. I'm just too fucking tired to breathe without some help."

"I'll call Jerry."

Shortly thereafter, Mark was sent down to the Pulmonary Unit for another bronchoscopy. The test confirmed what the doctor already knew, what we all knew. The drugs had not stopped the progression of the disease. Jerry told me that, unless something miraculous happened, Mark would probably die in the next two weeks. His deterioration was apparent, but I felt like I'd been socked in the gut. *Please God, not so soon.* I called his parents and said only that the PCP had not been arrested. I discouraged them from coming to Boston, saying that we wanted to see what his medical options were at this point and knew they were sending love and good wishes from Long Island. Mark was wearing the oxygen mask when I came back to his room. It had been a long day and we were exhausted when Jerry stopped by. I stood up. "What are you doing here so late?"

"I have some news for you," he said, looking at me.

I thought, *Oh my God, they've found a drug that will work on PCP!*

"When your test came back positive for HTLV-3, I was surprised. I don't know why, but I just couldn't take it at face value. The research is so new, there would have to have been some false positives and false negatives. So I called Gallo's lab and asked them to retest your blood sample."

I felt confused. *Isn't this about Mark?*

"It came back negative. You don't have the virus."

Mark pulled his mask back and tried to cheer, but ended up wheezing instead. He grabbed my hand and squeezed it hard. "Honey, I'm so relieved. I felt responsible, I was sure I'd given it to you." Looking at Jerry he said, "Tomorrow is my birthday. You just gave me the best present I could have gotten."

I remained confused, my mind spinning. Then I felt flooded with disappointment, as if Jerry had tricked me by saying he had news for me. *Mark was the one who needed a gift*, I thought, *not me.* Maybe I was in denial, but my diagnosis had never felt real. I said with false enthusiasm, "Wonderful, Jerry. Thank you so much!"

Chapter 18

The mood in the hospital room changed after the second bronchoscopy came back positive. As if in limbo, we had been waiting to see if the drugs could push back the *Pneumocystis*. On Friday the 13th, Mark's forty-second birthday, it became apparent that time was running out.

After Jerry had left the previous night, I asked the nurse if I could stay in Mark's room. She brought me a little roll-away bed and I pushed it right up next to Mark's. We wanted to cuddle but, because of the cumbersome size and shape of the new oxygen apparatus, we settled for holding hands. It was only eight o'clock but we were completely exhausted. I set up the cassette player and inserted our headsets into the dual plug I'd purchased, and we dozed off listening to Louise's voice. Neither of us slept well, constantly awakened by the lights being raised and lowered, nurses coming and going. Early in the morning we shared bits of our bizarre dreams after I washed my face in his bathroom. Each time he spoke, he would pull the mask away from his face to be understood. I told him his color was much improved, clearly the benefit of the mask.

"Dare I say happy birthday?" I asked. "There doesn't seem much to be happy about."

He smiled wanly. "Let's celebrate the fact that I'm still here. Surely that's something to remark on, if not celebrate." I rose as Cerise, his favorite food-service worker, arrived with his breakfast and set the tray on the bed table. She was from Haiti, round and plump, and gave him a million-dollar smile.

"Cerise," he said. "Today is my birthday. Did you bring me a present?"

She laughed and said, "*Joyeux anniversaire*, Mr. Mark. Be careful or I'll give you a birthday kiss." I left them to their banter and went home to shower and change clothes.

Mark had revised his will in New York in early June. When he finally received the documents for signing, he saw that some of the revisions were wrong. He was furious. He asked me to call David Latham, a friend and Boston attorney who specialized in wills and trusts. He said, "Ask him to come to the hospital

ASAP." David, God bless him, arrived in the Deaconess lobby, briefcase in hand, just as I was returning to the hospital. I had known him in several settings, mostly business, and felt so much relief at seeing him that I started crying.

"Oh honey," he said, "come here, come here!" He gave me a long hug while I tried to regain my composure. It felt good to be held tightly. He laughed and handed me his beautiful handkerchief. "Mop up, there's a dear. Are things that bad?"

"About as bad as they can be."

"What's the problem with the will?"

"I don't know. Mark's been trying to get something resolved for weeks with his guy in New York, the one who does the legal work for the building, and he's beside himself that it's not finished. I've tried to stay out of it. It feels awkward to insert myself into his legal business, especially now."

We talked as we made our way to the elevator and up to the 9th floor. As we came into the room Mark pulled back his mask and said, "David Latham, you are a prince! Thank you for coming so quickly."

David said, "For you, honey, the world. I have whatever we'll need with me, plus my notary seal, so if you know what you want, I'm your guy."

I stood by the door, taking in the scene: Mark looked like a character in a sci-fi movie with the mask, oxygen tank, and IVs. David, in a beautiful suit and tie, looked ready for the opera. I waved to both and said, "Breakfast time for me. I'll see you guys in a bit."

When I returned forty-five minutes later, two nurses were leaving the room and David was just packing up his briefcase. He turned to me and said, "We have the documents duly signed, witnessed, and notarized, Mike. I'm in town this weekend and can be reached on short notice if you need me. I'll get all this typed up *tout de suite*." He kissed Mark on the forehead, then stood in the doorway looking at us, side by side on the bed. "Love and luck," he said, and was gone.

The medical technicians began to take what we called "the dreaded blood gases." The procedure in July of 1984 was barbaric. The med tech would come into the room with a cart containing glass vials. She would numb the area around the radial artery on the inner wrist, then nick the artery and insert a needle to draw off the blood sample. From this they could determine how well the blood was oxygenated. Mark said the procedure hurt like hell, like a bad paper cut or a prick from a paring knife. Blood gases were drawn frequently over the next few days because the doctors needed to closely monitor his lungs' decreasing ability to maintain proper oxygenation.

Mark asked me to make a list, so I got paper and pen. Because of the mask, he had to speak, replace the mask for air, then speak again. "Number one. The will. Finished." He smiled. "At last. I was concerned about you having to pay the mortgage on the condo by yourself, so I've made some immediate provisions for you. The rest of my property will go into a trust, the interest from which will go to my parents and/or Pearl during their lifetimes. When they die, the trust will be dissolved and the estate disbursed, with a major share coming to you." He lay back on the pillows, out of breath. I sat watching him, wondering if we could really be having this conversation.

As if reading my mind, he said, "Don't say anything or I may cry, which I am loath to do. I would have been lost without you this last year. I can't imagine trying to deal with all that has happened without your support and love. What would my poor parents have been able to do?" He rubbed his eyes. "The list!" he continued. "Number two. Let's call Mom and Dad from here this morning so that they can wish me happy birthday. Don't tell them the test results yet, not today. I need to get my feet under me before I see them." He rested for several more minutes while I waited.

"Number three. We have to talk next steps with Jerry, ask if there is anything left to try."

After a pause, I said. "Is that it?" I could see that his energy was fading.

"One more thing. It's important. I want to be cremated. Jews don't do cremation, so we have to discuss this with my parents." His voice became tense. "I don't want to be buried with this fucking virus in my body. I want every last diseased cell burned away, so that all that's left of me is . . ." He closed his eyes. "Just me."

Jerry came in after lunch. Mark was dozing in bed, I was dozing sitting up. When I saw him I started to stand up and he waved me back into my seat. He gazed at Mark sleeping and folded his long frame into a chair by the door. We sat quietly for a few moments until Mark startled awake.

"How's the patient?" Jerry asked.

Mark said, "Breathing better with the mask, but feeling pretty depressed. Have you been here long?"

"Just a few minutes. I was sitting here thinking about the months I've known you. Almost a year now, yes?" Mark nodded. "You've been a model for so many men with AIDS, Mark. In the lab group, in the PWA group. You've had a tremendous impact, staying calm and steady." He stopped for a moment and then said dryly, "Even my staff is giving me hell for not coming up with something to keep you going." Mark laughed at this, both uncomfortable with and delighted by Jerry's praise. "I feel like I've failed you." When Mark started to demur, Jerry held up his hand and stood up.

"You've been adamant about not wanting to be intubated, and I appreciate that. However, there is a small chance, about one in ten, that another course of Pentamidine could keep you alive. The problem is the drug would take three days to take hold. You won't live three days with your oxygen levels as poor as they are, and it's going to take time to secure the drug. You'd need to be intubated. You're feeling better today because you're getting more oxygen. But the mask is a short-term solution." I felt the pressure of time, wanting to stop the clock. Three days without the respirator!

Mark closed his eyes for a moment, then looked at me. "What do you think, Mike?"

"Ugh. What a choice. I know how you feel about being put on a respirator." For his sake, I hoped he'd say no. But I felt mixed. What if the Pentamadine did work? What if a miracle was just around the corner?

Mark looked back to Jerry. "How much time will I last with this mask?"

"A couple of days at best."

"Can I put off deciding for now?"

"Yes. But it's urgent," he said softly.

Later, after Mark rested, we called his parents and let them sing their birthday wishes. Eddie's voice was as excruciating as his piano playing, but it brought a smile to Mark's face nonetheless. Bert also called, a surprise that pleased Mark enormously, and they spoke for several minutes. All family members got the same message: "There has been a shift from the cannula to the mask so that he can breathe more easily; things are not getting better; don't panic, we're looking at options." Ida asked me if they should come up that day and I said, "Let's wait until things are clearer."

Flowers arrived. Balloons. Cards were piled up on the window ledge.

I tried to run interference for him when people showed up to say happy birthday, telling most of them, "Five minutes, tops!" Richard and Patrick stayed a little longer, with Richard barely holding it together. He and Mark had been diagnosed a week apart. It was a unique friendship for Mark, who was as emotionally open and vulnerable to Richard as he was to me. Maybe more so. As a physician, Richard was aware of the prognosis at this point. He who had worried about "dying, to make three" with David and Pedro was now sitting with someone he loved who was much closer to death. Watching his face as he watched Mark broke my heart.

Fern arrived shortly before supper with Deborah Haynor. Deborah had brought lunch to Mark nearly every Friday for the duration of his illness. There was an ease in their relationship born of familiarity. Fern carefully opened a small cardboard box and removed a chocolate cupcake, its surface covered with tiny frosted flowers. Deborah reached into her shirt pocket and displayed a twist of tissue paper, which contained a candle.

"Don't panic about me lighting the candle, boys," she said, pointing to the oxygen tank. "It's made of candy!"

I stayed the night again. I tried to squeeze onto the bed on the side opposite the machine, but we couldn't get comfortable. More losses, unable to be physically close, unable to have any semblance of privacy. Even a moment of emotional intimacy was hard to create in the context of constant stimulation and chronic fatigue. I had stopped seeing my clients after July 4th and my entire universe seemed to be the Deaconess, not only Mark's room but the Pulmonary Unit in the basement, the cafeteria, even the small garden in front of the hospital where I would sometimes sit in the sunshine and attempt to quiet my mind.

Midafternoon of the day following Mark's birthday, he requested a "summit meeting."

"Who would you like to attend?" I asked, surprised by his announcement. He looked less pinched and gray than he had when he started using the mask, but already we were anxious about the slow but steady increase in the amplification of the oxygen. Time really was of the essence: soon he would not be able to breathe even with the mask.

Mark requested four men from different parts of our lives: David Latham, whom we knew was still in town; John Mazzullo, who had become a good friend to both of us; Larry Kessler; and Jerry Groopman. The topic: "extraordinary means." Eddie and Ida were going to arrive sometime the following morning and he felt it was important to have a plan in place.

Mark said he wanted to go home to die. The idea of being put on the respirator, of having a tube put down his throat into his lungs and a machine breathing for him, absolutely terrified him. What he wanted from the men assembled was counsel: Was it possible to go home? What would have to be done to set up the apartment? Were there legal ramifications? Of all the possibilities that had crossed my mind when he asked for this meeting, going home to die had never occurred to me. My first thought: *It's July! There's no air conditioning there!* How could we possibly take care of him?

The room felt close with so many people crowded in. Larry Kessler spoke first. "The AIDS Action Committee can get you whatever resources you need, Mark. Nurses, drugs, oxygen. We can be there with you 24/7."

David Latham spoke next. "There are no legal ramifications that I'm aware of, Mark. You are of sound mind and body and have the right to die wherever you wish. It's that simple."

Jerry Groopman cleared his throat. "But it's not medically simple, Mark. As the disease progresses, your lungs rigidify and fill with fluid. It's pretty terrifying. You then have the option of increasing morphine until the lungs stop functioning. Another option is to stay here in the hospital and let the disease take its course." Almost as an afterthought he added, "And I'm not advocating for intubation, but it does offer one more possible chance."

"What if I'm intubated and the Pentamidine fails?"

"Then you remain on the respirator until your heart gives out. It would probably take a few days."

I wondered if this would stop the conversation, but Mark soldiered on, his calm demeanor suggesting how utterly worn out he was. He had no energy for an emotional reaction.

Mark looked at John Mazzullo and said, "Anything to add, John?"

"I wonder if you could even make the transition home, Mark. Your condition is stable but very fragile. Consider this: getting you ready to be moved, moving your equipment with you, getting you up to the fourth floor in that tiny elevator, getting you set up and comfortable. I think it's a little late in the game, but it's your decision."

"Mike?"

I couldn't imagine how we could manage to move him physically, let alone how we'd take care of him in that suffocating apartment. But I said, "If you want to go home, I'll get behind it." At this point I felt overwhelmed by the events themselves and was doing my best simply to hang on.

David joined back in for a last word. "With all due respect to Larry, and while people have a strong emotional attachment to the idea of dying at home, I don't see how you'd survive the transition from here to there. I'm sorry."

The men sat back and several sighed. What could be said had been said. Mark thanked each person and asked Jerry if he could make it another day with the mask.

"Your blood gases are decreasing, Mark, but . . . it's possible you can live another day."

John Mazzullo asked when the senior Halberstadts were coming up and offered to have them stay with him, which brought a smile of relief to Mark's face. It was an unexpected and welcome offer. After goodbyes had been said, each man shook hands with Mark except David, who once again kissed him on the forehead.

Eddie and Ida arrived at the hospital late the next morning, relieved not to be staying in a hotel. John Mazzullo had met them at his condo in the Back Bay and gave them the master (and only) bedroom, relegating himself to the sofa in the living room.

Even in his diminished state, with anxiety high and time running out, Mark was calm and clear with his parents, who were frequently on the verge of tears. To his surprise they had no reaction to his desire for cremation, so he moved on to the next topic. "Mike will organize a memorial service here in Boston, and I would like something very simple at the burial of my ashes, just family and close friends." He paused, then added, "And I want a gay rabbi to lead the service at the graveside."

Eddie and Ida sat up straight. Eddie asked incredulously, "Where would we find a gay rabbi?"

"Mike will take care of it. We have Jewish friends in New York who can point us in the right direction."

Eddie said, "A gay rabbi," shaking his head in disbelief. "Imagine."

Ida looked at him and said with irritation, "Eddie, there are gay *everythings* these days!"

We put up a "No Visitors" sign when the Halberstadts returned to the Back Bay. After their long car trip and their grief at Mark's condition, they clearly needed rest. I suggested that they not return until the next morning and reassured them that I'd be with Mark and call if his condition became critical.

Mark and I looked at each other and he shrugged. There was nothing more to be done, and he sank into a fitful sleep almost immediately, visibly straining to breathe.

About 9:00 p.m. Mark woke me from a doze with the words, "I'm going to do it."

"What?" I mumbled, unsure I'd heard him correctly.

"I'm going to authorize the intubation."

I rubbed my eyes and tried to focus.

"Jerry said I'd only have one chance in ten on Pentamidine. But it's a chance, and I know the drug is in the hospital now, he told me yesterday. I can't give up now. This has been too hard. I can't quit."

My eyes filled with tears, and I turned my head away and said, "I'll set it in motion, sweetheart."

Still somewhat dazed, I buzzed for a nurse, who called the attending physician, a woman named Dr. James. She was in the room in less than five minutes, and I wondered if the staff had been waiting for this decision to be made. "I've notified Dr. Groopman, and Pulmonary is prepping now downstairs. It will take a bit to set up."

Shortly after Dr. James left, a young phlebotomist came in with the blood gas cart. Mark said, "Enough! I'm being intubated in a few minutes. Do I really need to suffer through this again?"

She said, "I'm sorry, Mark, but they need to know your exact level of blood oxygen right now." He winced and sighed as she tried to find a site on his lacerated wrists that was not scabbed. Finally she succeeded and got the vial filled, apologized and hurried out of the room.

Mark fell back on the bed, looking grimmer than I'd ever seen him. His struggle for breath was very apparent. I rubbed his neck, and he said, "I just want this to be over." I began to cry. I wanted desperately to put my arms around him, which was impossible with the IVs and oxygen mask in the way. There was so much that separated us now. "One of these days I'll join you in crying," he said, patting my arm clumsily. "You're lucky to be Irish. Tears don't come for me." He had not cried once in the ten months of his illness.

There was a knock at the door and the same tech was standing there with her cart, looking stricken. "Mark, I'm so sorry, honestly." She was fighting tears. "I dropped the vial when I was attaching the label and it broke on the floor. I have to get another sample. I'm so sorry."

Mark looked at me sadly. "Indignity follows indignity," he said.

I felt as if we were in a dream. Events began moving with breathtaking rapidity when two nurses arrived, already masked, and moved Mark onto a gurney for the trip to Pulmonary. My anxiety skyrocketed. I stood by helplessly and then walked quickly at his side, holding his hand as the nurses raced for the elevator. Soon he was taken into a small room in the basement that contained what looked like an operating table. I stood outside looking in through a window, paralyzed. The energy was fierce and very noisy, lights everywhere, the staff all seeming to talk at once. My fear and disorientation deepened. I realized I was going to be separated from him for the first time in days. I thought, *What if he dies?* We'd never acknowledged the possibility aloud. I felt a desperate need to speak to him once more. Screwing up my courage, I stopped a nurse who was entering the unit and said, "Please, could I have just one minute alone with him?" She started to say no but looked at my face and said, "Let me ask the doctor." She went into the room and spoke to the pulmonologist, who looked at me through the window and then spoke briefly to the staff. They streamed out of the room. "One minute!" the doctor said, patting my arm as he passed me.

Mark look confused when I came in. My panic made me short of breath. I looked at him on the table, new IVs already inserted, and struggled to remember what I needed so badly to ask him. As in a near-death experience, the last ten months flashed through my head. *Please God, what did I need to ask him?* Finally I sputtered, "Sweetheart, if you die— If you die—" I couldn't go on.

Mark brought up his hand and pulled the mask away. With great effort he glared and said, "I . . . am . . . NOT . . . going to die!" He replaced the mask and the room was suddenly swarming with people again.

These were the last words he ever spoke.

Chapter 19

Mark's initial response to the respirator was a nightmare for him and for us. The respirator was the size of a small cabinet, taller than it was wide, and covered with dials, plugs, lights, and gauges. Various alarms made intense and nerve-wracking beeping noises. Tubes ran from the machine in a loop over his shoulder and down his throat. The tubes were taped to his face, and his hands were tied to the side rails of the bed to restrain him from pulling them out. The respirator breathed for Mark, forcing air in and out of his lungs. The problem, of course, was that Mark had spent forty-two years breathing for himself, so he exerted every ounce of his will to regain control of his breath. His efforts threw the machine off. At the beginning it beeped almost continuously, while Mark's body bucked and convulsed as it tried to wrest back control of the breathing process. I felt frantic watching his suffering.

The technician said over and over, "Don't try to breathe, Mark, let the machine breathe for you."

Don't try to breathe? Who are you kidding? How can he not breathe?

The nurses medicated him to numb his reactivity and to paralyze his muscles. They began to administer the Pentamidine immediately. Over a period of hours, he stopped struggling. But he looked terrible: wild-eyed when conscious, corpse-like when not. Gradually he adjusted and they unbound his hands. They found a balance with the drugs that alleviated the anxiety but did not knock him unconscious. While it was difficult for him to follow conversations, given how both his body and mind were affected, he was determined to communicate. I got a yellow pad and pen, edged onto the bed between him and the respirator, and held the pad for him while he wrote. At first the lines were squiggles that made no sense to me.

"Thirsty? Does this mean you're thirsty?" I asked.

He shook his head no, waving the pen at me.

"I'm sorry, I can't read it, sweetheart. Try again."

Laboriously, patiently, he tried printing.

"What? Is the first word 'what'?"

He nodded, pointing to the next word.

"My? Is it 'my'?"

He rolled his eyes. I felt like a fool. He took the pen and carefully made the letter D, the printing of a four-year-old.

"Day? What day is it!"

Eyes crinkling in triumph, he released the pen.

"It's Monday, Mark. Today is Monday." I looked at my watch. "It's four in the afternoon."

He thought for a moment and then pointed once more to the pad. I repositioned myself and put the pen back in his hand. He squiggled again, but his effort was more successful and I was less anxious, so within two guesses I said, "Which day?" He nodded yes. Which day? What did he want to know? He looked at me expectantly and I tried to relax. He scrawled a large P on the pad. "Pentamidine?" He nodded. "Ah. It started early this morning. Jerry said it would take three days to know if it's working. You're almost through the first day."

His body seemed to sigh, the muscles in his face and shoulders relaxing, the effort to communicate having exhausted him. He closed his eyes, immediately drifting away. I dropped into the chair next to the bed and discovered I was sweating heavily despite the air conditioning. Swabbing the back of my neck with tissues, I thought, *God help me. God help us all.*

The second day on the drug was a nightmare of a different sort. Mark had adjusted to the respirator, but the battle between the medications and the disease ratcheted up. He vacillated between very high fevers and shuddering chills. When his temperature went up to 105, the staff brought in a "cooling blanket." He was stripped of his gown and laid out on something that looked like a thin blue mattress pad, only it was filled with a frozen substance. He was sweating profusely but was clearly uncomfortable on the icy blanket, in and out of consciousness, naked except for a small towel across his genitals. He looked like he was being tortured: shuddering, sweating, eyes wide with fright. The nurses were remarkable: always professional, always loving. They talked to him as if they'd known him forever.

Melanie, the charge nurse, said, "Mark, I know this is miserable. I'm sorry, but we have to break the fever. We want to do everything we can to support the Pentamidine taking effect. We know you can pull through. Your family is right here with you, supporting you. We're all with you." His parents and I took turns wiping his forehead with a cool washcloth.

When his temperature came down, they would remove the cooling blanket, bathe him and give him a clean gown, and rub lotion on him. He had several periods of complete lucidity on that day and was desperate to connect with us. He concentrated all his energies while I held the yellow tablet for him. By then he could write in a spidery cursive. After a particularly difficult episode on the cooling blanket, spasm after spasm shaking his body, he scrawled: *Terrible dream. In a big house on fire. Running from room to room but no way out, just kept running. SCARED.*

His parents and I were the only ones allowed in the room during the temperature spikes. At other times Fern would come in for a few moments, or Deborah or Mitch. Patrick was there every day, for me as much as for Mark. They would simply sit by the side of the bed and talk quietly to him.

Meanwhile other friends had gathered in the visitor's lounge. All sorts of people came and went, men from the PWA group, staff from the AIDS Action Committee, my colleagues from the office. Deborah organized a short list of people to be there during the day for several days in a row. They brought food for those of us who were at the hospital most of the time. Ida and Eddie had long conversations with the visitors. Someone told them about Mark organizing the men in the Gamma Interferon study and their reading of *Torch Song Trilogy*. Ida said to me repeatedly, "I had no idea Mark had so many friends. I had no idea how much love there was for him here. Why didn't he tell me more about his life?" There was little I could say to her in response. Decades of defenses that he had erected in childhood still stood between them.

On the third day, Mark's parents and I received a message that Dr. Groopman wanted to meet with us outside the ICU. I knew in my gut that he was going to tell us whether the Pentamidine was working. I didn't say anything to Eddie and Ida, just shepherded them in the direction of the lounge. Ida stopped to freshen her lipstick and fluff her hair. Jerry asked how Mark had passed the night. I watched him carefully, searching his face for clues.

Ida dove right in. "Is he getting better, Doctor? Is the medicine working?"

"I'm sorry, Mrs. Halberstadt, it's not working. It was a long shot, and I'd hoped that it would be more effective than the DFMO. But it's not." He looked at Eddie, then at me. I'd been holding my breath and let out a sigh.

Eddie cleared his throat and asked, "What else can you do?"

"There's really nothing else we can do, Mr. Halberstadt."

Despite all that I had witnessed since Mark had been hospitalized, the effort it took him just to pull himself into consciousness a few times a day in the ICU, I felt shocked. Some magical-thinking part of my brain had believed all along, as he had, that he was not going to die. The doctor put his hand on my shoulder.

"Is Mark awake now?" he asked, and I nodded yes. "Let's go in then." We filed back down the hall, no one speaking.

Mark was awake, eyes wide and bright. Awkwardly we lined up at the foot of his bed. The doctor cleared his throat and began to speak.

"Mark, you know that we've given you the full course of the Pentamidine." When Mark nodded, he continued. "I'm deeply sorry. You've been so committed in this fight. It was worth the chance of trying every possible course of action. But

I'm afraid it hasn't been effective."

Mark looked at me, then gestured for the yellow pad. I got it and sat next to him on the bed, but before he even grasped the pen, I asked Jerry, "Is there anything, anything at all, no matter how far out, that you could try now?"

He said only, "I'm sorry."

Mark held his gaze for a long moment, then looked at each of his parents. Ida was crying quietly, Eddie had his arm around her shoulders. Then Mark looked up at me, sitting beside him. He felt completely present to me, and for a long moment his eyes searched my face. Then he lifted his eyebrows and shrugged his shoulders. He might as well have said aloud, "I did my best." And he closed his eyes. By the time his parents and I had said our goodbyes to the doctor, Mark had slipped into a coma, where he remained for six days, coming out of it only once.

*

Early the following morning, Eddie and Ida arrived at the hospital. Both were beaming.

"Michael, you won't believe this!" Ida had not even asked how the night went with Mark, so I knew it was big news.

"Pearl is flying up to Boston this morning. Pearl's only been on a plane once, when her husband Sam was still alive and they went to Las Vegas. She said she has to come to Boston to talk to Mark."

"Did you tell her that Mark is comatose, Ida?"

"Of course I did, but you know my sister. She needs to see Mark for herself. There was no talking her out of it."

Eddie whistled tunelessly by the window, the respirator softly clicking and wheezing.

Ida continued. "By herself! For no one but Mark would Pearl get on a plane by herself!"

A few hours later, I heard Pearl's voice loud and clear, coming from the nurses' station.

"Darling, he's my nephew. He's like my own son. I don't have any children. Where's my sister? She'll vouch for me." I opened the door to the room and Pearl, in a large straw hat, had Melanie backed up against the counter. Melanie seemed at a loss for words.

"I just came from New York. That's a long trip for an old woman. I used to be afraid to fly." She laughed. "I talked to the lady next to me the whole way. She lives on Cape Cod! Can you imagine? I told her all about Mark." Pearl looked up and saw me in the doorway. Forgetting Melanie, she hurled herself at me. I was filled with relief to see her, to be engulfed in her warmth and aliveness. Ida and Eddie came out into the hallway and all three began talking at once. Melanie tried to shush them. "This is an intensive care unit," she stage whispered. "Mark is only supposed to have two visitors at a time." Ignoring her entirely, they moved as one into Mark's room.

I tried to see Mark through Pearl's eyes: IVs in both arms, the respirator tube taped to his face. There was a central venous catheter connected to a line in his chest, and the Foley catheter ran from under the sheet to a bag on the side of the bed. His face was pinched, forehead slightly wrinkled, as if he were having a troubled dream. I worried that Pearl would dissolve somehow, her grief so unbearable. But she took off her hat, put it and her enormous handbag on the window ledge, and carefully squeezed herself onto the edge of the bed next to Mark.

"Mark! Mark! Darling, it's Aunt Pearl. I came all the way from Kew Gardens to see you."

Her voice must have carried clear to the nurses' station outside the closed door, but Mark was immobile. I said gently, "Pearl, he can't hear you. He's been in a coma since yesterday."

Ignoring me, she leaned down next to his ear. Her voice quavered. "Mark, honey, can you hear me? I flew up here to see you. On an airplane! Can you believe that? I had to see you again. Can you hear me?"

Eddie, Ida, and I were lined up like statues at the foot of the bed, stock still. And then Mark opened his eyes. Not a flutter of eyelashes, but a full-out, open-eyed gaze right into Pearl's eyes. If the respirator had not been attached, I'm convinced he would have been grinning from ear to ear. Pearl grabbed his hand, squeezing hard.

"Darling, thank you for this," Pearl said. "I love you so, this is the happiest moment of my life. God bless you, Mark. I'm so lucky to have you."

Ida and I were both crying. Mark held Pearl's gaze a few more seconds, then his eyes fluttered briefly and closed again. Pearl leaned in and kissed him. "Thank you, darling. Thank you."

Chapter 20

After her whirlwind visit to the intensive care unit, Aunt Pearl had lunch with Eddie and Ida, then took a taxi to the airport. Mark's parents came back to be with him for the afternoon while I went home to shower and sleep for a few hours, then they left the hospital for the evening when I returned. Soon Fern came to spend a couple of hours with me. With her there was no need to talk. Mark was a small figure on the bed, the two of us flanking him in chairs, the respirator regularly making its *Whoosh! Hiss!*

During that night and the nights that followed, I felt intimately connected to Mark again, something that was impossible to experience during the long hours of the day when his parents were there, when friends came in briefly to sit with him and hold his hand, when nurses came in and out to check the machines, clean the respirator tubes, recalibrate the heart monitor. One of the nurses brought in a tiny radio, which I tuned to an easy-listening station. Lionel Richie's song "Stuck on You" was so popular at the time that disc jockeys played it repeatedly. Each time it came on, I felt a deep heartache at the line, "Needed a friend, and the way I feel now I guess I'll be with you till the end."

I talked to him as if he could hear me, sometimes asking, "What's going on in there? Can you hear what we say? Do you have any idea what's happening?" I'd tell him things I remembered, meals he'd cooked, a whole fish baked *en papillote*, rack of lamb. I reminded him of our "pilgrimage" to Julia Child's house in Cambridge, where he raced up to her porch and left a big bouquet of flowers at her door. Early in our relationship we had been in a Japanese restaurant in Manhattan, and he slipped off his shoe under the table and slid his stockinged foot up and down my calf, giving me goosebumps. Later we were walking in the Village and passed a small tobacco and magazine shop. The owner was standing outside speaking rapidly to another man in a foreign language. Mark, characteristically reserved, stopped and jumped into their conversation. Soon they were shaking hands and slapping each other on the shoulders. At the time I knew Mark had spent three years in Tunisia in the Peace Corps, but I didn't know he spoke three dialects of Arabic. The one these men were using was common in the mountain village where Mark had lived, and they chatted for several minutes before we moved on.

Over and over I went back to Fire Island in my head, September 2 nearly three years earlier, trying to recall every detail of our meeting: the shade of blue of his polo shirt, what photos he took when we wandered the boardwalk after meeting at Tea Dance, what we had for dinner that first night. When we stood on the widow's walk at the top of his rental, Mark felt lean and muscled when he tucked in to kiss me for the first time, his arms encircling my neck. For many years after he died I could remember the exact feeling of his hair, wiry and short, tickling my chin when I held him close.

There was my first trip to Fort Lauderdale to meet him after he helped move the *Skua* down to Jupiter from Bellport. I had only been with him three times before and wondered what we would feel, having not seen each other for a month. Our greeting in the airport felt awkward. He was housesitting for friends, and the place was lovely, cool, and spacious. There was a long sunken living room filled with comfortable furniture and a piano at the far end. I knew Mark could play both piano and harpsichord, but this was my first chance to hear him. I stretched out on a sofa and he blew me away, playing song after song from memory, Cole Porter, the Gershwins, on and on. He said as a kid he could hear something once and play it immediately from memory, delighting Hetty Levine, his piano teacher. His gift for mimicry showed up again when he imitated Hoagy Carmichael singing "The Nearness of You," goofing on it but also bringing tears to my eyes as I began to relax and remember how hard I had fallen for this man only two months earlier. We settled into a long and passionate weekend.

Whoosh! Hiss! Whoosh! Hiss! Periodically the respirator would need attention and begin beeping, interrupting my reverie. The night nurse on duty would come in, usually Patsy or Karen, and she would touch my shoulder as she passed to turn off the signal and adjust whatever control needed attention. I had developed an odd relationship to the respirator, habituating to the sounds it made. Sometimes I would think back to how desperate for breath Mark had been before he was intubated, and I felt gratitude to this weird little robotic device that gave him breath. But now we were in a kind of purgatory, waiting for his body to give out, his heart to fail, so that he could die. Once he was put on the respirator, there was no removing him. Day by day his body grew whiter and colder.

Chapter 21

The final three days of Mark's hospitalization felt as if they occurred outside of time. The doctor had said nearly a week earlier that "it would take a few days." On Monday morning the nurse said, "Only a few hours now." But time dragged on. Earlier I had felt delighted by Mark's tenacity, the power of his will to live. But now he didn't even look like Mark. The disease had rendered him unrecognizable. His left eye was partially open and rolled back in his head. His skin color was gray, cold and clammy. There was not a single sign of life in his body except for the rise and fall of his chest, mechanically generated by the respirator.

Our friends, who had crowded the visitor's lounge over the previous weekend, returned to their jobs and their normal lives. The visitors in the lounge now were there for other patients in the ICU. I stayed with Mark at night and left to shower, change clothes, and nap when Eddie and Ida arrived in the morning. I would return to the hospital a few hours later and they would go to the cafeteria to eat. Otherwise we remained in the ICU, usually all three of us in the room at once.

Eddie had two habits that made me crazy: ceaselessly pacing in a semi-circle, very slowly, from the corner on the far side of the monitors and respirator to the left of Mark's bed to the corner of the room on the right-hand side, where the window looked out onto the nurses' station. It was a journey of twenty-six paces, a journey he walked hundreds of times a day. While he paced, he whistled. Not loudly, but endlessly and tunelessly, hour after hour. Sometimes I would engage him in conversation just to stop the whistling, and he would hold forth on any subject I raised for as long as I wished. But as soon as the conversation stopped, it was walk and whistle, whistle and walk.

Ida, on the other hand, talked. Generally it was about her regrets: what they hadn't done right as parents, what she wished she could do over. Sometimes she was angry with Mark: Why hadn't he shared more, didn't he know how much pleasure they would have taken in knowing his friends? Why hadn't he let them help him? Surely that would have been better than worrying himself to death! She was beyond tears by then, as were we all, exhausted and simply waiting.

On Tuesday morning, July 24, Karen, one of the night nurses, stopped me in the hallway before she went off duty and told me that she thought she would not be seeing Mark again. She wanted to tell me goodbye.

"Why do you say that?" I asked. I wondered if she was going to go on vacation.

"You develop feelings in this work. I won't be back until tomorrow evening, and I really don't think Mark will live through another day. In our unit you see a lot of people get better, but you also see a lot of people pass on. There are patterns that we notice."

"Like what?"

"You know we work twelve-hour shifts, seven to seven. People often die at change of shift, more frequently in the evening than the morning. Maybe it's the tides and the moon, I don't know." She shrugged. "But it happens."

"It will be a relief, Karen. His parents and I are on our last nerve."

"It will be a relief for him too, Mike." She hugged me and went back to finish her paperwork.

Midafternoon, while Eddie paced and Ida talked, I excused myself and wandered the hallways, finding my way to the chapel on the first floor. Mark had been in the hospital for a month by now, and I had never even noticed that there was a chapel, let alone gone into it. I had left the Catholic Church at nineteen when I couldn't find a way to reconcile my sexuality with my religious beliefs. This chapel was lovely, small and quiet, with perhaps twelve pews to a side and a very simple altar, undecorated. It felt carefully nondenominational, with the exception of a cross etched into the single stained-glass window.

I sat down in the back for a few moments, then lay my forearms on the pew in front of me and rested my head on my arms. It was deeply relaxing to give way to the waves of fatigue that swept over me. I ached all over, so many nights of sitting up in chairs in the ICU, so many days of too much stimulation. I missed my clients, my colleagues, my normal life. I missed my privacy. I felt sick and empty. I knew Mark was never going to "come back." So why wasn't he letting go? I felt angry. He'd left me when the doctor said, "There's nothing else we can do, Mark." Six days later, I was still here.

After a few minutes I stood up and looked around the room, feeling a little lighter, aware of the ground beneath my feet. *I can do this on your terms*, I thought. *But Mark, I'm ready to let go when you are.* I returned to the vigil upstairs.

Around 6:00 p.m. Eddie, Ida and I started to discuss dinner. The three of us had never, in all these days in intensive care, left Mark alone to go have a meal together. I floated an idea by them: let's have dinner in a real restaurant, not the cafeteria, then I'll come back to the hospital and you can return to John Mazzulo's apartment. The idea seemed quite radical, but they thought it over and decided it would be a good change of pace for all of us. For a brief period Eddie paced while

Ida went to the ladies room to "put on her face." I took my seat in the chair next to Mark's bed, holding his hand, which was ice cold.

"Mark, we're going to dinner. We'll be gone an hour or more. I'll come back later and sit with you. I don't know if you can hear me, but . . ." I couldn't think of anything else to say that didn't sound stupid to my own ear. "I love you."

I glanced up at the heart monitor. It had been presenting the same pattern as regularly as his respirator pushed the breath in and out. But the pattern was elongating. I looked out the window at the nurses' station. Patsy smiled at me and nodded. Ida returned and joined Eddie and me at the head of the bed. The monitor showed a normal wave pattern, then a squiggle, a broken line, and another normal wave pattern. Patsy opened the door and said, "Maybe five more minutes."

I will be eternally grateful to Ida, who said to Eddie, "Let's give Mike a moment alone with our son." And they left the room. I pulled the chair close to the bed and held his hand, encouraging him to take the leap into whatever was next. I asked him for one thing: "As I have been here for you, be here for me when I have to make this transition. Offer me your hand on the other side." Eddie and Ida came back in and we stood with our arms around each other, sobbing. Within a couple of minutes the monitor went flat. His parents, on either side of me, folded into my chest, and Eddie wailed, "Our baby is dead." They felt as small as children, and their weeping was harsh and guttural. The floodgates were open at last. I stood still, holding them tightly, looking at Mark's face. I went numb. As their sobbing began to quiet down, I was aware only of this thought: *It's done.*

The one fear I had carried for months was of the moment when the staff would want to remove his body. The thought of it made me short of breath. How could I allow them to take him away? I had never been with anyone in the moment of their dying, but here with Mark, it was very clear that he simply wasn't in his body anymore. I felt a surge of energy and glanced quickly around the room, looking for something, anything that would tell me where he went. The room seemed abnormally bright as I searched. But the moment passed. Patsy came in to hug us and pull the sheet up over Mark's face. At last, the waiting was over.

It wasn't until I got the death certificate several days later that I saw the time of death: 7:00 p.m.

PART FOUR

Chapter 22

Ten days later Fern and I traveled down to Long Island to inter Mark's ashes, leaving Boston at 6:00 a.m. It was early August and hot. She drove while I held the urn on my lap. I couldn't imagine surrendering the ashes. I played Lionel Richie's "Stuck on You" over and over on the cassette deck. I smoked half a joint. I looked out the window.

"Do you want to talk?" she asked.

"If my mother were here, she'd say I was being dramatic." My voice was flat.

Fern put her right hand on my left and gave it a squeeze. I looked at the small brass box I was holding, filled with bits of bone and ash. I'd had it on the mantel of the new condo for a few days, and sometimes I talked to him out loud. This was all I had left. After the burial, I wouldn't have even that.

The Eastern part of Long Island is filled with Jewish cemeteries, mile after mile, New Montefiore, Mount Ararat, Maimonides. We were looking for Wellwood, which is south of Beth Moses on Pinelawn Road. We made several wrong turns and I was increasingly anxious, but we finally arrived at the entrance and passed through the imposing black iron gates. It's an enormous cemetery and the graves are very close together, with myriad paths stretching in all directions. We found the central office and parked behind the building. It was about 10:30 and the interment was scheduled for 11:00. I put on my suit coat and tightened my tie. I held the urn close as we made our way to the front of the building.

There were about twenty-five people milling about. There were family friends and relatives, plus some of Mark's friends from the city, and some of my friends and Mark's from Boston. The latter were conspicuously well-dressed. The Halberstadts were standing partway up the concrete steps that led to the office. Ida was wearing a navy blue dress, black shoes, and a small hat. She looked very tired but brightened up and waved when she saw us. Eddie moved toward Ida as we climbed the steps. He was wearing shiny polished cotton pants, yellow, the kind that older men often wear to the golf course, a bright green polo shirt, and a little straw fedora. Ida saw me in suit and tie, Fern in a dark suit, and started screaming at Eddie.

"Look at Michael and Fern, see how nice they look? I told you to wear your suit! Why don't you listen to me!"

"It's too goddamn hot for a suit. They can wear what they want. It's too goddamn hot!" Eddie's face was brick-red. He was perspiring heavily and trembling all over.

Aunt Pearl moved quickly to embrace us. She was wearing a flowered dress and a hat, quite large, with an artificial purple peony creating a lopsided effect. Her smile melted me. "Darling," she said, "I'm so sorry," giving me a crushing hug. I didn't know whether she was referring to Mark's death or his parents' argument, but for the first time that morning, I began to calm down. I felt compassion for Eddie and Ida, who decades earlier had buried their infant son, Clifford, in this cemetery. Now they were burying Mark, who abhorred public displays of any kind and would have been humiliated by their behavior here.

The Halberstadts and I went into the chapel office and met Rabbi Joan Friedman. A Jewish friend in New York who attended a gay synagogue referred her to us. Rabbi Friedman was quiet but present. She had laid out a simple service: a few brief words about Mark's life, the burial of the urn, and the saying of Kaddish. She handed us a printed Order of Service for our approval.

Ida asked her, "Do you have to say what he died of?" The rabbi paused and looked at me, and I shook my head no. She said to Ida, "Not if you'd rather I didn't." Ida said, "Rabbi, I have to tell you. I failed my son as a mother. He needed me to be more loving. I failed him." Eddie said, "Everyone knows you did the best you could, Ida. We need to get on with this." We stood and moved toward the door. The rabbi caught my eye, looking concerned.

Once outside, Rabbi Friedman gathered the group together and we proceeded along a path, passing monuments for Katzes, Shapiros, and Kittenplans, to the Halberstadt family plot, which is marked by a simple headstone. There was a small opening in the ground. Rabbi Friedman read psalms, said a few prayers in Hebrew, and then asked if anyone wished to speak. Ida said as loudly as she was able through her tears, "Mark, I'm sorry. I was a terrible mother. I failed you. I should have helped you more." Before she could continue, Eddie said, "Ida, stop it!" Then a friend of Ida's in the group cried out, "Ida, you were a wonderful mother!" Eddie clamped an arm around Ida's shoulders and looked at me. His face softened. "Mike will speak now. Mike was Mark's dear, dear friend." In fits and starts I said, "Mark was an extraordinary human being. He worked very hard in his life to make a difference, as a schoolteacher, as a friend, and as a patient." I paused for breath and then said, "He will be sorely missed by those who loved him." Eddie patted me on the back. A few others spoke, then Rabbi Friedman asked for the urn and I realized I was still clutching it under my arm. Fern looked at me and nodded. I handed it to the rabbi, realizing too late that I could have kept some of the ashes in Boston.

Mark's brother Bert placed the urn in the grave. He handed a shovel to Eddie, who put some soil in the ground, as did Ida and Pearl. Then Eddie said to Bert, "Give the shovel to Michael." I was grateful to be included with the family. I paused as I saw the urn for the last time, then put more soil on top. The sun was merciless. I felt lightheaded, sweat rolling down my face and my suit jacket stuck to my back. I moved to stand with my friends. As Bert handed the shovel to Ida's best friend, Martha, I heard a strangled sob. Sounding oracular, Martha cried out, "Mark, Mark, you left before your time!" Dropping the shovel, she lurched toward the hole in the ground, stumbling and falling to one knee. Nothing in my Irish Catholic background had prepared me for this. Suddenly I wanted to scream with laughter, to run away, to roar, "Please, God, let this be done!" Martha's husband, Irving, hauled her up off the ground, brushing the dirt from her knee. When the small grave was filled with soil, those who were Jewish recited Kaddish, first in Hebrew, then all of us read it in English from the back of the Order of Service. Mark had been remembered, and we were released.

The entire group was invited back to Kew Gardens to sit shiva at the Halberstadts' home. When Fern and I arrived there were perhaps twenty people, most familiar to me from the cemetery. The small living room and dining area were dimly lit, the lone air conditioner high in one window fruitlessly blowing cool air into an already stifling room. The venetian blinds were almost closed, creating the effect of dusk, though it was early afternoon. I noticed as I passed the upright piano that, in the sea of family photos on top, Eddie and Ida had recently added a four-by-six inch photograph of Mark and me on a sailboat, my arm casually around his shoulders. It felt like a small victory.

The table in the dining area, covered with a plastic tablecloth, was loaded with salads and meats and cheeses, pickles and olives, breads and bagels and lox and cream cheese. People were talking noisily as Fern and I entered. Ida was seated in a small chair by the air conditioner and looked crumpled from fatigue and grief. I knew Mark's friends from the city, including Barry Safran and the Garretts from the McIntyre Building. There were a handful of our friends from Boston and Long Island. Mostly, however, these were older people in their seventies and eighties, lifelong friends of Mark's parents. Though Mark and I had been together for three years, Aunt Pearl was the only person in their network I had met. Eddie moved Fern and me through the crowd to the table, introducing us to friends as we passed. His manner was jocular, more like the host of a Labor Day cookout than a funeral luncheon. I was bewildered by the scene, wondering what my role should be.

Martha and Irving stepped right up to meet us. I knew from conversation with Ida that each couple had been the witnesses at the other's wedding, which would have been nearly fifty years earlier. Martha was chatty, Irving pleasant.

"Such a hot day, I thought I would die at the cemetery," she exclaimed.

Irving poked her and said, "Don't make jokes!"

"I'm not joking, mister! I could have dropped dead from the heat!" No mention was made of her falling to the ground during the service.

Fern and I murmured sympathetically before Aunt Pearl, *sans* hat, elbowed her way into the conversation. Pearl's near deafness in the small and crowded space must have made it nearly impossible for her to understand any of the conversation. She compensated by shouting. "You must be starving! Eat something!"

We pressed on, hugging friends and smiling at strangers. Gerry Ente, both Jewish and a doctor, was highly sought after for advice by the elderly women. I elbowed him and muttered, "Stop having such a good time," as I passed by. I looked at the food and felt my stomach cramp, knowing that I must put something on my plate but unable to imagine eating. I finally took half a bagel, some lox, and some chips. Pearl appeared at my side and ladled potato salad onto my plate, then coleslaw.

"Stop, stop!" I said, and she laughed.

"Cookies? You'll want cookies," and piled up five or six.

As Pearl turned her focus to Fern, I moved quickly from the dining room through swinging doors into the kitchen, which was mercifully quiet. Leaving my plate atop a stack of bakery boxes on the counter, I entered the small bathroom by the back door. I was desperate for a moment alone to wash my hands and splash water on my face. I felt like part of me was still out at the cemetery, remembering the reddish soil on the little grave, wondering, *Is he OK?* I looked in the mirror and saw a tired, pale, forty-year-old man, tie askew, looking back. How odd, I thought, to be looking into this mirror, knowing that Mark is not in the other room waiting for me. I shook myself and said aloud, "Onward."

When I reentered the kitchen I picked up my plate, eying only the cookies, when a voice behind me said softly, "Michael?" Startled, I turned to see a lovely older woman, slim and beautifully dressed, a string of pearls standing out against a charcoal silk blouse, champagne blond hair swept into a chignon. "I'm Hetty Levine."

I recognized her name instantly. "You were Mark's piano teacher. He talked so much about you." Impulsively I hugged her, babbling briefly about his appreciation of what she brought into his life as a child, and later how supportive she was of his going to Paris at nineteen.

Her eyes were wet. She spoke with a slight Viennese accent. "He was one of my best students, ever. I know teachers say that all the time, but Mark was a brilliant student, so thoughtful, so disciplined. When he wanted to learn something, nothing stopped him. He was always my star at recitals."

Remembering Eddie plunking through "Edelweiss" on my first visit to the house, I asked, "Did Mark get the gift from his father?"

She laughed. "Definitely not! You can't start playing the piano at seventy-two and ever become very good." She said again, quietly, "Mark was my star." There was a pause, both of us suddenly aware of what had brought us together. "I'm sorry I couldn't be at the cemetery. I don't drive anymore, I'm eighty-two now." She took my hand. "This must have been terrible for you. Was he very sick from the beginning?"

I was on thin ice. *What does she know? What have Eddie and Ida told their friends?*

"AIDS is a frightening illness, so little is understood," she said.

I sighed with relief. "So you know?"

"Of course. We all do. His parents feel so much shame. We all pretend he died of pneumonia because they find the situation . . ." She searched for the word. "Unmanageable." I felt heartsick, then angry. They all knew. Everyone had known all along. She continued. "They couldn't accept the truth. They couldn't deal with his being gay, either. They come from a different time."

"The Dark Ages."

"Yes," she nodded. "The Dark Ages."

As if on cue, Ida pushed through the swinging doors into the kitchen. I almost dropped my plate, and Hetty and I looked guiltily at each other. Ida rushed past us to the bakery boxes and said, "Where are those *rugelach!* I told Pearl to put them out, but they're not on the table!" Hetty backed through the doors into the living room, giving me a little wave, and I turned to help Ida with her task.

Chapter 23

The following week I returned to my office for the first time in six weeks. When I joined the staff in September of 1979, I was given a large space that filled with sunlight by late morning. The room sat at an angle to the street and had an oversize picture window that looked out into Porter Square. I stood in the doorway and surveyed the room as if for the first time. Stacks of brightly colored floor pillows, piled against one wall, were used for therapy groups, whose members sat in a loose circle on the floor. A long sofa of indeterminate age had afghans crocheted by my mother draped across the back cushions. A wide desk sat squarely in front of the big window with a chair on wheels to one side, filing cabinets on the other, and bookcases along the back wall, jammed with books. The room definitely had a sixties feel. After all, it was Cambridge. It was a relief to be back, to experience the normalizing effect of work, having a role to play that felt so much less fraught than being the partner of a dying man.

I sat at the desk with my take-out coffee from the White Hen Pantry and surveyed the Square below, mostly buildings and shops that had a vintage feel. The office, the whole suite of offices, felt like part of the larger landscape, a little worn but very comfortable, a space one could relax into. I had half an hour before my first client session at 11:30, then a staff meeting at 12:30.

The session was with a couple I had been seeing for about six months. He was brilliant but passive; she was beautiful but hostile. They were challenging to work with, a challenge I enjoyed much of the time. But today, not having done therapy for many weeks, I felt off my game and very vulnerable. Still, I was glad to be back.

The couple, whom I will call Tom and Sofia, arrived in the waiting room a few minutes early. I could hear Sofia through the door, not her words but her sharp tone of voice. I opened the door and welcomed them into the office. They sat in their accustomed places on the sofa, and I sat in my rolling chair opposite them. I began, "I'm sorry I've been unavailable for so long. I had a family emergency that I needed to deal with, but it's resolved now and I don't plan to be away again for some time."

Sofia leaned forward slightly and smiled. It was not a pleasant smile, but reflexively I smiled back. She had been in the U.S. for at least ten years but her English was still heavily accented with her native Russian. She said, "You had a death in the family?"

"Yes," I replied. No additional details seemed appropriate. "What would you like to work on today?"

Tom remained silent, looking uncomfortably around, anywhere except at me. I began to feel uneasy. Something was up.

"Your friend, I think she was Fern? She called us in June to say you would be out of the office for a few weeks, then she called again in July to say you would not be back until August."

"Yes," I said, "she often does administrative work for me." I wondered if she was looking for an apology.

"Well," said Sofia, again with the strange smile, "I asked her, what's the problem, he's gone so long! Is he sick?"

Another pause. I could think of nothing to say.

"And then this Fern, she says, 'Oh, it's very sad. His partner died on July 24.' I said, 'His partner?' And she said, 'Yes, his partner, Mark.'"

I wished I had remembered to tell Fern not to share any details with this couple, with whom I had kept meticulous boundaries. But too many other things had needed my attention.

Sofia sat back and favored me with the full force of her smile. I suddenly had the image of a crocodile, rows of bright, sharp teeth. Tom was looking across the room and out the window, tapping his thumb over and over on the arm of the sofa. I wondered if he was listening to a piece of music in his head. For reasons I didn't understand in the moment, I felt like I was on thin ice. I said, "Yes. Mark was my partner. He died of AIDS." I stopped there, not trusting my voice to continue without breaking, and having no idea where the conversation was leading.

Sofia pounced. "So you're a homosexual!"

I almost laughed. Is that what this was about? "Yes," I said, "I am a homosexual."

"But you never told us that."

"I don't consider my sexual orientation to be anyone's business but my own. Most of the people I work with know that I'm gay, and it's never made any difference that I'm aware of."

"Well," she said, tossing her hair back, "it makes a difference to us." She turned to look at Tom, who had sunk miserably into the cushions. "Doesn't it, honey?"

"Yes," he said to her, not making eye contact with me. "Of course it does, Sofia."

I couldn't think of a single thing that I could say that would not cause me to lose my license. I simply sat and looked at her, wondering what kind of person would talk this way to someone who had just experienced the death of a loved one. But she wasn't done.

"The idea of you sitting here feeling desire for my husband disgusts me," she said. I sat up straight in my chair.

"What did you say?"

"I know you sit here wanting my husband." She shuddered theatrically.

Gathering what thoughts I could muster, I said, "Sofia, we clearly need to terminate this relationship. I'm sorry that you felt deceived by me. If a therapist's sexual orientation is important to you, you should probably ask them about it at the outset of treatment." I stood up. "I'm assuming you wish to end the session now?"

"Oh no," she said, looking at her watch. "We have thirty more minutes."

"How do you propose we proceed?" I asked.

"Maybe you could tell us what kind of work you think would be most helpful to us."

I sat down again and thought for a moment, discarding the hostile and hurtful statements I wanted to hurl at them. In a tone devoid of affect, I said, "In a termination session, I usually ask clients to tell me what they feel they've gained and what they believe they need to work on in the future."

"We can do that then. I want to use our time here, I don't want to waste it." She turned to Tom, putting her hand on his leg and softening her tone. "What do you think, honey?"

Tom looked bemused. "About what, Sofia?"

"What have we learned?" She stroked his leg. I refused to let my gaze drop to her hand and kept my eyes focused on her face. I moved from feeling numb to pure hatred.

Tom said, "I think we get along better now. We don't argue so much. Mike has encouraged me to speak up more, and I do that." Tom looked at me for affirmation but I would not make eye contact with him.

After a few more relatively banal exchanges, Sofia reached for her purse and pulled out a check, already written, and handed it to me. We stood. Instead of opening the office door as I usually did, I backed toward the desk. Tom moved toward me as if to shake my hand, our usual practice, and I turned my back, saying over my shoulder, "Good luck with your new therapist."

They left without another word, but I could hear Sofia saying, "You could have supported me!" as they went down the stairs. I felt like someone who had recently had abdominal surgery and then was unexpectedly kicked hard in the gut. I found my way across the hall to Mariel Kinsey's office for the staff meeting, carrying my cold coffee.

"Oh Michael, you look terrible. Come here!" Mariel said, and she gave me a long hug. Warren Brewer followed me in and closed the door. We usually began the meeting with a check in and I asked to be last, but they had both been affected by Mark's death and wanted me to begin. I fumbled through a few sentences and then said, "I feel completely psychotic. Clinically. My head is cracking open." Warren murmured something comforting and I said, "No, it's about something that just happened," and I told them about the session with Sofia and Tom.

Mariel leapt to her feet. "Damn her! Who does she think she is! What kind of a human being acts like that! Oh my God!"

She sat down next to me on the sofa and put both arms around me. I wanted to cry in the worst way, but there was too much dammed up. Her physical presence was a balm, however, and I began to breathe down into my belly, one to four, one to four. Warren went to the kitchen to make fresh coffee, and I slowly began to feel safe again.

Chapter 24

Before going to Long Island for the burial of Mark's ashes, I had written to Bill Coughlin at the *Boston Globe* and Sue Hyde at *Gay Community News*. I included a short piece I had written about Mark's life and death. They both called me within twenty-four hours and said they wanted to run stories and a picture. Sue Hyde said she would print essentially what I had sent her. Bill Coughlin asked me to come in for an interview, but I couldn't find a time before I had to leave for Long Island. We agreed that I would call him from New York and be interviewed on the telephone. Mark's parents would be interviewed as well. Both journalists were interested in his story primarily because of his involvement with the AIDS Action Committee and particularly the People With Aids group. Bill Coughlin said he'd "gotten a lot of flack" for how little the *Globe* had published about the gay community's struggle with AIDS and he wanted to do a substantial write-up to see how readers would respond. On Sunday, August 5, the *Boston Globe* published a long piece about Mark on the obituary page, including a very handsome picture. I was pleased at the thoroughness of the coverage and how Mark was praised for his community service.

As I read the article I wondered if Mark would have cringed. He had adored Claire Booth Luce's *The Women* and could quote chapter and verse. Whenever there would be a scandal of any sort, he would put the back of his hand dramatically to his forehead and quote the Countess De Lage, "*La publicité! La publicité!*" Would he scold and grimace if he were here?

All day people called to congratulate me on getting Mark's story into the *Globe*. "So powerful. So well deserved." I called Eddie and Ida and read the article to them, and Ida cried on the phone, saying repeatedly, "My son was such a fine man." Larry Kessler at the AAC called to say that the article was a breakthrough, and how happy he was that Mark had been honored in this way. More phone calls came later in the week when *Gay Community News* published its piece, with a large photo of Mark at the helm of a sailboat, squinting into the distance. *Bay Windows* published a piece that week as well, also with a photo. I told myself, "I didn't do this, really. It's the zeitgeist. It's time." Still, I felt uneasy, remembering Mark's reserve.

After sitting shiva in Queens, Fern and I spent the rest of the weekend planning Mark's memorial service on Long Island at Betts and Gerry's.

Fern had declined to be in the service ("No public speaking for me, thanks!"). Betts was going to speak, as well as Larry Kessler and Mitch Katz. Close friends of ours knew Yo-Yo Ma, who had offered to play the cello, and Martin Pearlman agreed to perform on the harpsichord.

"Please tell me it's not becoming a circus," I said to them. "All of a sudden it feels so public. I want it to be personal. Is it getting out of hand?" Betts and Fern reassured me it would be fine, that we would all make it personal, that the people who would be there would be people who knew Mark and cared for him.

The morning of the service, Sunday, August 12, I was up early and already exhausted. Eddie, Ida, and Pearl had come up the day before and were staying in the new condo, which at this point was still entirely devoid of furniture except for rented beds. When I had walked them up the four flights of stairs and shown them the beautifully clean and nearly empty space, Pearl searched for something on which to compliment me. Finally her eyes lighted upon the Sears dishwasher, and she exclaimed, "Oh, Kenmore! Very nice!"

That evening my friend Steven Holt hosted a potluck dinner at his apartment in Cambridge for a whole gang of people who had met the Halberstadts during Mark's hospitalization. I feared it would be sad, but the reconnection was joyful. Steven's apartment was filled with candlelight and good food and wine, and the buzz was steady for the entire evening. By the time I got the family back to the condo and returned to my apartment, it was late, and I was very wound up. I slept poorly.

At 6:00 a.m. I sat looking out the window, drinking coffee and filled with dread. Could I really pull this off? It felt so big, all those people, the church, the famous musicians, coffee and dessert in the social hall afterward. I had selected Emmanuel Episcopal Church because it had a beautiful, small chapel that seemed perfect to me. The rector had also been a gracious host to other families who had lost sons to AIDS.

I looked at my new suit hanging on the doorframe in its garment bag, the new shirt and tie. I felt a rush of pride in the beauty of the suit, how pleasurable it had been to go alone to Lord and Taylor's "All August Sale!" the previous week and search through the racks for something that would be appropriate for the service. A redheaded saleslady in four-inch heels sized me up and pulled four or five suits off the rack. I tried on the jackets one by one, turning to see the cut in the full-length mirror. When I told her it was for a memorial service, she murmured something sympathetic and then asked, "Are you speaking?" I nodded and she said, "Then you must look very nice!" As a boy with three older brothers from a blue-collar family, I wore nothing but hand-me-downs until I was in college. I remembered a photo of me in my brother Dan's overly large clerical suit, in a white shirt and tie, dressed for my junior prom. It hadn't fazed me at the time, but in the present circumstance, the young kid inside me wanted to look first-rate. We settled on a Hugo Boss navy blue pinstripe, subtle, beautifully made, and "only" $300 on sale. That seemed like a lot of money in 1984. Yvonne, the saleslady, said that the suit was "sophisticated without being funereal." Her opinion was good enough for me. But now, gazing at the suit in its garment bag, I was awash in anxiety. I felt like I was going to my execution. I reread the eulogy, which I'd already read aloud several times. It seemed trite. Too maudlin? Too sentimental? Too personal?

Fern called around 7:00. Hearing her voice brought me back to something like my normal self. We talked about the party at Steven's for a few minutes, then about the upcoming service. She ended by saying, "It's been a long road. Just remember to breathe and make eye contact with someone when you read the eulogy. It will ground you."

The memorial was scheduled for noon, so I had plenty of time for a run and a shower. Betts and Gerry had rented a room at the Ritz, which was next to Emmanuel Church. Bert Halberstadt had flown in that morning and was taking the family out to breakfast and bringing them to the service, so I was not needed anywhere before 11:30. I showed up at the Ritz about an hour before that, ate a little breakfast, drank a mimosa, and immediately regretted it, afraid I'd get foggy. Gerry laughed when I told him that and said, "Fat chance. You're going to be the center of attention of a hundred people in about an hour." They patiently listened to my reading of Mark's eulogy once more, and Betts read her piece. When Fern arrived, the four of us proceeded downstairs and out into a lovely, sunny morning. The Lindsey Chapel was open and people were gathering. I felt a little rush of excitement when I heard Martin Pearlman playing preludes on the harpsichord as I entered the church.

There were about 130 people. I stood by the door giving hugs and saying hello, dry-eyed until Frank Mahood, my former partner, showed up unexpectedly. The familiarity of his embrace, his simply murmuring "I'm sorry, I'm so sorry," made me cry. I had seen him only once since the Gay Pride March in New York and was deeply touched that he made the effort to come. There were guests from all parts of Mark's life, friends from New York, doctors and nurses who had taken care of him at the hospital, many PWAs and their partners, and staff from the AIDS Action Committee. The chapel was filled with flowers, and sunlight poured in through the stained-glass windows.

Larry Kessler gave the welcoming remarks, saying that we were there "to affirm that Mark's presence is still among us and that his unique spirit will continue to be with us for the rest of our lives." The Boston Gay Men's Chorus sang two versions of a short piece, *Cantate Domino*, one by Pitoni and one by Hassler. Then Mitch Katz and Betts each spoke and did a reading. Mitch focused on Mark's calming effect on other PWAs, his steady optimism, his commitment to not flinching or turning away when others were sick or dying. Betts shared stories of travels with Mark, his sense of humor and love of sailing. She said, "Michael's only competition in Mark's life was a sailboat." She paused. "Any sailboat!" And there was a great burst of laughter.

Martin Pearlman played once more, "Andante" from the *Italian Concerto* by Bach and "Les Barricades Mystérieuses" by Couperin. I had been sitting between Betts and Fern in the front row, and when Martin finished, I climbed up to the pulpit. As I looked out, I realized that the church was packed with people I knew and loved, people who had helped and supported Mark. Seeing Eddie, Ida, and Pearl in the front row made me deeply happy. Ida cried through my entire eulogy, which I managed to deliver without my voice breaking.

Initially I spoke about his diagnosis, how it had changed us in ways that we could never have predicted. I located his illness in the net of history in which we had been caught. I praised his courage. And I expressed gratitude for all of it, the whole three years of our relationship. Finally I read a passage from my journal, which I'd written on one of those long nights sitting by his hospital bed while he was still in a coma.

"There is no escaping the fact that you are dying, my dear. You have fought the good fight, and now you can let go. Despite the newspapers reporting on 'AIDS victims,' you are no victim. Your strength and intelligence have shown through in every step of this process, and in my eyes and the eyes of so many, you have become a model in our community, once again a teacher. Soon you will be released and this ordeal will be done. I promise to stay engaged in what looks to be a very long fight.

"I see your face so peaceful now. I remember the gravestone we saw together in Somes Sound, Maine. A lone sailor had been buried in a small, fenced-in plot on the side of a country road, and the inscription on the gravestone read, 'The sea is quiet tonight.' The sea will be quiet for many nights to come for you. I wish you peace on your journey, my love."

I felt a huge flood of relief when I descended from the dais and thought once more, *It's done.* For me, the service was complete. I resumed my seat.

There was silence for a few moments before Yo-Yo Ma played two pieces by Bach, "Prelude" from the *D Minor Second Suite* and "Allemande" from the *Sixth Suite in D Major.* The acoustics in the chapel were perfect, and he played with passion and gravity. The church was absolutely still when he finished. Then Jerry Groopman ascended the dais and spoke warmly of his relationship with Mark and how much he would be missed. Jerry ended by saying Kaddish, first in Hebrew, then in English. The Gay Men's Chorus closed the service by singing a passage from Walt Whitman:

Camerado, I give you my hand!
I give you my love, more precious than money.
I give you myself before preaching or law.
Will you give me yourself? Will you come travel with me?
Shall we stick by each other as long as we live?

Following the service, the hospice group from the AIDS Action Committee hosted a reception in the church library, an elegant room with wood paneling, high ceilings, and leaded-glass windows. I believe I greeted nearly every person who came into the room. It was wonderful to see Mark's nurses, Jeff and Karen and Melanie, to whom I had grown so close, and his buddies from the PWA group. I was happy to see Cesar across the room in an animated conversation with Fern. By the end of the reception my feet were killing me.

There were still dozens of people to thank and send on their way. Many of the guests were returning to other states and had hours of travel ahead. I stood outside the church saying goodbyes, then returned to the condo with Eddie, Ida, and Pearl to help them get organized and send them off. By the time I got back to the apartment, I had just enough time to shower, change, and put on sneakers before Mark's friends John Batson, Kirk Kirkpatrick, and Barry Safran showed up to take me to dinner. John was staying in a hotel for a few days and had promised to help me go through Mark's endless boxes of files and papers. Barry and Kirk would be flying back to New York after dinner.

By this time in the day I felt like I'd been run over by a bus. I was physically and emotionally tapped out. This particular trio of men felt like Mark's friends to me, not ours or mine. As much as I loved John in particular, I felt some distance from all of them. Kirk and John were big on teasing, reminding me unpleasantly of my older brothers, who were masters of using sarcasm like a scalpel. When we got to the restaurant we immediately ordered drinks, then more drinks. Food service was slow, but alcohol flowed. Initially the conversation buzzed around the day, then about the business of the McIntyre Building and when the co-op papers would finally be accepted by the city. A third round of drinks came. I faded in and out of the conversation until I heard Kirk say something sarcastic about "wondering who the service had been for." I looked at him.

"I missed that. What did you say?"

"I wondered where Mark was in the service. Who was this person that Betts described? When was he 'gifted on the harpsichord'? In his youth?"

I felt suddenly alert, sensing danger in his sarcasm.

"Kirk, he played the harpsichord in our living room. You heard him play."

"I know, but 'gifted on the harpsichord'? You made him sound like Igor Kipnis or something."

"I don't think I mentioned the harpsichord, Kirk."

"Oh Michael, you know what I mean."

Barry, who rarely had much to say, smirked and said, "I knew Mark for years. All he wanted was to get out of teaching and sail. How did he become a saint?"

Kirk said, "Really, Michael. Yo-Yo Ma? Where was the Mark I knew in that service? He wouldn't have recognized himself."

My head was fuzzy and I wanted desperately to mount a defense, but I felt powerless. There was rage deep inside that I'd learned long ago to repress. Those older brothers who delighted in sarcasm were also skillful at holding me down to slap my belly pink or locking me in a closet while I screamed and pounded on the inside of the door. The only way to get out was to give up and drop to the floor in silence. I would simply leave my body. So I left my body in the restaurant, retreating into numb silence as the food arrived. Full of self-hatred, I felt unmasked as a fraud. Maybe Kirk was right. It wasn't for Mark that I had done all this, it was out of my own grandiosity. I thought of the newspaper article in the *Globe*. Mark would have been mortified.

I wanted to flee the table, but dissociation is both a powerful and useful defense. I ate some of the dinner. After an awkward silence, the conversation shifted to John and Kirk's recent trip to Paris. I remember very little of the rest of the meal—I could feel a headache settle in. As we prepared to leave the restaurant, I said what I thought were the right things, thanking them for coming, thanking them for dinner. But I wished I were dead. And I was drunk, we all were.

I walked home, a distance of a couple of miles, hoping to wear off the effects of all the Scotch. I could hardly keep moving but knew better than to sit on a bench at a bus stop for fear of falling asleep. All I could think of was the night that Mark was intubated, how much I knew he dreaded the very idea of the procedure, how terrified he was, but how determined. I remembered the girl coming in to take his blood gases and dropping the vial, having to come back to cut him again. "Indignity follows indignity," he had said. My stomach hurt at the memory of what his wrists looked like, covered with tiny slits and scabs. I finally made it to our building and got into the apartment, kicked off my shoes, but couldn't sit down, my mind whirling with memories from the day, from the dinner, from the year of Mark's illness. I went into the kitchen to get a drink of water. As I was filling the glass, it slipped from my hand and shattered. I slammed my hand on the kitchen counter, making the silverware jump in the drawer beneath, and screamed, "Goddamn it! Goddamn it!" I saw Mark in the Pulmonary Unit waiting to be intubated, again felt my panic when I went in to see him one more time.

"Yeah. Right! You're not going to die. You're not going to die. Fuck you!"

Chapter 25

John Batson arrived at the apartment about 10:00 a.m. the next morning. I had gotten up at some point in the night and undressed, evidenced by my clothes, strewn across the floor between the bed and the bathroom. There were no signs of my having thrown up, which was a relief. I had a faint memory of taking aspirin during the night but took two more now for good measure. John regained my love when he opened a paper bag and took out a large cup of coffee, still hot.

"Drink your coffee, dear," he said. "We have a long day of work ahead sorting through the captain's priceless Delta Airlines collection. We'll need to dispose of most of it. Don't forget that you're moving to the condo in two weeks."

I drank a swallow of coffee, then another. "I need to shower first."

"I brought us something to eat," John said.

"I couldn't imagine eating anything, but thanks."

Fifteen minutes later, still suffering the after-effects of at least five Rob Roys, I sat with John at the kitchen table. He had removed the broken glass from the sink while I was in the bathroom. Neither of us mentioned it, nor the uncomfortable conversation at the restaurant.

We gazed into Hell, after two years still separated from the kitchen by those mismatched louvered doors. Thousands of dust motes danced in the sunshine that poured through the skylight. There were piles of clothes and random pieces of luggage, some open, and stacks of papers on the desk. But the room was still dominated by Mark's dozens of airline boxes, piled with no discernible organization against the left wall.

"Jesus," John said, taking in the full impact of what lay before us. "We could just drop them box by box from the window into the parking lot, then go down in the elevator and toss them into the dumpster."

"Yeah," I replied. "Or we could squirt lighter fluid on them, light it, and call the fire department."

"At least we'd get some firemen in here. Could we ask for young ones when we call 911?"

I laughed as I stood and stretched, feeling better. I began to chew on a cold toasted bagel with cream cheese. "Here's what I know. The really important papers, anything having to do with the McIntyre Corporation, the will, any insurance papers, are in that battered metal filing box. I don't know what the other papers are. As far as clothes are concerned, I'll give his dad anything good, since he's close enough to Mark's size, and we'll find someone to give his motorcycle jacket to." From the closet and luggage we removed what few articles of clothing we deemed new enough to pass along to Eddie (John referred to them as "holy relics") and piled them in the kitchen, putting the remainder into large green trash bags. Then we turned our attention to the battered boxes of papers. John wanted to start dumping them without even checking to see what was inside.

"John, we don't know what's important," I said impatiently.

He would have none of that. "Darling! You already said what was important was in the metal box! Most of this shit is about sailing. Given that you can barely swim, you're not likely to go get a sailboat. If you do, I'll buy you more manuals on knot-tying, OK?"

"Don't be so bitchy. I may surprise you." I began to feel better.

There were hand-scribbled notes relating to Mark's research in Arabic studies and a lot of complicated recipes cut from newspapers. There were articles in French about the Sorbonne, information on places to buy boats, tattered maps of nameless cities. "Oh look," I'd say, as John extracted things from my grip and put them into trash bags. "Do you think Kirk would like this article on 'Ten Ways to Prepare Escargot?'"

"Kirk loathes escargot," John said tartly, as he hauled another full bag to the elevator.

We ended by keeping only four of the boxes, mostly saving things that we believed would be meaningful to others. I kept two of his T-shirts, one from Charlie's Bar in Manhattan, one with a Suzuki motorcycle on it. They were his favorites and they took on a new identity in my T-shirt drawer: "holy relics." There were personal things, photos and objects from Mark's travels that I would move with me. But by late afternoon, after many trips to the basement in the elevator, we had half-filled the dumpster outside the building and considerably simplified my move to the condo. We were filthy, sweaty, and satisfied.

John poured us each a rum on the rocks to celebrate our success. I looked at the drink for a minute, wondering if I dared start up again. John raised his glass and said, "To the captain," so I saluted with my drink and took a sip. Once more at the kitchen table, we surveyed the interior room. I felt mildly guilty at the pleasure I took in seeing Hell nearly empty.

"I can't tell you how weird this feels, John, to have gotten rid of so much of his stuff. Thanks for being such a brick. I think I would have cried all day and ended up saving everything."

John said, "Did I ever tell you what Kirk and I did the last time we came to the hospital, right before Mark was intubated?"

I shook my head.

"He had that mask on, and he was panting. Panting, like a fucking dog! Kirk and I hadn't seen him that sick before, and I started going nuts. Mark was trying to talk to us but his mother kept interrupting him. Finally Mark pulls himself up in bed, yanks the mask away from his face, and says to his mother, "Shush! Shush!" John was laughing as he told the story, but there were tears running down his face. "Goddamn it, Mike. Kirk and I were so flipped out. We told you we were going to get coffee. We went out in the hall and into the stairwell, and we just stood there and bawled." By this time he was bawling, the first time I'd ever seen him cry, and my own amazement turned to tears. John got up and took a double length of paper towel, wiped his face and blew his nose, and said, "I've got an idea. You go take a shower. I'll go back to my hotel and shower, then we'll get something to eat and go to Chaps. I'm taking the widow dancing!"

And so he did. Pizza and salad seemed appropriately simple for day laborers, and we arrived at Chaps about 9:00. Monday night was not what you'd call busy at Chaps. John and I had had a few beers and smoked a joint before we went in. I was still feeling a little shaky from the day before, but John hauled me out onto the dance floor and, for the second time that day, we got sweaty. When I finally insisted on sitting down at the bar, John went to the men's room.

There were probably only twenty other patrons. I hadn't been in a bar, let alone a gay bar, in many months. It was comforting to realize that nothing in Chaps looked much different, mostly men over thirty, in jeans and T-shirts, drinking beer. It was like reentering an earlier lifetime: healthy-looking men, moderate cruising, a relaxed vibe. A man came through the side door, near where I was sitting, and looked over at me. He lifted his hand in greeting: Jeff Thomas, who had been one of Mark's primary-care nurses for nearly three weeks before Mark went into the ICU. I felt an impulse to run. I had seen him at the memorial service but we had not had a chance to talk. My desire to flee rose from embarrassment: What was I doing in a noisy dance bar three weeks after my lover had died? I began to wonder that myself. He came right over and gave me a quick hug.

"How are you doing?" he asked.

"I'm doing," I replied. "Maybe drowning my sorrows. How about you?"

"I'm well. I'm leaving the hospital. I was offered a good job at San Francisco General on their AIDS ward."

"Yikes. You're a brave soul, Jeff. Can I buy you a drink?"

"Just a beer, thanks. Bud Light. SF General is a great hospital and they're swamped with patients. It will keep me on my toes."

I was struck by the warmth of his smile, the easy way he held himself, unselfconscious. He slid onto the stool next to me. John came back to the bar and

I made introductions. Within a minute John moved away to talk to someone else at the bar, giving me a wink behind Jeff's back as he left. Jeff was easy to talk to, and we stayed with safe topics, where we'd gone to school, what he hoped for in San Francisco. He was thirty-five and had lived in Boston all his life, but he was "ready for a change." His relationship of four years had broken up ten months earlier.

We danced a few dances. I felt awkward in my body, not sure about how much eye contact to make or how close to get physically. The Mary Jane Girls song "All Night Long" came on, not fast, not slow. Without missing a beat Jeff moved closer and put his arms around me. "Let's make this a slow dance." I started to draw back, then relaxed in his arms. He was tall, nearly my height, and it felt odd to hold someone other than Mark. The lyrics were suggestive and we both laughed each time the refrain repeated, "I'm gonna give it to you/all night long." I pulled back a little and looked at him. "I think I need to sit down."

He shrugged and smiled. We returned to the bar and ordered another beer. John was nowhere in sight. Jeff said, "I thought the memorial service was amazing."

Remembering the chapel and the light through the stained-glass windows, I looked around the bar, which was dark and smoky. "So different from here, huh?"

"Yes. I wanted to talk to you at the coffee hour but there was a mob and I had a 3:30 shift to fill. I didn't get to tell you how much I loved working with Mark. He was such a sweet guy, solid, never complained. We could all see where it was going, but he stayed hopeful." He rested a hand on my shoulder. I had been looking away but brought my eyes back to his. Our knees were touching. I suddenly felt very sober. He continued. "I admired your relationship, how you were there for him, your love for him. I don't think I've ever felt love like that. Terry and I broke up because the relationship just didn't feel like it ever got deeper."

He held my gaze, and I was mesmerized by the intimacy of the conversation, the feel of his hand on my shoulder. He leaned in and kissed me, then said, "Maybe this is wrong to ask, but I'd really like to stay with you tonight. We don't have to have sex. I just want to hold you." The kiss tasted salty on my lips, and I shivered. I looked around for John, still didn't see him, and figured he'd gone back to his hotel. He was a big boy and could take care of himself. I hoped I could do the same.

"No guarantees that I won't freak out or ask you to leave as soon as we get to my place. But OK. And thank you."

Jeff had his car, and we were back at my apartment in fifteen minutes. We hardly spoke on the way home, but he kept his hand on my leg and I felt anchored. I wanted to start talking, to fill up the space with words, but I couldn't find my voice. So many things crowded my mind, memories, fears, critical thoughts about "this slutty behavior and Mark not dead a month!" I kept returning to Jeff's hand on my leg, the solidity of its weight. I thought, *This is a real person who is touching me, who wants to hold me. And I'm hungry to be held.*

Once inside the apartment we kicked off our shoes and moved to the window, looking at the lights of downtown Boston, the headlights from the cars on the Cambridge side making bright streaks on the river. He slipped his arms around me from behind and rested his chin on my shoulder. We were still for a moment. Hardly breathing, I turned and kissed him, a long kiss. The bed was in the alcove near where we were standing, and I led him to it and lay down, still dressed. He lay beside me, propped on one elbow. There was only the light from the windows, so his face was partly in shadow. "Are you doing all right?" he asked.

"I think so. I keep waiting to have a meltdown or something, but I'm just happy you're here. It feels good to be kissed like that. Mark had oral thrush for months before his diagnosis."

"You don't seem out of practice," he said, laughing. "Are you OK with me taking my clothes off?"

"Yes."

"And yours?"

"Maybe. Just kidding. But remember, no promises on performance."

He undressed slowly, standing in front of the window. He was lean and supple and very appealing in the half-light. He sat on the edge of the bed and I loved how slowly he moved, how gently he undressed me. He sat for a moment next to me, cross-legged, with his palm on my chest. My breathing slowed and I sank into the comfort and pleasure of the moment. Then he stretched out and we kissed, long kisses, followed by touching, exploring, staying close. It felt strange to be in bed with someone I hardly knew. It also felt completely natural. I was starved for physical contact and affection. I could feel months of contraction begin to loosen in tiny increments.

I don't think I ever got an erection. The experience felt delicious, more sensual than sexual, and all sorts of feelings and sensations arose that reminded me that I was alive. At some point Jeff was lying on top of me and said, "I'm going to come." When he finished he rolled over onto my outstretched arm and I held him, stroking his head. When he fell asleep I gently disengaged myself and moved to the window, pulling on my robe. I could see the shape of the dark blue sofa in the center of the room. Not so many months before, Mark had been lying on that sofa and I was standing here, in the same place near the window. We had talked about the increase of infections invading his body, *molluscum contagiosum*, *Giardia*, the ever-present thrush. He was clearly exhausted.

"I'm beginning to doubt that I'm going to make it," he said. "I'm getting worn down. I've been wondering how things might have turned out if I'd met you earlier."

"What do you mean?"

"I don't know. It's probably very Louise Hay, but I wonder if I might not have gotten sick. When I met you, I woke up. I had someone to live for. I seem to be taking an exit from our relationship much too early."

"You're not gone yet, Mark." I moved to the sofa and massaged his feet.

"I know. But I may not be here much longer. If I do die, I want you to know I'll watch out for you." Then he grinned and pushed at me with both feet. "And not just when you're in bed with another man!"

Suddenly I became aware of Jeff's breathing, and the image of Mark dissolved. I stretched out on the sofa and fell asleep. I was awakened a few hours later by the sound of the shower. Startled, I sat up, my heart racing, then saw Jeff's clothes neatly folded on the window ledge and it all came back. I called into the bathroom, "Do you have time for coffee?"

"I may be late as it is, Mike. Very bad nurse behavior!" He stuck his head out of the bathroom. "Rain check?"

"Of course." There was no awkwardness when he came into the kitchen, just some good-natured kidding about the consequences of living *la dolce vita*. A quick kiss and the promise of a phone call, and he was gone.

A week went by before I called and asked if I could buy him dinner. He picked a quiet restaurant near his apartment in the Fenway and we talked about the future, what we imagined it held for each of us. He was having second thoughts about moving so far away, but his former partner kept showing up in his life in Boston and he wanted a clean break. I had just read the newest statistics on AIDS in San Francisco. There were over 7,000 cases reported in the U.S. by this point and nearly 6,000 of those patients had died, the bulk of them in New York and San Francisco. The numbers were staggering.

"I shudder to think what you'll be facing when you move, Jeff. Are you really ready for this?"

I liked that he didn't answer immediately, took his time and had a sip of wine. "The truth is, I won't know until I get there. This sure looks like an epidemic."

"Do you think there will ever be a vaccine or a cure?" I asked.

"I'm a realist, Mike. At this point it all feels like a crapshoot. But I have a high tolerance for being with sick people, really sick people."

"I was impressed with how you took care of Mark," I said. "With all the anxiety he had about his breathing, the shift from the cannula to the mask to the respirator, you were kind and reassuring. And unflappable. I always felt like you knew what you were doing."

"Thank you." He smiled. "Mark's here with us again, isn't he?"

My eyes filled up. "He's never very far."

The waiter interrupted to ask if he could clear our plates, and we ordered coffee. We returned to more mundane topics, when the moving truck was coming, where he would stay until he found an apartment. Finally he said, "I know the answer to this question, but I have to ask it. There's no point in my staying here now, is there?"

I looked at him, not sure what he was asking but getting the seriousness of his tone. The waiter saved me by bringing the coffee. Then I understood.

"You mean, for you and me?"

"Yes, to put it baldly." Though he laughed, I could see it took some courage to put this on the table so directly.

"No, Jeff. Not now. The night we spent together was a godsend for me. The timing was perfect and you were just the right guy, someone I trusted and felt secure with, but didn't really know."

"Not biblically, anyway."

"Wise guy! But you're recovering from your breakup with Terry, and I—" My voice faltered. "I have a long row to hoe before my life will feel balanced again."

We said our goodbyes on the street and I walked back to Bay State Road, my thoughts shifting to the packing boxes at the apartment and the work that lay ahead.

Epilogue

On Friday, June 26, 2015, the Supreme Court of the United States ruled that the Constitution guarantees same sex-couples the right to marry. On that morning I was in a meditation retreat. We had just finished a session but were directed to remain in silence on our break. About fifteen of the eighty-five participants were gay or lesbian, and we had been waiting for weeks for the decision. One person felt his cellphone vibrate in his shirt pocket and looked at the screen. In the deep silence of the meditation hall, he cried out, "We won. Gay marriage is legal in the United States!" Pandemonium ensued, people hugging each other, laughing and weeping. For those of us who had been involved in the gay rights movement since the early seventies, the victory was bittersweet. Many of our loved ones had not lived to celebrate this day. In just thirty years, gay Americans had gone from the government's seeming indifference to the plague that was annihilating our community to a legal ruling that same-sex couples could marry, with all the rights and privileges that heterosexual couples enjoyed, including the right to raise children.

How far we had come, and how far I had come. Following in my father's footsteps, I "put down the drink" eleven months after Mark died. I used pot occasionally for several more years, finally finding my way into the halls of AA, where I have been an active and grateful member ever since. I honored my pledge to Mark and became involved with the AIDS Action Committee, first running support groups for men who had lost partners, then for many years leading a weekly support group for the counseling and social work staff. AIDS informed my world, both personally and professionally, for the next decade.

In 1988, I met Maurice "Moe" Melchiono at the Thirteenth Annual Gay and Lesbian Health Conference. The lone workshop at this gathering that was not health related was called "Being Mr. Right." Most people, myself included, interpreted this to mean "Meeting Mr. Right," and eighty men showed up to a conference room set up for forty. When we were asked by the group leaders to break into groups of four, then two, to do exercises on emotional vulnerability,

Moe stepped in front of another person in order to partner with me. The rest, as they say, is history. We had a commitment ceremony after eleven years together, attended by seventy family members and friends. When the Massachusetts Supreme Judicial Court ruled that the state's ban on same-sex marriage was unconstitutional, Moe and I joined thousands of celebrants at Cambridge City Hall on the evening of May 16, 2004. Those who wished to obtain licenses lined up at midnight. Ours was granted at 3:30 a.m., one of 262 licenses issued that day. We married on June 9, having already been a couple for sixteen years.

Ida Halberstadt asked me in nearly every conversation after Mark's burial, "So. Have you met someone yet?"

I'd say, "Ida. It's complicated."

"It's not complicated," she would reply. "You shouldn't be alone." She was thrilled when I met Moe and insisted that I bring him down to Queens to meet them. Of course Eddie made his famous burgers on the grill, and Pearl and Ida continued to disagree with each other. Loudly. Moe was utterly charmed and we saw them at least once a year. Pearl died first, in 1997, Ida in 1999, and Eddie in 2002, outliving his son by eighteen years.

Despite Ida's protestations, it *was* complicated. I remained in therapy for years. I knew no one who worked within the AIDS community who hadn't suffered from PTSD. Any potential connection with a man was fraught. "Have you been tested?" "Are you positive?" I had three brief relationships before I met Moe, and two of those men eventually were diagnosed. I began attending yoga classes at the Kripalu Center in Stockbridge, Massachusetts, and enjoyed it so much I became certified to teach. I continued to take meditation classes and did weekend retreats. After a time I found a place inside myself, sober and quiet, in which I could abide. My life felt simpler as a single man.

Moe changed all that. I told my friends, "This is just a little romance." But one of Moe's many qualities, evidenced in his behavior at the "Mr. Right" workshop, is determination. When I found out he was thirteen years younger than me, I said, "I can't date you. You're too young."

He replied, "You'll be surprised. I'm very grown up for my age!"

Many months later, as the relationship deepened, my friend Betts pointed out that I still had half a dozen framed photos of Mark in my apartment. She asked how Moe felt about that. I was ashamed to admit that I hadn't given it a thought. Mark was so much a part of my consciousness, I couldn't imagine packing him away in a box. But the question bothered me, and I finally raised the issue with Moe, very much afraid he would say he hated seeing the photos in every room. Instead he said, "You wouldn't be who you are if you hadn't loved Mark. I love who you are. Mark's photos don't take anything away from me." Reassured by his openheartedness, I found the freedom to put away most photos, keeping out only one, a snapshot of Mark on the *Dancing Bear*, grinning into the camera with shaving cream on his face.

I have survivor's guilt. I still wonder, thirty years later, why I didn't get HIV when so many others did. My sexual behavior was no different from anyone else's. I want to believe that I survived for a reason: to be useful, to contribute, to be a vehicle for change. In the nineties I gave up leading my AIDS Action group and helped to found an organization called The Shared Heart. Forty young people were featured in an exhibit of photographs, each of which was accompanied by text describing the subjects' experience of coming out to family and friends. The exhibit was shown in schools across Massachusetts, and a book of the same name was published by William Morrow in 1997. This book, which won the American Library Association's GLBT Task Force Nonfiction Award in 1998, was sent to every high school library in the state and had a major impact on the passage of the Safe Schools Act in Massachusetts in 2014.

I have been asked many times, "What do you think would have happened to your relationship if Mark had not gotten sick?" Given the complexity of the circumstances and our very different life goals at the time, it feels insincere to say, "Oh, I'm sure we would have worked things out." A more compelling question, to me, is "What do you think would have happened if there had been a cure for AIDS and Mark had survived?" Given the intensity of the bond we forged during the year of his illness, I think many of the things we had initially considered problems would have been cast in a different light.

I hold dear the memory of Mark saying to me, "I'll watch out for you." My life since his death has been blessed, filled with loving relationships and meaningful work. Many books and movies about AIDS have been produced, and each one validates some part of my experience. The most poignant film, however, is *Longtime Companion*, particularly its final scene, when all those who died are resurrected on a boardwalk in the Pines just like the one Mark and I walked so many times. As they rush to the beach, laughing and talking, it's easy to imagine my friends' faces in the crowd, Mark's most of all. As the main character Willy says at the end of the film, "I just want to be there."

Acknowledgments

For lifelong love and support: my late parents, Aloysius Joseph and Anna Mary Ward, and late brother, Tom; and my siblings, Joe, Dan, Judy, Jeanne, John, and Jeff.

For quiet space in which to retreat and write in peace: George and Maggie Bartlett, Meryl Friedman, and Peaked Hill Trust.

For early and late readings: Shira Block, Betts Cassady, and Beverly Simon.

For inspiration and encouragement: Helene Atwan, David Lennon, Catherine Parnell, and Joan Wickersham.

For help and support, both then and now: Fern Ganley, Jerome Groopman, Steven Holt, and Mitch Katz.

For patient, thoughtful, precise instruction in writing, and for his friendship: Ken Harvey.

For our commitment to each other as writers, and for always being there when I needed them: Liz Gray and Holly Hartman.

For creative and effective publicity and marketing: Michele Karlsberg.

For excellent editorial assessment and direction: Don Weise.

For cover design and typesetting: Linda Kosarin of The Art Department and Raymond Luczak, respectively.

For reading every word of every chapter countless times, giving brilliant feedback, and pushing me when I needed it: Rosanne Annoni.

For providing whatever I needed whenever I needed it: I couldn't have done it without you, Moe Melchiono!

About the Author

Michael H. Ward received his B.A. and M.A. in English Literature from the University of Nebraska at Omaha. He taught composition and literature on military installations in the North Atlantic for the University of Maryland Overseas Program and then became Director of Freshman English at Tuskegee Institute, Alabama. In 1971 he joined the test development staff at Educational Testing Service and stayed for eight years. While at ETS he went into therapy in New York City and loved it so much he enrolled in a training program to become certified as a Transactional Analyst. He moved to Boston in 1979 and began a private practice in psychotherapy, which he maintained for more than thirty years. In retirement he began to write this book out of a need to memorialize the events of the early AIDS epidemic in Boston.

CPSIA information can be obtained
at www.ICGtesting.com
Printed in the USA
LVOW12s1552030117

519573LV00001B/313/P